D1566167

The Pianist as Orator

GEORGE BARTH

THE PIANIST AS ORATOR

Beethoven and the Transformation of Keyboard Style

Cornell University Press

Ithaca and London

Copyright © 1992 by Cornell University

All rights reserved. Except for brief quotations in a review, this book, or parts thereof, must not be reproduced in any form without permission in writing from the publisher. For information, address Cornell University Press, 124 Roberts Place, Ithaca, New York 14850.

First published 1992 by Cornell University Press.

International Standard Book Number 0-8014-2411-9
Library of Congress Catalog Card Number 92-52743
Printed in the United States of America
Librarians: Library of Congress cataloging information
appears on the last page of the book.

♾ The paper in this book meets the minimum requirements
of the American National Standard for Information Sciences—
Permanence of Paper for Printed Library Materials, ANSI Z39.48-1984.

Contents

Acknowledgments

I owe my earliest insights about the ways of the musical orator to the inspiration of my mentors and friends from Wesleyan University in Connecticut, especially Jon Barlow, Peter Armstrong, and Richard Winslow. It was they who prepared me for my studies with John Kirkpatrick, one of the most profound musical orators I have had the privilege to know. I wish to thank the scholars and performers with whom I had the good fortune to work while at Cornell University—in particular Neal Zaslaw, Malcolm Bilson, James Webster, Roger Parker, John Hsu, and Sonya Monosoff—for their much-needed criticism and encouragement, and their warm responsiveness to my research and to the performances in which I tested my beliefs. Sonya Monosoff was also an inspiring participant with Lynden Cranham in those performances, and Edward Murray and Martin Hatch provided new perspectives on all our work in progress.

When I arrived in California, William Meredith, Patricia Elliott, and the staff at the Ira F. Brilliant Center for Beethoven Studies at San Jose State University proved eager to make available at a moment's notice rare materials that have been of inestimable value. I am indebted to them for permission to reproduce excerpts from early editions and copies of manuscripts in their holdings. A summer study grant from the National Endowment for the Humanities (NEH) enabled me to complete the first round of revisions, during which time my colleagues Thomas Bauman and Martha Feldman lavished their attention on the manuscript. As the book continued to take shape, Steven Lubin, Leonard Ratner, Jean Pang, and Jonathan Bellman contributed many helpful thoughts, and Alejandro Tkaczevski worked with saintly patience to reproduce in the annotated musical examples every retrievable nuance of the early editions.

From the very first days of this venture Robert Winter has offered his enthusiastic support, his sage advice, and his warm friendship, for which I am deeply grateful. I am also specially indebted to Sandra Rosenblum, who encouraged me, kindly supplied me with both manuscript updates and page proofs of her definitive work on performance practices in classic piano music, and offered some excellent suggestions as this book neared its final stages. My friends, my family, and my wife, Sharon, provided the love and support that made all the rest possible.

G. B.

The Pianist as Orator

Introduction

One evening several years ago I attended a concert in which a world-renowned European trio performed early chamber works by Beethoven on instruments much like those that he would have known. As it happened, I had received an advance copy of their program, and since I was coaching some of my students in the work that was to be the evening's finale, I had tucked my silent electronic metronome into the pocket of my jacket so I could take some notes on the performers' tempi. The concert began, and to my surprise what I heard in the very first movement—not the work I had planned to check—made me reach for the metronome. The players were performing in a style that I knew Beethoven's pupil Carl Czerny had described not long after his teacher's death: a tempo so mechanically exact that it coincided perfectly with the blinking light on my metronome for minutes on end. But as those minutes passed I became more and more uncomfortable. While it was obvious to me that all three players recognized the character of the piece, they seemed resigned to presenting it within the intractable confines of mechanism, and the effect gradually made it more and more difficult for me to breathe.

"Czerny needs another look," I told myself. "He has had an enormous impact." I knew what he was after: unity, cogency, a tempo whose profile would be powerfully recognizable throughout a movement. He wanted players to avoid exaggeration. But if this was the way he intended to achieve cogency, his method was not working. The piece itself seemed to me to be playful, sometimes gleeful, and occasionally rough or even downright coarse, but what I was hearing masked all that in what seemed to be a parody of "classic" values and "classicistic" performance. I was struck by the atmosphere of reverence and caution, with the concern for the "projection of form," but all this seemed out of keeping with the character of the piece, an application of "classical restraint" as a kind of overlay. Why pin Beethoven, young or old, to only one side of Hellenic culture? Surely he and his circle steeped themselves in antiquity for more reasons than this.[1] I mused about what Beethoven might have done with us had he been on stage. Then I turned my thoughts to a metaphor that seemed to hold an answer, something I remembered from my teens when a friend introduced me to the playing of Ornette Coleman: "You gotta hear this," he had said. "He can talk with his horn!"

"Music is a language" had been a pervasive metaphor centuries before Beethoven. Music and rhetoric had already been linked in the great works of the ancient Greek and Roman orators—Aristotle's *Rhetoric,* Cicero's *De inventione,* Quintilian's *Institutio oratoria*—and many thoughtful critics in Beethoven's day were tired of the link and thought it at best a tenuous one.

But it must have seemed tenuous in ancient days, too. The Greeks and Romans associated music mainly with the art of rhetorical delivery. Only in the Middle Ages, when musical rhetoric began to assume a position of major importance, did theorists begin to draw musical analogies when they analyzed arrangement and style. The passion for codifying musical figures and applying rhetorical devices in composition reached its height in the Baroque era, rhetoric's "golden age," when theorist and composer alike had at hand musical analogues for almost every technique of classical rhetoric.[2]

---

[1] Eleanor Selfridge-Field, in her essay "Beethoven and Greek Classicism," points out that "order" and "form" were by no means the only concerns, and may not even have been the central concerns of eighteenth-century musicians who revived the ancients. She draws attention to "the Dionysiac aspects of antiquity cherished in Beethoven's day," and comes to the conclusion that Beethoven, far more than either Mozart or Haydn, manifested a real interest in the revival of Hellenic culture, including its concern with "sublimity," "profound simplicity," and, of course, "sense of destiny" (*Journal of the History of Ideas* 33 [1972]: 577–78, 594).

[2] Christopher C. Hill, "Rhetoric," *New Harvard Dictionary of Music,* 698.

Then, with the fading of the high Baroque style in the eighteenth century, interest in the art of rhetoric began to wane, at least so far as its conscious cultivation was concerned. The whole approach might have died out had it not been for the fact that at midcentury, some twenty years before Beethoven's birth, there was a sudden resurgence of interest in the art of delivery.³ And with that, rhetoric's decline came to resemble, ironically enough, an inverted version of its origins: only in discussions of delivery had the ancients mentioned *music,* and now, among musicians in the latter part of the eighteenth century, the art of delivery was just about the only context in which anyone mentioned *rhetoric.* Johann Joachim Quantz gave it his special attention:

> Musical execution may be compared with the delivery of an orator. The orator and the musician have, at bottom, the same aim in regard to both the preparation and the final execution of their productions, namely to make themselves masters of the hearts of their listeners, to arouse or still their passions, and to transport them now to this sentiment, now to that. Thus it is advantageous to both, if each has some knowledge of the duties of the other.⁴

The musician as orator—any soloist served to gain from an image like this, but for some reason when the idea was taken up by the champions of the newest keyboard instrument, the fortepiano, it became especially compelling to the musical public. Emanuel Bach set

³George J. Buelow, "Rhetoric and music," *New Grove Dictionary of Music and Musicians* 15.802.

⁴"Der musikalische Vortrag kann mit dem Vortrage eines Redners verglichen werden. Ein Redner und ein Musikus haben sowohl in Ansehung der Ausarbeitung der vorzutragenden Sachen, als des Vortrages selbst, einerley Absicht zum Grunde, nämlich: sich der Herzen zu bemeistern, die Leidenschaften zu erregen oder zu stillen, und die Zuhörer bald in diesen, bald in jenen Affect zu versetzen. Es ist vor beyde ein Vortheil, wenn einer von den Pflichten des andern einige Erkenntniß hat" (Johann Joachim Quantz, *Versuch einer Anweisung die Flöte traversiere zu spielen* [Berlin, 1752], 100; translation from Edward R. Reilly in Johann Joachim Quantz, *On Playing the Flute,* 2d ed. [New York: Schirmer Books, 1985], 119). Reilly notes that in 1754 the Dutch translator of Quantz's treatise, J. W. Lustig (a pupil of J. S. Bach), found the term *Vortrag* new enough to remark that "the expression . . . , which is often used by the author, deserves to be admitted as a new and concise technical term signifying *the manner of performance*" [een nieuw en bondig konstwoord, *de wyze der uitvoering* betekenende].

the stage for those who would capitalize on the image of the *pianist* as orator. In his *Versuch über die wahre Art, das Clavier zu spielen* of 1753—a treatise Beethoven was to study decades later under his teacher Christian Gottlob Neefe—Bach described the art of fantasy as one in which "the keyboardist, before all other musicians, is especially able *all alone* to practice the declamatory style, that astonishingly swift flight from one affect to another."[5] "Keyboardist" (*Clavieriste*) was the generic word he used, and in those days the fortepiano still seemed to him primitive compared to the clavichord.[6] But Beethoven read Bach's treatise knowing his later reputation as an enthusiastic promoter of the fortepiano, a reputation reflected in the much more favorable comments about the instrument that appeared in the second part of his *Versuch*.[7] Though he may have continued to prefer the clavichord, by 1762 Bach recognized and welcomed the fortepiano as an elegant tool for the most sensitive artists.

By the 1780s the fortepiano was enjoying a spectacular ascent to popularity, but with each passing year, the idea that music was a language faced more and more resistance from critics and aestheticians. The very utterance of the one who "spoke in tones" at the keyboard was being hailed by some as "emancipated from language."[8] Even before he moved to Vienna in 1792, Beethoven was becoming a pivotal figure in all this. His instrument of choice was the Viennese fortepiano; with it he gained an early reputation as a consummate performer, and was admired especially for the wealth and

[5]"[E]in Clavieriste . . . das Sprechende, das hurtig Ueberraschende von einem Affeckte zum andern, *alleine* vorzüglich vor den übrigen Ton-Künstlern ausüben kann . . . " (Carl Philipp Emanuel Bach, *Versuch über die wahre Art, das Clavier zu spielen,* part 1, 1st ed. [Berlin, 1753], 123–24).

[6]Carl Philipp Emanuel Bach, *Essay on the True Art of Playing Keyboard Instruments,* trans. William Mitchell (New York: W. W. Norton, 1949), 35–36, §11; and 112, §36.

[7]Ibid., 172, §6; 369, §6; and 431, §4.

[8]Daniel Gottlob Türk gives a late-eighteenth-century description of "the tones [becoming] as it were a language of the feelings" in his *Klavierschule* (Leipzig and Halle, 1789), 332: "Wer ein Tonstück so vorträgt, daß der darin liegende Affekt (Charakter &c.) auch bey jeder einzelnen Stelle auf das Genaueste ausgedruckt (fühlbar gemacht) wird, daß also die Töne gleichsam zur Sprache der Empfindung werden, von dem sagt man, er habe einen guten Vortrag." For a brief account of "the emancipation of music from language," see John Neubauer's *The Emancipation of Music from Language: Departure from Mimesis in Eighteenth-Century Aesthetics* (New Haven: Yale University Press, 1986), 1–2.

power of his ideas. He was, as Carl Ludwig Junker observed, a musician "for the heart—equally great . . . as an *adagio* or *allegro* player."[9] Yet Beethoven brought to the instrument a manner of playing markedly unlike the detached, short-slurred styles of Emanuel Bach, Haydn, and Mozart. To the Viennese instrument—designed originally for the articulate brilliance of a "speaking music," with rapid decay of sound, quick and efficient damping, and variation of timbre from one register to another—Beethoven brought a style characterized by flawless legato, so overwhelming in its effect that his generation and the next began to look upon the "old manner of performance" at first as "choppy," and finally as entirely unsuited to the fortepiano.[10]

Admittedly this was not the first time earlier keyboard music had been described as choppy. In 1804 an anonymous reviewer for the *Allgemeine musikalische Zeitung* reported that the adjective *zerhackt* had been applied to Emanuel Bach's compositional style "in his own time . . . , and not unjustly." But one gets the impression that in Bach's day the term was more descriptive than pejorative: the reviewer explained that Bach's listeners, less offended by the absence of "flowing melodies," were accustomed to this kind of playing.[11] By Beethoven's time it was another matter: tastes were changing, and fortepianos began to reflect the desire for flowing melodies as they grew from the five-octave versions of the 1770s to the six- or six-and-a-half-octave pianos most common in the 1820s.[12]

Where does Beethoven belong in the history of musical rhetoric? Did he abandon it or transcend it? Did his style mark the death of one

[9]Beethoven continued to prefer Viennese instruments even after receiving an English instrument from Broadwood (William S. Newman, *Beethoven on Beethoven: Playing His Piano Music His Way* [New York: W. W. Norton, 1988], 45–57). Carl Ludwig Junker vividly recalled Beethoven's projection of musical "ideas" (*Thayer's Life of Beethoven,* ed. Elliot Forbes, 2 vols. [Princeton: Princeton University Press, 1964], 105).

[10]Carl Czerny, "Recollections from My Life," trans. Ernest Sanders, *Musical Quarterly* 42 (1956): 307.

[11] Review of the Variations H. 14 (Wq. 118, no. 7), *Allgemeine musikalische Zeitung,* ed. J. F. Rochlitz (1769–1842) 6, no. 15 (11 January 1804): cols. 243–44.

[12]For a clear and detailed account of the development of the fortepiano, see Sandra P. Rosenblum's *Performance Practices in Classic Piano Music: Their Principles and Applications* (Bloomington: Indiana University Press, 1988), 31–52.

language and the birth of another, or something more subtle, like the emergence of a new dialect?

The modern musician who tries to answer these questions faces several difficulties. First there is a problem of perspective. We look back to Beethoven's time from a century that knows comparatively little about oratory. But Beethoven lived to see the burial of a tradition he had known in many ways from his youth. He had begun studying the treatises of Johann Mattheson, Johann Philipp Kirnberger, and Emanuel Bach while still in Bonn, and knew partly through them and partly through his reading of the Greek and Roman writers some of the theory of the ancient rhetoricians.[13] Perhaps because he was largely self-taught, he was bold enough about his own accomplishments to write that "there is no treatise that would be too learned *for me; without* making the least claim to actual scholarship, I have labored since childhood to grasp the *meaning of the better and wise* of every age. Shame on any artist who does not consider it his duty to bring himself at least this far."[14]

And what meaning did he encounter in the works he studied? From

[13]Beethoven's study of Mattheson's *Der vollkommene Capellmeister* and Kirnberger's *Die Kunst des reinen Satzes in der Musik* is probed in Richard Kramer's "Notes to Beethoven's Education," *Journal of the American Musicological Society* 28 (1975): 72–101. His concern with declamation is addressed in Kramer's "Beethoven and Carl Heinrich Graun," *Beethoven Studies*, vol. 1., ed. Alan Tyson (New York: W. W. Norton, 1973), 18–44, especially 22–24. See Rosenblum, *Performance Practices*, 14–15, for a description of Beethoven's early training under Christian Gottlob Neefe (in particular his introduction to Emanuel Bach's *Versuch*) and the scope of his library, which included works of the Greek and Roman writers as well as Daniel Webb's *Observations on the Correspondence between Poetry and Music* (London, 1769) in its German version, *Betrachtungen über die Verwandschaft der Poesie und Musik* (1771). For an account of his general reading habits see Karl-Heinz Köhler's "The Conversation Books: Aspects of a New Picture of Beethoven," *Beethoven, Performers, and Critics*, ed. Robert Winter and Bruce Carr (Detroit: Wayne State University Press, 1980), 157. See also Albert Leitzmann's "Beethovens Bibliothek," *Ludwig van Beethoven: Berichte der Zeitgenossen, Briefe und persönliche Auszeichnungen* (Leipzig: Insel-Verlag, 1921), 379–83.

[14]"Es gibt keine Abhandlung, die sobald zu gelehrt *für mich* wäre; ohne auch im mindesten Anspruch auf eigentliche Gelehrsamkeit zu machen, habe ich mich doch bestrebt von Kindheit an, *den Sinn der Bessern und Weisen* jedes Zeitalters zu fassen. Schande für einen Künstler, der es nicht für Schuldigkeit hält, es hierin wenigstens so weit zu bringen" (Ludwig van Beethoven, *Ludwig van Beethovens sämtliche Briefe und Auszeichnungen,* ed. Fritz Prelinger [Vienna: C. W. Stern, 1907], 213; the letter is to Breitkopf und Härtel in Leipzig and is dated 2 November 1809).

Mattheson through Emanuel Bach and Friedrich Wilhelm Marpurg to Kirnberger and Daniel Gottlob Türk, the theoreticians of the eighteenth century used the terminology of classical oratory to describe music as gestural art, to systematize its elements, and to illuminate the ways in which these elements cohered in eloquent musical discourse. They consciously cultivated the art of musical declamation, the "speaking style," in its widest sense, finding in the consistent use of linguistic analogues a means of awakening in themselves and their listeners a stronger, clearer sense of their expressive intent.

But what of Beethoven? While it is tempting to infer ideas of *his* practice from the theory he read, that approach is dangerous, because his manner of using "the meaning of the better and the wise" was at times most peculiar. In studying the theorists, Beethoven often pursued lines of inquiry that had little to do with their arguments.[15] That he drew inspiration and enlightenment from his reading is plain enough, but the effects on his practice are not so obvious. We can draw from his sources a sense of the tastes and issues of their day and from his comments about them a sense of his opinions—both provide grounds for speculation. But only occasionally can we link these with documentary evidence to uncover really significant clues about Beethoven's approach to performance.

Beethoven's cultivation of the image of the self-made man further obscures his practice from our view. There were times when he insisted that his genius put him above the influence of others, as when he declared of Haydn, with whom he studied for just over a year beginning in 1792, that he "had never learned anything from him"—a claim weakened by the records that remain of those studies, by the reverence he showed for Haydn in later years, and not least of all by Beethoven's music itself.[16] How should we deal with one who took such delight in hiding and denying influences?

[15]Kramer, "Beethoven's Education," especially 84–86 and 91–92.

[16]The comment about Haydn is related by Ferdinand Ries and recorded in Franz Gerhard Wegeler and Ferdinand Ries, *Biographische Notizen über Ludwig van Beethoven von Wegeler und Ries,* ed. Alfred C. Kalischer, 2d ed. (Berlin: Schuster and Loeffler, 1906), 103. Beethoven's Haydn studies are described in Kramer, "Beethoven's Education," 91–92, and the personal relationship between Beethoven and Haydn in Maynard Solomon's *Beethoven* (New York: Schirmer Books, 1977), 67–77.

On the one hand, it seems wise to respect this facet of Beethoven's character. That he could apparently forget the source of an idea was in a sense a great strength, for what inspired him became so much "his own" that he could use it freely to serve his creative ends.[17] On the other hand, much of what he brought forth had its origins—as he sometimes acknowledged—in the work of his musical forebears, work that he appreciated and assimilated. So however much we stand in awe of the way he could give old things an entirely new look, we gain something from recognizing a commonplace when we see one.[18] Part of the interpreter's task is to discern and then express both the ancient thing and the freshness of its new appearance.

Yet when we aim to distinguish old from new in Beethoven's practice, that, too, is complicated. Much of what we know about his way of playing comes to us through the accounts of his students Ferdinand Ries (1784–1838) and Carl Czerny (1791–1857), and from the writings of Anton Schindler (1795–1864), who assisted him in his final years. Beethoven, the man of extremes, seemed to draw from his interpreters extreme responses; they saw his new guises for the old sometimes as prophetic, sometimes as reactionary, and sometimes, curiously, as both. They left us a treasury of documentary evidence and reminiscence, but it is a treasury of divergent views, biased, personal, and full of veiled or explicit attempts to instruct us.

Especially daunting is the fact that Beethoven had little to say directly about his place in the history of keyboard technique, aesthetics, or notational practice. His reticence compels us to read between the lines, using the traditional tools: his own music and writings, the theoretical and practical works we know that he studied, the reminiscences and advice of his interpreters, and the other influential works of his day—and while this may at first seem like a wealth of material,

[17]John Neubauer reminds us that in the history of musical aesthetics "creative work occasionally shapes the theory, whereas at other times theoretical reflection inspires creativity" (*Emancipation*, 3).

[18]On the notion of a commonplace, see, for example, Leonard G. Ratner's explication of "topics" in the finale of the *Eroica* Symphony, Op. 55, in his *Classic Music: Expression, Form, and Style* (New York: Schirmer Books, 1980), 258–59. For an account of Beethoven's delving into more obscure traditions in order to fashion them anew, see Warren Kirkendale's "New Roads to Old Ideas in Beethoven's *Missa Solemnis*," *Musical Quarterly* 56 (1970): 665–701.

it provides no more than a basis for informed experiment for the performer, who must integrate knowledge, intuition, and conviction into a persuasive whole.[19]

I want to promote that integration while stressing that it is never enough to apply generalizations. In the chapters that follow I present a picture of the rhetorical tradition among musicians in the years preceding Beethoven's creative work and then suggest reasons for the differences between his keyboard declamation and that of those who came both before and after him, especially as regards matters of tempo and character.

The core of the book is in three parts. The first part, on musical time, contrasts two ways of apprehending time and illustrates ways in which each affects the perception of music's content. The second part, on music's character as described by three of the theorists Beethoven studied, begins with Mattheson's establishment of the art of gesture as the basis for musical rhetoric, describes Emanuel Bach's influence in freeing rhetorical theory from the confines of Enlightened French rationalism, and concludes with Kirnberger's application of the theory to levels below the musical surface. Other important theorists active in Beethoven's day, whose works we have no evidence that he studied, are also considered—whenever their speculations on rhetoric and musical structure seem particularly lucid, interesting, or controversial. The third part, on Beethoven's keyboard practice and his use of the metronome, highlights the opposing views of Czerny and Schindler on tempo and character in his music.

These three discussions serve as a foundation for several analyses, including an interpretation of tempo, gesture, and articulation in the first movement of the Sonata in F major for Piano and Violoncello, Op. 5, no. 1, and a study of tempo flexibility in the Variations on an Original Theme, Op. 34. In these works, recorded performances serve as additional tools for the critique of theoretical advice.

[19]Because translation of the documentary evidence raises so much controversy—for example, Ries's comment that Beethoven played his own compositions "sehr launig" has been translated by reputable authorities variously as "very spiritedly," "very moodily," "most capriciously," and even "very freakishly"—I have retained the original language of almost all translated material in the notes. Unless otherwise credited, translations are my own.

When Beethoven wrote to Ignaz von Mosel in 1817 hailing the arrival of the metronome, he distinguished between tempo and character by analogy: time or tempo, he suggested, "is really more the body," while "words that describe the character of the piece" were meant to refer "to the spirit."[20] In music, of course, tempo and character are interdependent; we come to know music's "body" through its "spirit," and vice versa. But there is good reason to believe that the eclipse of rhetorical thinking and the gradual acceptance of the metronome profoundly changed music's "body" during Beethoven's life and immediately afterward. Since the metronome has played a central role in most discussions of tempo and character in Beethoven's music from his day to ours, we will begin by contemplating its contributions, and what it may have been like in a world without metronomes—a world Beethoven inhabited for his first forty-seven years.

[20]"Der Tact eigentlich mehr der Körper ist, [den Karakter des Stückes bezeichnenden Wörter] aber schon selbst Bezug auf den Geist des Stückes haben" (quoted in Alexander Wheelock Thayer, *Ludwig van Beethovens Leben,* 5 vols., trans. Hermann Dieters, ed. Hugo Riemann [Leipzig: Breitkopf and Härtel, 1907], vol. 4, 67).

1 *Time: The Body*

Time knows no equality of parts.
    —Victor Zuckerkandl, *Sound and Symbol*

The Experience of Time: Cyclic Continuum versus Abstract Unit

Music operates in the nonspatial continuum of time; whatever space it may be said to contain—between its high and low tones, for example, or between the sounding of its tones—is a conceptual space, a space without dimension.[1] Yet nowadays we describe music's realm, the realm of time, in dimensional terms, much as we speak of the dimension of length, as if time comprised units like those on a measuring stick. In measuring time we remain silent about its nonspatiality; we speak only of bodies in motion, as the Russian mathematician Lobachevski did in his elegant definition: "The motion of one body, if it is taken as the measure of the motion of another body, is called time."[2]

Because we measure time this way, our perception of time depends on the nature of the motion with which we measure it. Take, for example, the way we measure the passage of days. At the beginning

---

[1]See Victor Zuckerkandl's discussion of the space of tones in *Sound and Symbol: Music and the External World*, trans. Willard R. Trask, Bollingen Series 44 (New York: Pantheon, 1956), 267–362.

[2]N. I. Lobachevski's definition of time is quoted in Zuckerkandl, *Sound and Symbol*, 154.

of recorded history we waited for the coming of dawn; the sunrise was our practical and symbolic marker. The *American Heritage Dictionary* suggests that we chose it because it is "a regularly recurring event."[3] But the expression "regularly recurring event" is paradoxical. We waited for the sunrise and it came. How did we know its arrival was "regular"? Were we all the while secretly using some other "regular" motion by which we tested each appearance of the sun?

Well, let us enter the regress: we can appeal to astronomy and proclaim that the sunrise is *not* regularly recurring, that it is in a word "irregular" (through the cycle of the year).[4] Now we are measuring with a new tool: with the astronomers we have chosen a celestial event of greater magnitude than the sunrise, whose motion we are dividing into "equal" parts. We call these abstract units "seconds," "minutes," "hours," even "days," and we group them in ways that suggest rough correspondences with events we know, like parts of the day or the sunrise. But because the correspondences are *rough,* our new way of measuring makes us sense a kind of "temporal dissonance," a tension between the vivid envelope of our experience (the sunrise) and the counting of abstract units (twenty-four hours, a "day").

Before it was practical to use a machine to measure time in musical performance, was the application of "accurate" time anticipated as a bearer of such dissonance? Was anyone expecting an analogue to the play of time already well known as *rubato,* the play among orders of cycles ordinarily experienced in music making? From most accounts it appears unlikely. Instead of being associated with dissonance, the application of "accurate" time seems to have been anticipated among musicians as a bearer of concord and clarity. Many seemed to assume that their sense of "strict time" in music would correspond to the ticking of a simple machine. Indeed, there is a tendency that persists to this day to associate "classical" tempi with the regularity of machines.

---

[3]*American Heritage Dictionary of the English Language,* s.v. "time."
[4]The perspective here is intentionally European; the irregularity of the sunrise cycle is more marked in temperate zones than at the equator.

And yet in a way this assumption about strict tempo ought to provoke suspicion. Admittedly there was a widespread fascination with clockwork in the eighteenth century, but even then a very great part of that fascination had to do with the way in which machines could be made to imitate things that were not mechanical. It was, in a sense, the irregularity of the sunrise they wanted to capture—the effect of the eccentric orbit—and so their most sophisticated machines were capable of imitating eccentricity. In the realm of music, for example, the most advanced barrel organs and music boxes were pinned to re-create the subtle nuances of dance rhythms or inflections in song.[5]

In contrast, the machine developed for time measurement among musicians, the metronome, was one of the simplest, and it reflected the mechanisms at work in the natural world with the simplicity of abstraction, that is, only in the most rudimentary way. It seems ironic that it was adopted by musicians of stature at the dawn of the Romantic era—a period we generally associate with the rise of individualism—during an age when the rhetorical analogies that had shaped musical time for centuries began to fall into disuse.

Did those who anticipated the salutary effects of mechanically measured time find their experience in working with machines entirely fulfilling? In particular what of Beethoven, who was always concerned with the problem of conveying information about musical tempo and character? When he first endorsed the metronome he spoke as if the problems of musical time and tempo were susceptible to solution by mechanical means, but as is well documented, his subsequent remarks clouded that impression considerably. Is it likely that he, or *any* musician of his day, was really conscious of the effect that changing metaphors for time would have on musical perception? To lay the groundwork for some further speculation, let us trace part of the history of musical timekeeping, beginning with one of the theorists Beethoven studied and admired.

[5]For some varied and thought-provoking examples, see David Fuller's *Mechanical Musical Instruments as a Source for the Study of Notes Inégales* (Cleveland Heights, Ohio: Divisions, 1979); for a broader perspective, see his "Notes inégales" in *New Grove Dictionary of Music and Musicians* 13.420–27.

The Measure of Time: Some Theoretical Accounts

In his *Der vollkommene Capellmeister* of 1739, Johann Mattheson pondered a "regularly recurring event" that was often used for the measurement of duration in music: the pulse of the human body. He described it as a wave form with two distinct parts:

> The principal character of the mensuration is established once and for all on the fact that each mensuration, each segment of the time-measure, has only two parts and no more. These have their source or their basis in the arteries, whose pulsations and relaxations are called *systole* and *diastole* by experts in medicine.
>
> Musicians as well as poets have taken such qualities of the body as a model, and arranged the time-measures of their melodies and verses accordingly, but they have called the ebb and flow in the beat *thesis* and *arsis.*[6]

Mattheson was primarily interested in envelope, in the shape of time's measure, and concerned himself little with its reliability or "accuracy." In contrast, Johann Joachim Quantz, in his *Versuch einer Anweisung die Flöte traversiere zu spielen* of 1752, was one of several eighteenth-century writers sensitive to the variation in human pulse. He related disposition and personality type (according to the theory of temperaments current in his day) to variation in pulse, and this in

---

[6]"Das Haupt-Wesen des Tacts kömmt einmahl für allemahl darauf an, daß eine iede Mensur, ein ieder Abschnitt der Zeit-Maasse nur zween Theile und nicht mehr habe. Diese nehmen ihren Ursprung oder ihren Grund aus den Pulsadern, deren Auf- und Niederschläge bey den Arzeney-Verständigen *Systole* und *Diastole* genennet werden. "Sothane Eigenschafften des menschlichen Leibes haben nun sowol die Ton-Künstler als Dichter für ein Muster angenommen, und die Zeitmaasse ihrer Melodien und Verse darnach angeordnet, die Nahmen aber des Niederschlages und Aufhebens im Tact *Thesin* und *Arsin* geheissen" (Johann Mattheson, *Der vollkommene Capellmeister* [Hamburg: Christian Herold, 1739; facsimile, Kassel: Bärenreiter-Verlag, 1954], 171–72; translation from Ernest C. Harriss, *Johann Mattheson's "Der vollkommene Capellmeister": A Revised Translation with Critical Commentary* [Ann Arbor, Mich.: UMI Research Press, 1981], 365). Mattheson is speaking here of "beat" prior to metric considerations.

[7]Johann Joachim Quantz, *On Playing the Flute,* 2d ed., trans. Edward R. Reilly (New York: Schirmer Books, 1985), 288–89.

turn to varieties of character and tempo in music.[7] Leopold Mozart, in his *Versuch einer gründlichen Violinschule* of 1756, seems to echo both Mattheson and Quantz in his discussion of systole and diastole, thesis and arsis, and the effect of the character of the performer on his sense of tempo.[8] But whereas the human pulse is one of the most ancient standards for musical time measure, Marin Mersenne referred as early as 1636–37 to a fixed, abstract unit from the astronomical frame of reference, the length of a second, as he reflected on the limits of performers:

> . . . [I]t is necessary to establish a definite and determined time for the measure, if one wishes to know how many sounds can be made, that is, how many notes one can sing in the time of a measure. And because the astronomers have divided each *minute* of time into sixty parts, and each sixtieth part of a minute, which they call a *second,* is equal to one ordinary pulse beat, as I have already said, I now assume that a measure lasts one second, and say that there is no hand so quick that it can play more than 16 times one or more strings, nor any voice which can sing more than sixteen notes, or double crotchets, in a second's time, and consequently that those who use thirty-two notes to the measure employ two seconds for the measure, and that those who make 64 use a measure of four seconds or four pulse beats.[9]

[8]Leopold Mozart, *Versuch einer gründlichen Violinschule* (Augsburg, 1787), 27 and 32; translation from *A Treatise on the Fundamental Principles of Violin Playing* (based on the first and third editions of *Versuch einer gründlichen Violinschule* [Augsburg, 1756 and 1787, respectively]), trans. Editha Knocker, 2d ed. (London: Oxford University Press, 1951), 31 and 34–35.

[9]"Il est necessaire d'establir vn temps certain & determiné pour la mesure, si l'on veut sçauoir combien l'on peut faire desons, c'est à dire combien l'on peut chanter de notes dans le temps d'vne mesure: & parce que les Astronomes ont diuisé chaque *minute* de temps en 60 parties, & que chaque 60 partie de minute, qu'ils nomment *seconde,* est esgale à vn battement ordinaire du poux, comme i'ay desia dit ailleurs, ie suppose maintenant qu'vne mesure dure vne seconde minute, & dis qu'il n'y a point de main si viste qui puisse toucher plus de 16 fois vne mesme chorde, ou plusieurs, ny voix qui puisse chanter plus de 16 notes ou doubles crochuës dans le temps d'vne seconde minute, & consequemment que ceux qui font 32 notes à la mesure employent 2 secondes dans la mesure, & que ceux qui en font 64 font la mesure de 4 secondes ou de 4 battemens de poux" (F. Marin Mersenne, *Harmonie universelle, contenant la théorie et la pratique de la musique* [Paris, 1636; facsimile, Paris: Éditions du Centre national de la recherche scientifique, 1975], 138; translation from F. Marin Mersenne, *Harmonie*

Mersenne's association of the second with a pulse beat was not unusual. Even eighteenth-century theorists who recommended mechanical devices precisely *because* they were unaffected by physique and temperament, retained a vocabulary rich in pulse imagery.[10] In his *Klavierschule* of 1789, Türk followed a qualified recommendation of Quantz's rule for use of the pulse (against which "many objections can be raised") with the suggestion that a pocket watch be used as a basis for determining tempo.[11] Nevertheless in Türk's view the dissimilarity of thesis and arsis remained essential to musical time:

> When in a succession of several tones of outwardly equal duration, one gives more emphasis to some of these than to others in a steadily maintained order (uniformity), then there arises through these accents the feeling we call meter. . . .
>
> Each meter has *good and bad beats* . . . , that is, although, for example, all crotchets are alike in terms of their outer value or their duration, . . . yet one receives more emphasis (internal value) than is given to the other. For everyone feels that in *a,* of two, and in *b,* of three crotchets, the first [crotchet] is more important than the second, etc.

> For this reason, the good beats are also called *internally long, struck* or *accented,* etc. In beating time, they occur at the time of the beat (*thesis*).
>
> The bad beats one also calls *internally short, passing, unaccented,* etc. They are performed during the lifting of the hand, which in technical language is called *arsis.*[12]

universelle: The Books on Instruments, trans. Roger E. Chapman [The Hague: M. Nijhoff, 1957], 190–91).

[10]For a brief account of theorists who suggested the use of machines for measuring musical time, see *New Harvard Dictionary of Music,* s.v. "metronome."

[11]Daniel Gottlob Türk, *School of Clavier Playing or Instruction in Playing the Clavier for Teachers and Students,* translated by Raymond H. Haggh (Lincoln: University of Nebraska Press, 1982), 108 (111–12 in original).

[12]"Wenn man, bey einer Folge mehrerer äußerlich gleich langen Töne, einigen derselben, in einer gewissen anhaltenden Ordnung, (Einförmigkeit,) mehr

Türk makes it clear that in a metric context, notes of outwardly equal value are not alike. And although it may at first seem that he might be speaking only about emphasis and not duration, his further comments suggest that he is aware of durational difference brought about by the privilege of metric placement. This need not be associated with the practice of *notes inégales,* an expression best saved for describing a particular convention in the performance of French music.[13] Rather, his explanation indicates a sensitivity to much more universal principles of musical time—principles that were often associated with poetry and dance, as is evident when he continues by describing the beats within a triple meter, in which "the first one is, strictly speaking, the good beat, however, now and then the third also gets an emphasis, just as in a few cases the second is internally long and therefore the third becomes short"—a virtual catalog of the varieties of agogic accentuation common among the triple-time dance meters.[14] Not surprisingly, when Türk later defines agogic accent, he includes

---

Nachdruck giebt, als der andern: so entsteht schon durch diese Accente das Gefühl, welches wir *Takt* nennen. . . .

"Jede Taktart hat *gute und schlechte Takttheile* . . . , das heißt, obgleich z. B. alle Viertel, ihrem äußern Werthe oder ihrer Dauer nach, einander gleich sind, . . . so liegt doch auf Einem mehr Nachdruck, (innerer Werth,) als auf dem Andern. Denn Jeder fühlt das bey *a)* von zwey, und bey *b)* von drey Vierteln jedesmal das erste wichtiger ist, als das zweyte, &c.

"Aus diesem Grunde werden auch die guten Takttheile *innerlich lange, anschlagende, accentuirte,* &c. gennant. Beym Taktschlagen fallen sie in die Zeit des Niederschlagens. (*thesis.*)

"Die schlechten Takttheile nennt man sonst auch *innerlich kurze, durchgehende, unaccentuirte* u. s. w. Sie werden im Aufheben der Hand, vorgetragen, welches in der Kunstsprache *arsis* heißt" (Türk, *Klavierschule* [Leipzig and Halle, 1789], 88, 91–92). Unlike Mattheson, Türk is observing "beat" within a metric context. While he is clearly referring here to conducting (*beym Taktschlagen*), the "striking" he associates with thesis, and the "lifting of the hand" he ascribes to arsis suggest chironomic techniques used by keyboard players as well.

[13]I make this distinction in response to Raymond Haggh, who argues that Türk is using the expressions *innerlich lange* and *innerlich kurze* to describe "emphasis rather than duration," since "throughout the *Klavierschule* there is a stress on exactitude that occasionally verges on the pedantic, and the text and examples give no reason to believe that the practice of *notes inegales* [*sic*] is implied here" (*School of Clavier Playing*, 446n.101).

[14]"In den dreytheiligen Taktarten ist eigentlich nur der erste Takttheil gut; indeß erhält auch dann und wann der dritte einen Nachdruck, so wie in einigen Fällen der zweyte innerlich lang, und dafür der dritte kurz wird" (Türk, *Klavierschule,* 92).

among tones that are subject to such emphasis those "that fall on a good beat."[15] By his own admission he found the very idea of a time measure based on unity to be repugnant:

> If indeed this generally accepted theory is correct, then all meters must consist of several beats. . . . However, let us now inquire whether beats consisting of equally long internal values which do not allow themselves, even in thought, to be divided into smaller parts, could arouse in us the feeling which we call meter? Or, if that were possible, whether such a meter would have any appeal for us? I am very much inclined to answer this question with "no." In poetry, no one has yet introduced as desirable a meter which consists of nothing but one-syllable feet.[16]

The Introduction of the Metronome

When Johann Nepomuk Mälzel copied, modified, and popularized a machine invented around 1812 by Dietrich Nikolaus Winkel of Amsterdam, musicians who hankered after "accuracy" were at last granted their wish: composers, performers, and teachers rallied to underwrite a device that produced paired mechanical beats visibly, audibly, and incessantly, in close proximity to the musician.[17] Prior to Mälzel's success, at least a dozen other eighteenth-century inventors tried to market chronometers (as they were then called) designed for musicians, but although some of their machines worked quite

---

[15]Ibid., 335, 337, and 338.

[16]"Wenn anders diese allgemein angenommene Theorie richtig ist, so müssen alle Taktarten aus mehreren Zeiten bestehen. . . . Uebrigens wäre nun zu untersuchen, ob Zeiten von gleich langern innern Werthe, die sich nicht einmal in Gedanken in kleinere (Zeiten) abtheilen ließen, das Gefühl, welches wir Takt nennen, in uns erregen könnten? oder wenn das möglich wäre, ob eine solche Taktart Reiz für uns haben würde? Ich bin sehr geneigt diese Fragen mit nein zu beantworten. In der Poesie hat man noch kein Metrum von lauter einsilbigen Füßen einzuführen für gut befunden" (Türk, *Klavierschule*, 91; translation adapted from Haggh, *School of Clavier Playing*, 445–46n.99).

[17]*New Harvard Dictionary of Music*, s.v. "metronome."

well, none was marketed as well as Mälzel's metronome.[18] Like most of his rivals, Mälzel promoted his device as a tool for communicating correct beginning tempi, stressing that mechanical rigidity had little to do with musical tempo; but somehow he could not resist voicing the popular notion that paralysis of expressive tendencies was acceptable for beginners: "We do not contend that an accomplished musician should perform an entire piece according to the metronome; for all expression would be paralyzed by such enslavement. But for the beginner it is otherwise: the metronome should be his most reliable guide in gaining a true feeling for the time [of a piece]."[19] Students, of course, were a favorite target for sales. In the fourth volume of his *Vollständige theoretisch-practische Pianoforte-Schule,* Op. 500 of 1846, Carl Czerny wrote: "We presuppose that each *pianist* possesses the indispensable *Mälz[e]l metronome* (of the better, loud-beating sort), and uses it according to our instructions in the 3rd volume of this school."[20] In the third volume, he describes the proper use of the new device: "When, for example, the indication M.M. ♩ = 112 is found, . . . one plays each *crotchet* exactly with the audible beats of the metronome."[21]

Before the metronome, the durations marked off by machines were used as a starting point, and were usually associated with the shapes of traditional units of measure: heartbeats, paired syllables, or steps in

[18]See Rosamund Evelyn Mary Harding, "The Metronome and Its Precursors," in *Origins of Musical Time and Expression* (London: Oxford University Press, 1938), 1–35.

[19]This is an excerpt from a pamphlet published by Mälzel, "Information on the Metronome by J. Mälzel / May 1818," trans. Fritz Rothschild (who lists it as a holding of the library of the Gesellschaft der Musikfreunde in Vienna) in *Musical Performance in the Times of Mozart and Beethoven: The Lost Tradition in Music, Part 2* (New York: Oxford University Press, 1961), 103.

[20]"Da wir voraussetzen, dass jeder *Pianist* den unentbehrlichen *Mälzl-schen* Metronom, (von der bessern, lautschlagenden Art,) besitzt, und nach uns'rer Angabe im 3ten Theil dieser Schule benutzt . . . " (Carl Czerny, *Über den richtigen Vortrag der sämtlichen Beethoven'schen Klavierwerke* [Vienna: Diabelli, 1846; facsimile, ed. Paul Badura-Skoda, Vienna: Universal, 1963], 27). Page numbers cited here always refer to those of the Universal edition (bottom center of each page) rather than to the original numbers.

[21]"Wenn daher zum Beispiel die Vorzeichnung vorkommt: M.M. ♩ = 112, so . . . spielt [man] jede *Viertelnote* genau nach den hörbaren Schlägen des *Metronoms*" (Carl Czerny, *Vollständige theoretisch-practische Pianoforte-Schule,* Op. 500 [Vienna: Diabelli, 1839], vol. 3, 49).

a dance, as Mersenne and Türk had suggested. One sensed for a moment the ticking and tocking of a watch as one had formerly sensed the systole and diastole of one's pulse, in an effort to relate one's sense of tempo to a standard. But after the metronome had appeared, a profoundly different practice arose: many musicians began to equate metrics and even rhythm with the ticking of the machine.

The canonization of the metronome represented a giant step toward what might be called the "equalization" of time measure in music, for while the machine's pendulum (and to some degree even its sound) allowed the image of thesis and arsis to linger, the image itself was undermined by its manner of application: the performer of music in a triple meter, for example, played to paired beats. Thus not only did subtle differentiations between the parts of the beat begin to be overlooked but the characteristic shapes of the various meters began to be homogenized. Gradually the marks on the metronome's scale gained a more independent life, until at length designations like "M.M. ♩ = 112" seemed more compelling to some musicians than the envelopes suggested by paired syllables, the pulse, or changes in the character of a discourse. The machine fostered in effect precisely what Türk had found so offensive: "a meter which consists of nothing but one-syllable feet." As we shall see, musicians enlightened by this mechanical metaphor began to refer to the new device in deferential and sometimes almost reverential terms: only the greatest artists could approach in performance the unsurpassable "accuracy" of the metronome. There was resistance, of course, and some of it from the greatest nineteenth-century composers and performers; but especially among pedagogues the machine continued to be highly valued, and the effect of their support was to a high degree pervasive.

In determining Beethoven's part in all this, we must again ask whether he was troubled by "temporal dissonance" when music was made to conform to mechanically measured time. This was a question over which some of his followers disputed bitterly. Czerny used the metronome habitually and, as we have seen, recommended it as a practice tool for all students of Beethoven, but Anton Schindler insisted he was terribly mistaken in so doing. Although it may be easy to dismiss Czerny as one who was at heart a pedant, we must remember that he was not alone in his allegiance to the machine. But neither was Schindler alone in objecting to its use as a device with which to play. As we search for evidence that clarifies Beethoven's relationship to the older standards of measurement by pulse, step, speech rhythm, and poetic meter, we must try to determine whether Czerny's use of the metronome revealed an aesthetic at odds with Beethoven's, as Schindler claimed, or in harmony with it, as Czerny believed.

2 *Character: The Spirit*

Music's Character as Mattheson Taught It

An eighteenth-century teacher of oratory usually began by offering instruction in grammar as a foundation for the study of rhetoric. But Johann Mattheson, who taught musical orators, wanted first of all to show that music and rhetoric were deeply related. He began by instructing his students in a soundless art, that of gesticulation:

> *Cassiodorus* writes on this thus: Our ancestors called the art of gesticulation silent music, because with the mouth closed, the hands and certain gestures alone say things which can hardly be uttered as clearly with the tongue or the written word.
>
> Now though *pantomimes,* people who presented everything merely through gestures without singing or speaking, are no longer common; still one can . . . see that the art of gesticulation indeed pertains to music, and constitutes today, as it did in ancient times, an essential part of it: though now it is coupled with song and playing.[1]

[1]"*Cassiodorus* schreibet hievon also: Unsre Vorfahren haben die Geberden-Kunst mit dem Nahmen der stummen Music beleget, weil man bey geschlossenem Munde nur die Hände und gewisse Leibes-Stellungen solche Dinge für sich reden läßt, die kaum mit der Zunge, oder mit geschriebenen Worten so deutlich gegeben werden mögten.

"Ob nun gleich die *Pantomimen,* welches Leute waren, die alles durch blosse

The musician in Mattheson's day plied an art of evocative gesture, an art served by the science of chironomy, which was in essence a science of rhythm. Mattheson believed chironomy had "greater force than all words":

> It is, so to speak, a derivative branch or subpart of rhythm or mensuration from which three other things evolve, namely the oratorical, which directs the movement of the body; the histrionic, which belongs to plays and requires much stronger gesturing than the first; and the saltatorial, which deals with all kinds of steps and leaps.[2]

Through chironomy the hands of the keyboard player attained musical "speech," the coherence of which depended in part, just as in speech, on the correct articulation of properly formed syntactic units. For this reason Mattheson chose as the analogical basis for his "musical grammar" the structure of language:

> Every idea, be it verbal or written, consists then in certain *word-phrases,* or periods; but every such phrase also consists in smaller caesuras up to the close with a period. A whole *structure* or paragraph is developed from such phrases, and from various of these paragraphs a main part of a chapter is finally developed. That very

---

Geberden, ohne Singen oder Reden, vorstelleten, nicht mehr gebräuchlich sind; so siehet man doch hieraus, daß die Stellungs-Kunst allerdings mit zur Music gehöret, und sowol noch heutiges Tages, als vor Alters, ein Haupt-Stück derselben ausgemacht hat und noch ist: unangesehen man sie bey uns mit Gesang und Klang ausübet und vergesellschafftet" (Johann Mattheson, *Der vollkommene Capellmeister* [Hamburg: Christian Herold, 1739; facsimile, Kassel: Bärenreiter-Verlag, 1954], 33; translation adapted from Ernest C. Harriss, *Johann Mattheson's "Der vollkommene Capellmeister": A Revised Translation with Critical Commentary* [Ann Arbor, Mich.: UMI Research Press, 1981], 132).

[2]"Sie sey, so zu reden, ein abgeleiteter Zweig und Gesencke von der Rhythmic oder abgemessenen Bewegungs-Kunst, woraus drey andre entspringen, nehmlich die rednerische Sprosse, welche die Leibes-Wendungen anweiset; die histrionische, welche zu den Schauspielen gehöret, und weit stärckere Geberden erfordert als jene; und die Tanz-mäßige, welche von allerhand Schritten und Sprüngen handelt" (Mattheson, *Capellmeister,* 34; translation from Harriss, *Johann Mattheson's "Der vollkommene Capellmeister,"* 132, 133).

briefly is the stepwise outline or *climax* of all that which can really be spoken, written, sung, or played.[3]

This was certainly not a new idea, but Mattheson's whole approach to musical rhetoric is at once more playful and more detailed than those found, for example, in the keyboard methods of Michel de Saint-Lambert or Marpurg, partly because he borrows liberally from many earlier writers on the subject.[4] Especially important to him is the theory of the *diastolica* (from the Greek *diastole*, dilatation, separation), which explains how speech is made intelligible by the modulating influence of punctuation.[5] In his chapter entitled *Von den Ab- und Einschnitten der Klang-Rede* (which might be loosely translated "On the Sections and Caesuras of Tone-Speech") he introduces the *diastolica* as a tool for shaping melody:

> This theory on incisions, which one also calls *distinctiones, interpunctationes, posituras,* etc., is the most essential in the whole art of composing melody . . . ; however, it is so neglected that hitherto only the smallest rule has been given thereupon or the slightest instruction: indeed, one does not even find it in the most recent musical dictionaries.[6]

[3]"Ieder Antrag, er geschehe mündlich oder schrifftlich, bestehet demnach in gewissen *Wort-Sätzen,* oder Periodis; ein ieder solcher Satz aber wiederum in kleinern Einschnitten, bis an den Abschnitt eines Puncts. Aus sothanen Sätzen erwächst ein gantzer *Zusammensatz* oder Paragraphus, und aus verschiedenen solchen Absätzen wird endlich ein Haupt-Stück oder Capitel. Das ist aufs kürtzeste der stuffenmässige Entwurff oder *Climax* alles dessen, so ordentlich geredet, geschrieben, gesungen oder gespielet werden mag" (Mattheson, *Capellmeister,* 181; translation from Harriss, *Johann Mattheson's "Der vollkommene Capellmeister,"* 381).

[4]Mattheson describes some of his research in Harriss, *Johann Mattheson's "Der vollkommene Capellmeister,"* 492n.99.

[5]In modern usage, the word *diastole,* from Greek and Latin prosody, indicates the lengthening of a normally short syllable. See the Appendix for a chronological selection of excerpts on the *diastolica* from eighteenth-century treatises (including Saint-Lambert and Marpurg).

[6]"Diese Lehre von den Incisionen, welche man auch *distinctiones, interpunctationes, posituras* u. s. w. nennet, ist die allernothwendigste in der gantzen melodischen Setz-Kunst . . . ; wird aber doch so sehr hintangesetzet, daß kein Mensch bishero die geringste Regel, oder nur einigen Unterricht davon gegeben hätte: ja man findet nicht einmahl ihren Nahmen in den neuesten musicalischen Wörterbüchern" (Mattheson, *Capellmeister,* 180–81; translation from Harriss, *Johann Mattheson's "Der vollkommene Capellmeister,"* 380).

Then he begins his study of melody—in this case, an aria—by considering first the paragraph (the aria as a whole) and then the sentences that make it up (its musical periods), so that he can immediately link the largest units with formal harmonic closes, the largest antecedent-consequent pairings:

> The concept of a period obliges me not to make a *formal* close in the melody before the sentence is finished. But the concept of a paragraph prohibits me from using a *full* cadence anywhere except at the end. Both cadences are *formal:* but the first is not *full.*[7]

Having dealt with the large units, he next describes the effect of punctuation marks within the sentence:

> *Lipsius* describes their force thus: *Comma sustinet,* the *Comma* makes a little pause; *Colon suspendit,* the *Colon* delays longer; *Periodus deponit,* brings the sentence to rest. In short, the *Comma* is a little part of the sentence through which the discourse obtains a little caesura, though there is not a rhetorical but only a grammatical and imperfect meaning: for very often a single word requires its own comma.[8]

Because ordinary punctuation—the comma, semicolon, colon, and period—serves only some of music's expressive ends, Mattheson next describes the force of the more extraordinary marks—the question mark, the exclamation point, and the parenthesis—and their realization in musical terms. The question in musical speech can occur with or without a "raising of the voice"; doubt is its essential ingre-

---

[7]"Die Erkenntniß eines Periodi verbindet mich, ehender keinen *förmlichen* Schluß in der Melodie zu machen, als bis der Satz aus ist. Die Erkenntniß aber eines Paragraphi verbietet mir irgend sonstwo, als am Ende desselben, einen *gäntzlichen* Schluß anzubringen. Beide Schlüsse sind *förmlich;* der erste aber ist nicht *gäntzlich*" (Mattheson, *Capellmeister,* 182; translation from Harriss, *Johann Mattheson's "Der volkommene Capellmeister,"* 383).

[8]"*Lipsius* drückt ihre Krafft so aus: *Comma sustinet,* das *Comma* macht einen kleinen Einhalt; *Colon suspendit,* das *Colon* schiebet länger auf; *Periodus deponit,* der Satz bringt zur Ruhe. Kurtz, das *Comma* ist ein Stücklein des Satzes, dadurch die Rede einen kleinen Einschnitt bekömmt; ob gleich noch in den Worten kein rhetorischer, sondern nur ein grammatischer und unvollkommener Verstand ist: denn es erfordert sehr offt ein eintzelnes Wort sein eignes Comma" (Mattheson, *Capellmeister,* 184; translation from Harriss, *Johann Mattheson's "Der volkommene Capellmeister,"* 384).

dient, and melodically this can be expressed especially well through imperfect consonance. The exclamation depends on "melodic vehemence," often attained through strikingly rapid gestures and extraordinary intervals. The parenthesis is the kind of interpolation that can be achieved, for example, by breaking off the sound of a whole choir for an aside by a single voice.[9]

Although much of his discussion of punctuation concerns text setting, Mattheson applied diastolic theory to purely instrumental music with an ease that bespoke a highly developed Baroque sense for "transfer of idiom": the "word-phrase" applied to "all that which can really be spoken, written, sung, *or played*" (italics mine).[10] Instrumental music, then—Mattheson's *"speech in tones* or *oratory in sound"*— required that the composer "know how without the words to express sincerely all the emotions of the heart through selected sounds and their skillful combination in such a way that the auditor might fully grasp and clearly understand therefrom, as if it were actual speech, the impetus, the sense, the meaning, and the expression, as well as all the pertaining divisions and caesuras. It is then a joy! Much more art and a better imagination is required if one wants to achieve this without, rather than with words."[11] Though he cites the eighteenth-century principle that "all that is played is merely an imitation of

---

[9]Mattheson, *Capellmeister,* 183 and 192–95 (383 and 398–404 in Harriss). Later in the century Friedrich Wilhelm Marpurg described both ordinary and extraordinary punctuation in his *Kritische Briefe über die Tonkunst* (Berlin: Birnstiel, 1764; facsimile, Hildesheim: Georg Olms, 1974), vol. 2, 309–10. See also Johann Philipp Kirnberger, *The Art of Strict Musical Composition,* trans. David Beach and Jurgen Thym (New Haven: Yale University Press, 1982), 416–17 (vol. 2, 152–53 in original), where Kirnberger, at the close of a discussion characterizing effective melodic invention as "an intelligible statement from the language of sentiments" suggests that young composers setting texts "carefully read" Mattheson's *"Von den Ab- und Einschnitten der Klang-Rede,"* from which my observations on punctuation here are drawn.

[10]My thanks to Neal Zaslaw for this observation.

[11]". . . [W]ahrhafftig alle Neigungen des Hertzens, durch blosse ausgesuchte Klänge und deren geschickte Zusammenfügung, ohne Worte dergestalt auszudrucken wissen, daß der Zuhörer daraus, als ob es eine wirckliche Rede wäre, den Trieb, den Sinn, die Meinung und den Nachdruck, mit allen dazu gehörigen Ein- und Abschnitten, völlig begreiffen und deutlich verstehen möge. Alsdenn ist es eine Lust! dazu gehöret viel mehr Kunst und eine stärckere Einbildungs-Krafft, wenns einer ohne Worte, als mit derselben Hülffe, zu Wege bringen soll" (Mattheson, *Capellmeister,* 208; translation from Harriss, *Johann Mattheson's "Der volkommene Capellmeister,"* 425).

singing," Mattheson is not proposing a theory of imitation: for him music's communication is immediate; it can move the listener directly because of the "'isomorphic relationship' between the inner nature of the emotions and music."[12] He points out with relish the special qualities and powers of instrumental music and energetically defends them: instrumental melody has "more fire and freedom," it can be more "impetuous," it can perform "many-tailed notes, . . . arpeggios, . . . broken chords . . . counterpoints, fugues, canons, . . ." and in all this it can speak clearly to the heart.[13] Mattheson seemed to believe his conviction was shared: "Harmony can *express, personify,* and *articulate* everything, even without the help of words. [Jean Baptiste Louis Gresset,] *Discours sur l'Harmonie,* p. 76, Paris, 1737. From this one sees that the intelligent French are also of my opinion in this respect: as if we had agreed on it."[14]

But he may have retracted his remark on the "intelligent French" had he been able to foresee the influence of the Enlightened Rationalists. For between the publication of his *Capellmeister* in 1739 and the writings of the *Frühromantiker* of the 1790s, German aesthetics faced a veritable invasion of French writings, many of which appeared to strike at the very heart of the theory of musical rhetoric. For the French, music's primary value lay in its ability to "paint," "imitate," and "express" the natural; hence it was regarded as occupying a lesser position than that enjoyed by poetry or painting, which were seen as "the most natural imitations of nature."[15] That music needed to be "dominated" by declamatory principles was a sign of its weakness as a means of imitation. Yet if music were to have any power at all, it was to remain close to declamation. Instrumental music was judged by its

[12]The term is Bellamy Hosler's; see her *Changing Aesthetic Views of Instrumental Music in 18th-Century Germany* (Ann Arbor, Mich.: UMI Research Press, 1981), 217.

[13]Ibid., 217 and Harriss, *Johann Mattheson's "Der volkommene Capellmeister,"* 420, 422, 423.

[14]"L'Harmonie sçait *exprimer, personnifier, articuler* tout, & même sans le secours des paroles. *Discours sur l'Harmonie, p. 76. à Paris, 1737.* Woraus man siehet, daß auch die klugen Franzosen hierin meinen Gedancken beipflichten: als wenn wirs abgeredet hätten" (Mattheson, *Capellmeister,* 208; translation from Harriss, *Johann Mattheson's "Der volkommene Capellmeister,"* 492).

[15]Maria Rika Maniates, "'Sonate, que me veux-tu?': The Enigma of French Musical Aesthetics in the Eighteenth Century," *Current Musicology* 9 (1969): 121, 123.

distance from declamation of a text, and genres that seemed more abstract came to be held in especially low esteem. Blainville labeled these *harmonico* and *sonabile* (referring in particular to the music of Locatelli and Vivaldi), and in contrast to his *genre cantabile* they were "meaningless."[16] Not long after the publication of *Capellmeister,* claims as bold as Mattheson's for the power of instrumental music had vanished from German criticism.[17]

Emanuel Bach and the Limits of the Word-Tone Relationship

By midcentury there were a number of German apologists for French views, and among those who supported strict adherence to a narrow interpretation of the theory of imitation was Johann Christoph Gottsched, whose statements on the matter could be particularly acerbic:

> We hear that music without a text or dance is a dead thing, is only a body without a soul. Why? One can understand or guess only halfway at the most what is being played, if neither gestures nor words are joined which explain more distinctly what the tones are supposed to be saying. . . . Music by itself is soulless and unintelligible when it doesn't cling to words, which must speak for it, so that one know what it means.[18]

---

[16]Ibid., 124. I stress those expressions of French opinion that were most likely to trouble Germans such as Mattheson. Maniates gives a well-balanced view of the scope of the debate that raged over the issue in France; it was far from one-sided.

[17]Hosler, *Changing Views,* 85.

[18]"Wir hören, dass eine Musik, ohne Text, oder Tanz, nur ein todtes Ding, nur ein Körper, ohne Geist ist. Warum? Man versteht oder erräth es vielmehr nur halb, was gespielet wird; wenn nicht entweder Gebärden, oder Worte dazu kommen, die das deutlicher erklären, was die Töne sagen sollen. . . . Die Musik allein aber ist unbeseelet und unverständlich, wenn sie nicht an Worte hält, die gleichsam für sie reden müssen, damit man wisse, was sie haben will" (Johann Christoph Gottsched, *Auszug aus des Herrn Batteux schönen Künsten aus dem einzigen Grundsatze der Nachahmung hergeleitet. Zum Gebrauch seiner Vorlesungen mit verschiedenen Zusätzen und Anmerkungen erläutert* [Leipzig, 1754], 202, 207; translation from Hosler, *Changing Views,* 116–17).

What had seemed perfectly clear to Mattheson seemed preposterous to Gottsched. How could tones *comprise* gestures when they themselves stood in need of clarification, in need of some pairing with words or physical gestures that would make their "meaning" clear? By this time matters had reached an impasse among the Enlightened *Kenner und Liebhaber* of Germany. Faced with the conflict between French instrumental culture with its emphasis on the primacy of imitation in art, and their own growing fondness for "meaningless" German and Italian instrumental works (so thoroughly despised by the French), they refused to budge: "Despite the obvious and seemingly irreconcilable clash of mimetic theory and nonrepresentative instrumental music, German music-lovers were willing neither to abandon the principle that human emotions were the proper content of music nor to constrict the spirit of the specifically musical for the sake of principle."[19]

Few personified the split so clearly as Frederick the Great. Although he was one of the century's most avid Francophiles, when it came to music his taste was incontrovertibly German and Italian.[20] His court may well have been the scene of Emanuel Bach's experiment in musical questions, answers, and exclamations: his programmatic *Sanguineus und Melancholicus* Trio Sonata in C minor (Wq. 161, no. 1), written in 1749 and published in 1751. The work, in Bach's words,

> tries as it were to represent a conversation between two persons, one sanguine and the other melancholic, who in the very first movement almost through to the end of the second movement, argue with each other, each trying to persuade the other to his point of view, until they become reconciled at the end of the second movement, when Melancholicus finally concedes and accepts the hypothesis of the other. . . . In the final movement they are and remain in complete agreement.[21]

[19]Hosler, *Changing Views*, 32. See also E. Eugene Helm's *Music at the Court of Frederick the Great* (Norman: University of Oklahoma Press, 1960), 73–74.
[20]Hosler, *Changing Views*, 32.
[21]"Es soll gleichsam ein Gespräch zwischen einem Sanguineus und Melancholicus vorstellen, welche in dem ganzen ersten, und bis nahe ans Ende des zweyten Satzes,

The idea of "instrumental discourse" was very popular at this time in France, and chamber works frequently appeared under titles like "conversation."[22] In the preface to his work Bach provides—only for those "who have inadequate insight into the musical expressions"[23]— a commentary on the first two movements in which over forty "important points" in the "conversation" are explained.[24] Each point is assigned a letter corresponding to a letter in the score itself.

Perhaps the piece seemed to Bach a natural outgrowth of Mattheson's "art of gesticulation," that "silent music" in which "certain gestures alone say things which can hardly be uttered as clearly with the tongue or the written word."[25] Yet it proved highly controversial, and Bach seems to have foreseen that it would: in the preface he asks "in anticipation, that one should desist from mockery."[26] Why the fear of mockery? Maybe because he already suspected that music's referents—if that is what they are—do not point back into the world of language in quite this way. His own account of the "conversation" reads like a description of an exchange heard through a wall, a record based more on tone of voice than on content:

(a) means, because of the half-cadence on the dominant, a question: whether the cheerful man agrees with the melancholy man at this point. That one [the cheerful man], however, at (b), lets it be known clearly enough—through the difference in tempo as well as in the entire content of his answer, and even by beginning in a totally

---

mit einander streiten, und sich bemühen, einer den andern auf seine Seite zu ziehen; bis sie sich am Ende des zweiten Satzes vergleichen, indem der Melancholicus endlich nachgiebt, und des andern seinen Hauptsatz annimmt. Im lezten Satze sind, und bleiben sie auch vollkommen einig" (Carl Philipp Emanuel Bach, *Sonata c-moll: "Sanguineus und Melancholicus"* [Wq. 161, no. 1], for two violins and continuo, ed. Klaus Hofmann, Stuttgarter Bach-Ausgaben, series E: Carl Philipp Emanuel Bach, Ausgewählte Werke, 4. Gruppe: Kammermusik, trans. Derek McCulloch [Neuhausen-Stuttgart: Hänssler-Verlag (1980)], 2, 4).

[22]Maniates, "The Enigma of French Musical Aesthetics," 130.

[23]"[W]elche noch nicht genugsame Einsicht in die musikalischen Ausdrücke besitzen . . . " (Emanuel Bach, *Sonata c-moll*, 2).

[24]Ibid., 2, 4. Bach's terms are *"Hauptstellen"* and *"Gespräch."*

[25]Harriss, *Johann Mattheson's "Der volkommene Capellmeister,"* 132 (33 in original).

[26]"Man verbittet zum Voraus, alle Spöttereyen . . . " (Emanuel Bach, *Sonata c-moll*, 6, 4).

different key [E-flat major instead of the melancholy man's C minor]—that he is of a quite different mind.[27]

Charles Burney was one critic who could not under the circumstances resist mockery; he roundly criticized Bach for his experiment: "That truly great musician, Emanuel Bach, some years ago, attempted, in a duet [i.e., for two violins and continuo], to carry on a disputation between two persons of different principles; but with all his powers of invention, melody, and modulation, the opinions of the disputants remained as obscure and unintelligible, as the warbling of larks and linnets."[28]

Burney's complaint was really part of an attack on another programmatic work, Geminiani's *The Enchanted Forest:* "Music has never had the power, without vocal articulation, to narrate, or instruct; it can excite, paint, and soothe our passions; but it is utterly incapable of reasoning, or conversing, to any reasonable purpose."[29] Was the experiment Bach's idea? His musical language for clavichord or fortepiano was certainly conducive to mimetic gesture: the so-called ordinary touch of his day was syllabic, short slurs predominated, and melodies were often shaped to sound like passionate speech.[30] But given that Frederick's court was a place where the German struggle with French rationalism could be felt so acutely, one wonders whether Bach may have been assigned the task by Frederick himself.[31]

[27]"(a) Bedeutet, wegen des halben Schlusses in die Quinte, eine Frage, ob der Sanguineus mit dem Melancholicus hierinne einig sey. Jener aber giebt (b) Durch die Verschiedenheit des Zeitmasses sowohl, als durch den ganzen Inhalt der Antwort, und noch über dem, durch den Anfang in einem ganz andern Ton, deutlich gnug zu erkennen, daß er ganz anderes Sinnes sey" (Ibid., 8; translation from Eugene Helm, "The 'Hamlet' Fantasy and the Literary Element in C.P.E. Bach's Music," *Musical Quarterly* 58 [1972]: 292).

[28]Helm, "'Hamlet' Fantasy," 292. The Burney quotation is from his *A General History of Music* (originally in 4 vols., London, 1776, 1782, 1789, and 1789), 4 vols. in 2, ed. Frank Mercer (New York: Harcourt, Brace, 1935; reprint, New York: Dover, 1957), vol. 2, 992 (vol. 4, 643 in original).

[29]Helm, "'Hamlet' Fantasy," 293.

[30]Idem, "Carl Philipp Emanuel Bach," *New Grove Dictionary of Music and Musicians* 1.851.

[31]The possibility is mentioned by William S. Newman, *The Sonata in the Classic Era,* 2d ed. (New York: W. W. Norton, 1972), 422.

Perhaps this trio was one of the works composed to fulfill the "ridiculous instructions" Bach complained of in his autobiography: "Because I have had to compose most of my works for specific individuals and for the public, I have always been more restrained in them than in the few pieces that I have written merely for myself. At times I even have had to follow ridiculous instructions, although it could be that such not exactly pleasant conditions have led my talents to certain discoveries that I might not otherwise have come upon."[32]

We do know that Bach had doubts about the piece years later, as did his brother Johann Christoph Friedrich (1732–95).[33] In fact it was Friedrich who expressed perhaps the most important point about the work in a reply to the poet and playwright Heinrich Wilhelm von Gerstenberg, who had engaged in a lively exchange with both Bachs on the subject of the limits of the word-tone relationship. Friedrich noted that any programmatic work such as his brother's trio "would actually go no further than [any] characteristic fantasy." And although he was willing to admit that "the clavier can intelligibly convey general character and general passions, in a certain way," he summarized the effect of the trio much as Burney had: "In spite of the great deal of trouble he took with it, one would not feel the meaning of each movement if he had not carefully indicated his intention in words."[34] Significantly, Friedrich likens the trio to the characteristic fantasies: neither the trio nor the fantasies have the power to narrate a verbal text.

Emanuel Bach knew when to stop testing; in his reply to Gerstenberg he insisted that "words remain always words, and the human voice remains pre-eminent."[35] But was this, for Bach, an admission

[32]"Weil ich meine meisten Arbeiten für gewisse Personen und fürs Publikum habe machen müssen, so bin ich dadurch allezeit mehr gebunden gewesen, als bey den wenigen Stücken, welche ich bloß für mich verfertigt habe. Ich habe sogar bisweilen lächerlichen Vorschriften folgen müssen; indessen kann es seyn, daß dergleichen nicht eben angenehme Umstände mein Genie zu gewissen Erfindungen aufgefordert haben, worauf ich vielleicht ausserdem nicht würde gefallen seyn" (Charles Burney, *Tagebuch einer musikalischen Reise durch . . . Hamburg . . . 1772/1773;* facsimile, ed. Richard Schaal [New York: Bärenreiter, 1959], vol. 3, 208; translation from Newman, *Classic Era,* 422).

[33]Newman, *Classic Era,* 422–23.

[34]Helm, "'Hamlet' Fantasy," 291n.20.

[35]Ibid., 291.

of defeat that implied a disdain for the rhetoric of the hands? Did he abandon the declamatory style as merely illusory? By no means, as his later compositions attest. Like Mattheson he trusted in music's affective power, that "isomorphic relationship" that would enable him somehow to transcend the boundary between word and tone, to create music that would indeed *speak without words*.[36]

Bach seems to have emerged from the representationalist controversy a wiser man; his approach was now more than ever an analogical one that left him free to contemplate structural cohesion in abstract terms, and so language remained a useful paradigm. Given the German predisposition for the analogical view, it comes as no surprise that Bach's reputation was not severely damaged by unfavorable criticism of his trio. Indeed his music continued to be admired by many, and late in the century was still described as "so communicative that one believes he is perceiving not tones but an understandable language that sets and keeps our imagination and feelings in motion."[37]

Kirnberger's Rhetoric of Large-Scale Form: "Rhythmic Harmony"

Despite his lucid awareness of the function of harmony, Mattheson applied the metaphor of punctuation only to melody. He felt so strongly that melody was preeminent and harmony merely its derivative that he branded the opposite assertion "false, misleading and pernicious."[38] In this sense, he focused mainly on the musical fore-

---

[36]Ibid., 293, and Hosler, *Changing Views*, 85.

[37]"Die mehresten derselben sind so sprechend, daß man nicht Töne, sondern eine verständliche Sprache zu vernehmen glaubt, die unsere Einbildung und Empfindungen in Bewegung setzt, und unterhält" (from a description of Emanuel Bach's sonatas by J.A.P. Schulz in the article "Sonate," from Johann Georg Sulzer's *Allgemeine Theorie der schönen Künste*, enlarged 2d ed. [Leipzig, 1792–94], vol. 4, 425; translation from Sandra P. Rosenblum, *Performance Practices in Classic Piano Music: Their Principles and Applications* [Bloomington: Indiana University Press, 1988], 11n.63).

[38]"Daß die Melodie aus der Harmonie entspringen soll, ist ein falscher, verführischer und schädlicher Satz . . . " (Mattheson, *Capellmeister*, 22; translated in Harriss, *Johann Mattheson's "Der volkommene Capellmeister,"* 56–57).

ground. But in a time when such an attitude confined most other eighteenth-century theorists to discussing only local events when they used analogies with rhetoric, Mattheson was an exception. In spite of his preoccupation with melodic detail, he ventured to analyze entire movements and even multi-movement works in rhetorical terms.[39] Indeed for Mattheson melody revealed the key to large-scale form.[40]

But a later theorist whose work we associate with Beethoven's studies took a subtly different approach, one that emphasized the application of syntactical analogies at deeper levels. Kirnberger, in the first volume of his *Die Kunst des reinen Satzes in der Musik* (1771), describes the relationship between music and language in the following way:

> Chords are in music what words are in language. Just as a sentence in speech consists of several words that belong together and express a complete idea, a harmonic sentence or period consists of several chords that are connected and end with a close. And just as a succession of many sentences constitutes an entire speech, a composition consists of a succession of many periods.[41]

[39]David Schulenberg, *The Instrumental Music of Carl Philipp Emanuel Bach* (Ann Arbor, Mich.: UMI Research Press, 1984), 26.

[40]Leonard Ratner finds his "method of using a single principal figure and its variants to carry out the phrases of the rhetorical discourse" "typically baroque," while Schulenberg insists that it "somewhat resembles that of the nineteenth century, since it is based on an *Inventio* or *Haupterfindung,* that is, a theme in the literal sense, which is developed or expounded upon in the course of the work" (Leonard G. Ratner, *Classic Music: Expression, Form, and Style* [New York: Schirmer Books, 1980], 94; Schulenberg, *Instrumental Music of Emanuel Bach,* 26). As we shall see, this is one sense in which Beethoven shares an aesthetic ideal with Mattheson, and of course with J. S. Bach.

[41]"Die Accorde sind in der Musik das, was die Wörter in der Sprache: wie aus etlichen zusammenhangenden und einen völligen Sinn ausdruckenden Wörtern ein Satz in der Rede entsteht, so entsteht in der Musik ein harmonischer Satz, oder eine Periode aus einigen verbundenen Accorden, die sich mit einem Schluß endigen. Und wie viel mit einander verbundene Sätze eine ganze Rede ausmachen, so besteht ein Tonstück aus viel verbundenen Perioden" (Johann Philipp Kirnberger, *Die Kunst des reinen Satzes in der Musik* [Berlin and Königsberg, 1776–79; facsimile, Hildesheim: Georg Olms, 1968], vol. 1, 91; translation from Beach and Thym, *Strict Musical Composition,* 109).

Corresponding to the word in speech is the *chord,* not the figure or gesture. Kirnberger's version of the analogy carries us one step further from the mimetic—from preoccupation with the melodic surface as it depicts "passionate utterance"—toward something more attenuated, but still bearing an analogy to the sound and sense of language. He equates harmonic motion with the points of repose in language that reflect degrees of summation or completion; in this sense harmony is essentially rhythmic:[42]

> Whoever has even a moderate sense of hearing will have noticed the greatest strength of music comes from its rhythm. Through rhythm the melody as well as the harmony of several measures are bound together into a single phrase so that the hearing grasps them all at once. And then several short phrases are again gathered together into a larger whole, forming one main sentence at the end of which comes a point of rest which enables us likewise to understand these several phrases all at once. . . . Just as in spoken discourse only at the end of a sentence has one grasped its meaning, and through this meaning one is more or less satisfied according as it is a more or less complete sentence, so it is with music.[43]

Kirnberger's description of the *diastolica* is very much like Mattheson's except for the fact that he stresses a harmonic rather than a melodic frame of reference:

---

[42]His view is well expressed by Putnam Aldrich in "'Rhythmic Harmony' as Taught by Johann Philipp Kirnberger," *Studies in Eighteenth-Century Music: A Tribute to Karl Geiringer on His Seventieth Birthday,* ed. H. C. Robbins Landon and Roger E. Chapman (New York: Oxford University Press, 1970), 40.

[43]"Wer nur einigermaßen ein Gehör hat, wird bemerkt haben, daß die größte Kraft des Gesanges von dem Rhythmus herkommt. Durch ihn wird so wol der Gesang, als die Harmonie von mehreren Tackten in einen einzigen Satz zusammen verbunden, den das Gehör auf einmal faßt, und etliche kleine Sätze werden wieder als ein größeres Ganzes in einen Hauptsatz verbunden, an dessen Ende ein Ruhepunct ist, welcher uns verstattet, das wir ebenfals diese einzeln Sätze zusammen auf einmal zu fassen im Stande sind. . . . Wie man in der Rede erst am Ende eines Satzes den Sinn desselben gefaßt hat und dadurch nun mehr oder weniger befriediget ist, nachdem dieser Sinn eine mehr oder weniger vollständige Rede ausmacht; so ist es auch in der Musik" (Kirnberger, *Kunst des reinen Satzes,* vol. 2, 137 and 138; translation from Aldrich, "Rhythmic Harmony," 38–39).

A principal section of a composition always ends with . . . a perfect cadence. Therefore it may be likened to a paragraph in speech which concludes a succession of sentences that are individual yet related by a central topic, after which the speech pauses for a moment.

Just as a paragraph in speech consists of segments, phrases, and sentences that are marked by various punctuation symbols such as the comma (,), semicolon (;), colon (:), and period (.), the harmonic "paragraph" can also consist of several segments, phrases, and periods.[44]

Kirnberger's terms *Einschnitt, Abschnitt,* and *Periode* (interpreted here as "segment," "phrase," and "period") describe successively larger formal units in music and in speech, though his use of the terms is somewhat free.[45] He uses them to describe musical articulation:

Each period generally consists of a greater or smaller number of phrases, which are not cut off or separated from each other as they would be by cadences, but are nevertheless divided from each other by smaller points of repose. These small points of repose are marked in the melody by caesuras or rests, but in the harmony they are produced by restful chords, especially by dominant chords. Whenever the little point of repose occurs, at least a new consonant chord must be heard. One can also use cadence chords, but they must be weakened by inversions or dissonances so that the pause will not be

---

[44]"Durch eine [solche] vollkommene Cadenz wird allemal ein Haupttheil eines Tonstücks geendiget; sie stellt also das vor, was in der Rede ein solcher Abschnitt mit dem sich eine Folge einzeler, aber zu einer Hauptvorstellung gehöriger Sätze endiget, nach welchem die Rede etwas ausruhet.

"Wie aber in der Rede ein Hauptabschnitt aus kleinern Einschnitten, Abschnitten und Perioden besteht, welche man durch verschiedene Zeichen, als das *Comma* (,) das halbe *Colon* (;) das *Colon* (:) und den *Punkt* (.) andeutet; so kann auch der harmonische Hauptabschnitt aus mehrern Einschnitten Abschnitten und Perioden bestehen" (Kirnberger, *Kunst des reinen Satzes,* vol. 1, 96; translation adapted from Beach and Thym, *Strict Musical Composition,* 114).

[45]Compare his use of the terms in his discussion of rhythm in the chapter entitled "Tempo, Meter and Rhythm" in Beach and Thym, *Strict Musical Composition,* 403–17 (vol. 2, 137–53 in original).

too noticeable and the ear will maintain its anticipation of the harmony that is to follow.[46]

Thus, in describing the character of musical discourse, Kirnberger,
like Mattheson, focuses on phrases within a period, but unlike Mattheson he distinguishes the caesuras that articulate the melodic surface
from the degrees of repose that articulate the deeper harmonic structure as consonance is delayed or weakened by dissonance or inversion.[47]

The theories of Mattheson, Emanuel Bach, and Kirnberger represent three North German contributions to Beethoven's heritage: a
rhetoric of gesture, an analogical basis for theory, and a rhetoric of
deep form. All three exemplify well the eighteenth-century delight in
analogical abstraction. But beyond that, the metaphors that bring
them to life serve to relate music's character (its spirit) to its temporal
nature (its body). In the tradition Beethoven knew, the performer
mastered rhythmic gesture, and through the play between melodic
surface and harmonic depth his music "spoke" and was apprehended
as "oration." But as the eighteenth century drew to a close,
Beethoven and some of his English contemporaries began to trans-
form both surface and depth, and not a few critics began to wonder
whether the old analogies were not better forgotten.

[46]"Jeder Abschnitt bestehet gemeiniglich aus einer größern oder kleinern Anzahl
Einschnitte, die durch kleinere Ruhepunkte, als die Schlüße geben, von einander,
zwar nicht abgeschnitten oder getrennt, aber doch etwas abg[e]sondert sind. Diese
kleinen Ruhepunkte werden in der Melodie entweder durch melodische Clauseln,
oder durch Pausen, in der Harmonie aber durch beruhigende Accorde, besonders
durch Dominanten-Accorde, bewürkt: wenigstens muß allemal da, wo der kleine
Ruhepunkt seyn soll, ein neuer consonirender Accord gehört werden. Man kann auch
Schluß-Accorde dazu brauchen, aber sie müssen durch Verwechslungen oder durch
Dissonanzen geschwächt werden, damit die Ruhe nicht zu merklich sey und das
Gehör in naher Erwartung des folgenden unterhalten werde" (Kirnberger, *Kunst des
reinen Satzes,* vol. 2, 142; translation from Aldrich, "Rhythmic Harmony," 39).
[47]Aldrich, "Rhythmic Harmony," 39.

3 Inflection: The "Speaking Style" Transformed

The Paradoxical Metaphor of "Speaking in Tones"

During the common practice period analogy was used by many teachers and performers with remarkable conviction, apparently because the relationship between linguistic and harmonic syntax seemed to them to be "direct and clear."[1] But analogy is a paradoxical tool: in clarifying correspondences between things that are otherwise dissimilar, it can obscure important distinctions.[2] For example, if the way a question is intoned seems like the best guide for shaping a rising antecedent musical phrase, we can get that point across by giving the musical phrase a new metaphoric name: "musical question." But in so doing we risk losing touch with qualities that set a "musical question" apart from language, qualities that point up music's very different ways of "meaning."

Quantz, Emanuel Bach, Türk, and others invoked the great orators

---

[1]John Kirkpatrick, "New Looks at Old Music" (revision of an informal talk at a reception given by the Alberta Registered Music Teachers Association for examiners of the Royal Conservatory of Toronto and of the Western Board of Music, at Edmonton, Sunday, 11 June 1972) typescript, 2.

[2]George Lakoff and Mark Johnson, *Metaphors We Live By* (Chicago: University of Chicago Press, 1980), 10–13, 163.

when they began to teach the art of "speaking in tones," fully confident that great music, like great rhetoric, could speak directly to the heart. But when questions of music's "meaning" arose, their claims often became far more modest. Friedrich Bach grew noticeably uncomfortable when he was questioned about the viability of portraying the history of Cleopatra in a composition for solo keyboard. At first he cautioned that the "otherwise reasonably adequate clavier" was "not yet sufficient as a means of very perceptively expressing such a wordless painting"—almost as if there were some problem with the instrument itself that might be solved with further development. Then he got to the point: such a piece, like his brother's programmatic trio, would amount to no more than a "characteristic fantasy," which he viewed as limited to conveying those "general" characters and passions of which he spoke.[3]

The brothers Bach were cautious for good reason. Obviously they were both attracted and puzzled by the paradox of music as language. Music seemed to cohere, seemed to have meaning, it could even be "topical" in using or referring to well-known musical cues or styles, but it would not yield to translation, would not in fact have truck with language except in senses that were "analogous to that of tone of voice or inflection in ordinary speech . . . necessary but never sufficient for conveying meaning."[4]

Yet we must be careful not to infer from all this that acceptance of the "speaking style" was somehow hindered by music's apparent inability to refer as language does, as with the imagined musical discourse about Cleopatra. The Bachs' caution really had nothing to do with the limits of music's evocative power; it had to do with their sense that whatever it was that music communicated, it did it in a way that language did not.

While controversy about what music could and could not say continued to rage, the declamatory style assumed a life of its own. Haydn—who felt sure that anyone who knew him well would realize

[3]Eugene Helm, "The 'Hamlet' Fantasy and the Literary Element in C.P.E. Bach's Music," *Musical Quarterly* 58 (1972): 291.
[4]Janet M. Levy, "Texture as a Sign in Classic and Early Romantic Music," *Journal of the American Musicological Society* 35 (1982): 483.

that he owed "a great deal" to Emanuel Bach, having "understood him and . . . studied him diligently"—was one of the next to endure censure for "trying to solve the problem of expressing clearly in instrumental music, without words, the meaning of the words."[5] Yet he came to be praised far and wide for the effectiveness of his musical rhetoric; in England, for instance, he was referred to as "the Shakespeare of music," and "this *Shakespeare* of composers."[6] Why? Because his music did not leave his listeners with the impression that it was limited to conveying "general character"; they found in this "language of the feelings *without* words" something that could couple up to human experience in ways that were utterly particular, intimate, and detailed.

Is it any wonder, then, that the young Beethoven was strongly attracted by the dramatic possibilities of keyboard oratory? From his earliest studies under Neefe, who introduced him to the works of Emanuel Bach, Beethoven found Bach's mode of expression natural to him, being temperamentally suited to soliloquy and the other dramatic stances of the orator. For the rest of his life he passionately pursued what Emanuel Bach and Haydn had mastered.[7] Yet it is no less true that he joined the ranks of the pianistic orators with something of a foreign tongue. Earlier in the century—with the style of Emanuel Bach, and to a great extent with the styles of Mozart and Haydn as well—syllabic nonlegato had been the norm, bar lines were relatively inviolable, and slur groups within the measure were generally short. In those days articulation clarified both meter and gesture,

---

[5]G. A. Griesinger, *Biographische Notizen über Joseph Haydn* in *Haydn: Two Contemporary Portraits,* trans. Vernon Gotwals [Madison: University of Wisconsin Press, 1968], 12; and Albert Christoph Dies, *Biographische Nachrichten von Joseph Haydn* in ibid., 105. Bach acknowledged Haydn's sensitivity to his work: A. C. Dies relates that he considered Haydn "the only one to understand his writings completely and to know how to make use of them" (ibid., 96). Haydn's description of his plan to express texts through instrumental music appears in ibid., 106n.35.

[6]H. C. Robbins Landon, *Haydn: Chronicle and Works,* vol. 2: *Haydn at Eszterháza 1766–1790,* 597, 598, quoting reports in the *Gazetteer and New Daily Advertiser* of 17 January 1785 and the *Morning Post* of 23 November 1786, respectively.

[7]Kenneth Cooper makes the claim for Beethoven's "direct" inheritance of style from Emanuel Bach; see his *The Clavichord in the Eighteenth Century* (Ann Arbor, Mich.: University Microfilms, 1972), the abstract and the third and sixth chapters, especially 120.

and the analogues from poetic speech involving syllables, words, and word phrases did indeed seem "direct and clear." Beethoven's forte-piano touch changed all that.

Beethoven's Keyboard Touch and the Analogies of Musical Grammar

In 1753 Emanuel Bach described in detail his approach to notation in the chapter of his treatise entitled *Performance*. There he recommended that moderately paced notes without marks of articulation—"normal" notes—be sounded for up to half their notated length. But by 1789, Türk felt the need to redefine common touch, and took the time to explain why he disagreed with Bach:[8]

> For tones which are to be played in customary fashion (that is, neither detached nor slurred) the finger is lifted a little earlier from the key than is required by the duration of the note. . . .

> Bach says . . . : "The notes which are neither detached nor slurred nor to be sustained are held down as long as one half of their value." But taken in general, this kind of playing does not seem to me to be the best. For (1) the character of the composition necessitates a variety of restrictions in this respect; (2) the distinction between the tone which is actually detached and that which is to be played in the customary manner is practically abolished; and (3) the execution would probably become too short (choppy) if every note not slurred was held for only

---

[8]Türk's description is particularly applicable to common touch on the clavichord, his preferred keyboard instrument, but his desire for more duration within note value is in accord with the general trend toward legato playing. See the discussion of Marpurg, Nicolo Pasquali, Vincenzo Manfredini, Nicolas Joseph (or Joseph Nicolas) Hüllmandel, Milchmeyer, and especially Muzio Clementi (who in his 1801 tutor recommended "[adhering] chiefly to the LEGATO") in Sandra P. Rosenblum, *Performance Practices in Classic Piano Music: Their Principles and Applications* (Bloomington: Indiana University Press, 1988), 149 and 152–54.

half of its value, and consequently the second half would be a rest.[9]

Although Türk used the increasingly popular invective "choppy," he continued to recommend a syllabic common touch, though now with a ratio of roughly three-quarters sound to one-quarter silence. He was soon radically outdone: by the century's end Beethoven was creating a sensation with his general application of a legato touch at the fortepiano, something that had formerly been associated mainly with organ playing.[10] Mozart's style, which had seemed to listeners of his own generation to be ideally articulate and expressive, now seemed in retrospect unduly disjointed, and, according to Czerny, Beethoven began to characterize it as "delicate but choppy, . . . with no legato."[11] At this point, however, a curious practice emerged,

[9]"Bey den Tönen, welche auf die gewöhnliche Art d. h. weder gestoßen noch geschleist, vorgetragen werden sollen, hebt man den Finger ein wenig früher, als es die Dauer der Note erfordert, von den Tasten. . . . Bach sagt . . . : 'Die Noten, welche weder gestoßen noch geschleist noch ausgehalten werden, unterhält man so lange als ihre Hälfte beträgt &c.' Allein im Ganzen genommen scheint mir diese Spielart doch nicht die beste zu seyn. Denn 1) macht der Charakter eines Tonstückes hierbey verschiedene Einschränkungen nothwendig; 2) würde dadurch der Unterschied zwischen den wirklich abzustoßenden und nur auf die gewöhnliche Art zu spielenden Noten beynahe ganz aufgehoben; 3) möchte der Vortrag doch wohl zu kurz (hackend) werden, wenn man jeden nicht zu schleifenden &c. Ton nur die Hälfte seiner Dauer aushielte, und folglich die zweyte Hälfte pausirte . . . " (Türk, Klavierschule [Leipzig and Halle, 1789], 356; translation from Daniel Gottlob Türk, School of Clavier Playing or Instructions in Playing the Clavier for Teachers and Students, trans. Raymond H. Haggh [Lincoln: University of Nebraska Press, 1982], 345).

[10]In January of 1778, Leopold Mozart mentioned having heard this organlike style from "[Josef] Reicha, the 'cellist, who plays the clavier very well and who had also previously been playing very legato [and] organlike on our harpsichord . . . " [Reicha der Violozellist, der recht gut das Clavier spielt, und dann auch auf dem flügl recht bündig orgelmässig vorhero spielte . . .] (W. A. Mozart, Wolfgang Amadeus Mozart: Briefwechsel und Aufzeichnungen, ed. E. H. Mueller, 2 vols. [Vienna: Verlag Franz Perneder, 1949], vol. 2, 313–14).

[11]Czerny reported this to Otto Jahn in 1852, adding that Beethoven found Mozart's touch "very strange, since he [Beethoven] was accustomed to treat the pianoforte like an organ" (Rosenblum, Performance Practices, 24). The charge of "no legato" seems highly unlikely, given Mozart's frequent references to playing that "should flow like oil." See, for example, his letter of 23 October 1777, in The Letters of Mozart and His Family, trans. and ed. Emily Anderson (London: Macmillan, 1985), 339 [letter 228b].

revealed here in Czerny's description of Beethoven's teaching and playing:

> Then he went through the practice pieces in [Emanuel Bach's] treatise with me, making me particularly aware of the legato of which he had such an unrivalled command, and which all other pianists at that time considered unfeasible at the fortepiano; choppy and smartly detached playing was still in favour then (as it had been at Mozart's time). (Beethoven told me in later years that he had heard Mozart play several times; since the fortepiano was in its infancy then, Mozart had acquired a manner of playing on the spinet, which was much more common, that was in no way suited to the fortepiano. Later I met several people who had studied with Mozart, and I found that their way of playing confirmed Beethoven's remark.)[12]

While Beethoven's legato made a strong impression on the young Czerny—perhaps stronger than the content of Bach's studies—he seemed not at all surprised that his teacher was applying this revolutionary technique to works in the "choppy and smartly detached" style. What was happening to the "syllables"? How was Beethoven clarifying the syntax without articulation? Had he some other means

---

[12]"Hierauf ging er mit mir die zu diesem Lehrbuch [Emanuel Bachs] gehörigen Übungsstücke durch und machte mich vorzüglich auf das Legato aufmerksam, das er selber in einer so unübertrefflichen Art in seiner Macht hatte, und das zu jener Zeit alle andern Pianisten auf dem Fortepiano für unausführbar hielten, indem damals (noch von Mozarts Zeit) das gehackte und kurz abgestoßene Spiel Mode war. (Auch hat mir in späteren Jahren Beethoven erzählt, daß er Mozart mehrmal spielen gehört und daß dieser, da zu seiner Zeit die Erfindung der Fortepiano noch in ihrer Kindheit war, sich auf den damals mehr gebräuchlichen Flügeln ein Spiel angewohnt hatte, welches keineswegs für die Fortepiano paßte. Auch hatte ich in der Folge die Bekanntschaft mehrerer Personen gemacht, welche bei Mozart Unterricht genommen, und fand in ihrer Spielweise diese Bermerkung bestätigt)" (Carl Czerny, *Erinnerungen aus meinem Leben,* ed. Walter Kolneder [Strasbourg: Éditions P. H. Heitz, 1968], 15–16; translation adapted from "Carl Czerny, Memoirs [Excerpts]," in *On the Proper Performance of All Beethoven's Works for the Piano* [London, 1846; facsimile, ed. Paul Badura-Skoda, Vienna: Universal, 1970], 5).

of making sense of the tones? And if so, was there anything left of the character that Emanuel Bach may have imagined?

These are questions for speculation, of course, but we can deepen our grounds for speculation if we determine what prompted Beethoven's cultivation of a bound touch in the first place. What was he after? Czerny seems convinced that Beethoven was after some of the effects popularized by Johann Baptist Cramer (1771–1858), who was famous for his broad legato style: "When Cramer was in Vienna around 1800, he caused a great stir by his playing and by three sonatas dedicated to Haydn (the first of which, in 3/4, was in A flat Major). At that time, Beethoven (who did not appear to get along well with him) wrote his Sonata in A flat Major, Op. 26, whose Finale is intentionally reminiscent of the Clementi-Cramer passage-work manner of Finale. The so-called 51st Sonata in F Major is from the same period, and its Finale is in the same manner."[13] But Czerny is focusing on texture, as he does when he describes Cramer's "style" as "that uniform, perpetually moving style [jener gleichmässig bewegt fortlaufenden Manier]," hence the "influence" of Clementi and Cramer at that time may have had little to do with touch.[14] Sandra Rosenblum suggests that Beethoven's early study of both violin and organ contributed to his preoccupation with legato playing on the fortepiano. She also points out the possibility of Clementi's influence as early as the Bonn years (some of his sonatas were available in Simrock's shop there) and notes that Beethoven was evidently cultivating a legato common touch well before 1800, citing his annotation on the piano part of the song "Klage" (WoO 113, probable date 1790): "Throughout, the notes must be smooth, sustained as much as possible, and

    [13]"Als um 1800 Cramer in Wien war und ebenso durch sein Spiel wie durch die dem Haydn gewidmeten 3 Sonaten (wovon die 1te in As dur 3/4 Takt) großes Aufsehen erregte, schrieb Beethoven (der sich mit ihm nicht sehr gut zu vertragen schien) die As Sonate op. 26 in welcher das Finale absichtlich an die Clementi Cramersche laufende Manier des Finale erinnert. Die sogenannte 51ste Sonate F dur ist aus selber Zeit und auch da das Finale in gleicher Manier" (Carl Czerny, *Über den richtigen Vortrag der sämtlichen Beethoven'schen Klavierwerke* [Vienna: Diabelli, 1846; facsimile, ed. Paul Badura-Skoda, Vienna: Universal, 1963], 16; translation from Carl Czerny, *Proper Performance,* 9). For both sources page numbers cited here always refer to those of the Universal edition (bottom center of each page) rather than to the original numbers.
    [14]*Proper Performance,* 38; and *Über den richtigen Vortrag,* 42.

slurred together."[15] Rosenblum claims that greater use of the legato touch was principally a function of "increased breadth of cantabile lines."[16] That might at first seem a sufficient explanation, but especially in Beethoven's case the expression "cantabile lines" needs more definition.

Beethoven and "Cantabile Lines"

Although Carl Czerny might simply have described Beethoven as a melodist, he said instead that in Beethoven's works "the melody, the musical *idea,* everywhere predominates," because "each of his pieces expresses some particular and persistently held mood or point of view, to which, even in the smallest details, it always remains true."[17] The observation is a sensitive one. That Beethoven was not primarily bent on lyricism is a fact that alone distinguishes his work from that of many of his followers, even the greatest of whom, according to Brahms, cultivated sonata form "in a lyric spirit that stood in contradiction to its innermost dramatic nature."[18]

In his use of cantabile Beethoven was aiming especially for dramatic breadth, and Czerny knew it. He sensed that for Beethoven the fragment, the rustic melody, the rudimentary tune all served his larg-

---

[15]"Durchaus müssen die Töne geschliffen und so sehr als möglich ausgehalten und zusammengebunden werden" (quoted in Johann Baptist Cramer, *21 Etüden für Klavier: Nach dem Handexemplar Beethovens aus dem Besitz Anton Schindlers,* ed. Hans Kann [Vienna: Universal, 1974], Preface, iii; translation from Rosenblum, *Performance Practices,* 152). Kann's title is misleading; according to Alan Tyson there is no evidence that a "Handexemplar" from Beethoven exists in the material we have received from Schindler concerning Cramer. See Tyson's review of Kann's edition in *Music and Letters* 58 (1977): 247–49.

[16]Rosenblum, *Performance Practices,* 151.

[17]"Jedes seiner Tonstücke drückt irgend eine besond're, konsequent festgehaltene Stimmung oder Ansicht aus, der es auch selbst in den kleinsten Ausmahlungen treu bleibt. Die Melodie, der musikalische *Gedanke* herrscht überall vor" (Czerny, *Über den richtigen Vortrag,* 25).

[18]Brahms's comment to Gustav Jenner is recorded in Oswald Jonas, *Introduction to the Theory of Heinrich Schenker: The Nature of the Musical Work of Art,* trans. and ed. John Rothgeb (New York: Longman, 1982), 142n.19.

est designs, wherein microcosm and macrocosm are deeply related. This was something Czerny so admired that he tried again and again to attain it in his own sonatas, but his approach was, unfortunately, superficial. William S. Newman emphasizes "how little [his] ideas develop and how often the modulations lead to no clear goal in the initial, 'sonata-allegro' movements. The ideas themselves show Czerny to be even less of a creative melodist than Ries. They are usually no more than slight melodic fragments reiterated sequentially or in place."[19] In light of Beethoven's success with melodic fragmentation, surely Czerny's attempts were a kind of emulation.

Beethoven's way of achieving breadth, his way of "persistently holding" onto the "particular," links him with the aesthetics of the rhetorically based tradition of the earlier eighteenth century. Leonard Ratner, for one, sees Beethoven bringing that tradition to its culmination:

> The changes in musical style that took place around the turn of the 19th century were so profound that this time might well be considered the beginning of the romantic era. Were it not for Beethoven, this view would be entirely valid; significant trends after 1800 were more consistent with later than with earlier styles. These new trends included . . . extension of the range and amplification of the sound of the piano, greater emphasis upon mechanical virtuoso skills, richer tone color due to mechanical improvements in instruments, . . . and a broader sweep of melodic line. Also, by 1800 the presence of a lyric *middle* theme in a sonata or symphony movement had been fairly well established. These devices tended to focus the listener's attention upon immediate effects, to please quickly; as a consequence, the grand thrust of rhetoric essential to classic sonata form was interrupted.
>
> Beethoven assimilated all these new elements into a line of structure that maintained the periodicity of 18th-century rhetoric. The works of his maturity, in this sense, represent the final embodiment of classic principles, raised to even a higher power than that reached

---

[19]William S. Newman, *The Sonata since Beethoven* (New York: W. W. Norton, 1972), 183.

by Haydn and Mozart. This apotheosis of structure was not achieved by any later work, although facets of his style were imitated for more than a century afterwards, so that in retrospect, much of Beethoven's music seems to have a romantic flavor.[20]

So it was that Beethoven carried the declamatory style into the new century with articulative tools that were markedly unlike those of his forebears. And somehow his cherished innovations—the legato style, the slurs that more frequently crossed bar lines to subsume points of arrival, the lengthy passages of unarticulated figuration—all of which seemed on the surface to undermine the very linguistic analogies on which the projection of musical rhetoric depended, became part of "the formulations and syntheses that added a final and greater dimension to the classic style."[21] We know something of his prowess at the piano, how in improvising he could "produce such an effect upon every hearer that frequently not an eye remained dry, while many would break out into loud sobs."[22] But we need to determine how his dramatic rhetoric was unlike the rhetoric of his contemporaries and followers. And to understand that we must explore further the relationship of tempo to the sounding of musical structure, to articulation.

Beethoven and the Metronome

Beethoven began using the metronome in 1817. Thayer writes that he was "at first not well disposed to the instrument, notwithstanding he had joined Salieri and the other composers in strongly recommending the 'chronometer' in 1813." Mälzel apparently admitted that the composer's first response to his pressure for endorsement was

---

[20]Leonard G. Ratner, *Classic Music: Expression, Form, and Style* (New York: Schirmer Books, 1980), 422.
[21]Ibid.
[22]Carl Czerny quoted in *Thayer's Life of Beethoven*, ed. Elliot Forbes, 2 vols. (Princeton: Princeton University Press, 1964), 185.

indignant refusal: Beethoven dismissed the whole project as "silly stuff; one must feel the tempos."[23] Nevertheless, before long Beethoven had been persuaded to join the growing ranks of musicians convinced of the metronome's usefulness, and in 1817 he wrote to Ignaz von Mosel:

> It heartily delights me that you share my opinion with respect to the terms for tempo that originated in the barbaric ages of music; because, to take one example, what can be more nonsensical than *Allegro,* which of course means *cheerful,* and how far removed we often are from the understanding of this tempo, so that the piece itself says the *opposite of the indication.*—As for these 4 chief movements, which by no means have the reality or accuracy of the 4 chief winds, we gladly *put them aside;* it's a different matter with the words that describe the character of the piece; these we can't give up, since time is really more the body, *whereas these have more to do with the spirit of the piece.*— —As for me, for a long time I've thought of abandoning these nonsensical descriptive terms *Allegro, Andante, Adagio, Presto;* Mälzel's metronome offers us the best opportunity. I give you *my word* that I'll *never use them again* in my new compositions—it's another question whether by doing this we are aiming at bringing the M[etronome] into *universal use;* I hardly think so! That we'll be shouted down as *tyrants,* that I don't doubt; if the cause were served by this it would still be better than to be accused of feudalism—That's why I think it best, especially in our countries where music has now become a national need and every village schoolmaster will have to promote the use of the metronome, that Mälzel try to sell a certain number of metronomes by subscription at higher prices, and as soon as this number defrays his expenses he will be in a position to supply the metronomes required by the national need so cheaply that we can surely expect to achieve the greatest *universal use and distribution.*—It's self-evident that someone must take the lead in this in order to whip up enthusiasm. You may

---

[23]The admission is contained in a letter to Thayer dated 21 May 1873 from Mr. Joseph J. Mickley of Philadelphia, where Mälzel had lived for some time before his death in 1838 (ibid., 687).

count on me to do whatever I can, and I await with pleasure the post to which you will hereby assign me—[24]

For the public, Beethoven cosigned with Salieri an endorsement that appeared in the Vienna *Allgemeine musikalische Zeitung* on the fourteenth of February, 1818:

Mälzel's metronome

is here! The usefulness of his invention will be proved more and more; moreover, all the composers of Germany, England, France have adopted it; we think it necessary on the strength of our convic-

---

[24]"Herzlich freut mich dieselbe Ansicht, welche Sie mit mir theilen in Ansehung der noch aus der Barbarei der Musik herrührenden Bezeichnungen des Zeitmaaßes, denn nur z. B. was kann widersinniger seyn als *Allegro* welches ein für allemal *lustig* heißt, und wie weit entfernt sind wir oft von dem Begriffe dieses Zeitmaaßes, so daß das Stück selbst das *Gegentheil der Bezeichnung* sagt.—Was diese 4 Hauptbewegungen betrifft, die aber bey weitem die Wahrheit oder Richtigkeit der 4 Hauptwinde nicht haben, so geben wir sie gern *hindan,* ein Anderes ist es mit den den Karakter des Stückes bezeichnenden Wörtern, solche können wir nicht aufgeben, da der Tact eigentlich mehr der Körper ist, *diese aber schon selbst Bezug auf den Geist des Stückes haben—* —Was mich angeht, so habe ich schon lange drauf gedacht, diese widersinnigen Benennungen *Allegro, Andante, Adagio, Presto* aufzugeben; Mälzls Metronom gibt uns hiezu die beste Gelegenheit. Ich gebe Ihnen *mein Wort,* daß ich sie in allen meinen neuen Compositionen *nicht mehr* gebrauchen werde—eine andere Frage ist es ob wir hiedurch die so nöthige *Allgemeinheit* des M. bezwecken werden, ich glaube kaum! Daß man uns aber als *Zwingherren* ausschreien wird, daran zweifle ich nicht, wäre nur der Sache selbst damit gedient, so wäre es noch immer besser als uns des Feudalismus zu beschuldigen—Daher glaube ich, das beste sey besonders für unsere Länder, wo einmal Musik Nationalbedürfniß geworden, und jedem Dorfschulmeister der Gebrauch des Metr. gefördert werden muß, daß Mälzel eine gewisse Anzahl Metronome auf Pränumerazion suche anzubringen zu den höheren Preisen und sobald diese Zahl ihn deckt, so wird er im Stande seyn, die übrigen nöthigen Metron. für das musikalische Nationalbedürfniß so wohlfeil zu geben, daß wir sicher die größte *Allgemeinheit und Verbreitung* davon erwarten können—Es versteht sich von selbst, das sich einige hierbey an die Spitze stellen müssen, um Aneiferung zu erwecken. Was an mir liegt, so können Sie sicher auf mich rechnen, und mit Vergnügen erwarte ich den Posten, welchen Sie mir hierbey anweisen werden.—" (Beethoven quoted in Alexander Wheelock Thayer, *Ludwig van Beethovens Leben,* 5 vols., trans. Hermann Dieters, ed. Hugo Riemann [Leipzig: Breitkopf and Härtel, 1907], vol. 4, 66–67 [emphasis restored]). The date "Vienna, 1817" is "noted on the autograph in another hand" according to Emily Anderson, trans. and ed., *The Letters of Beethoven,* 3 vols. (New York: St. Martin's Press, 1961), vol. 2, 727 (letter 845).

tion to recommend it also to all novices and students, whether in
song, the pianoforte or any other instrument, as a useful, indeed
indispensable aid. Through its use they will discover the easiest way
to grasp note values and to learn to practice, and in the shortest time
they will reach the point where they can without difficulty perform
fluently with accompaniment; for since a student receiving proper
preparation and *guidance from the teacher must not in the [teacher's]
absence capriciously sing or play out of tempo,* with [the metronome] his
feeling for the beat will so quickly be guided and corrected that such
things will give him scarcely any more difficulty. We believe that
this universally useful invention of Mälzel's must also be promoted
on this account, because it seems that in this respect it hasn't yet
been warmly enough received.
    Ludwig van Beethoven.
    Anton Salieri. [25]

    In this vigorous campaign Beethoven expressed two hopes for the
metronome: most important to him was the promise it seemed to
hold for the accurate communication of tempo in his works; sec-
ondarily he reiterated the popular notion that students would benefit.
But while both letters made clear his enthusiasm for the new device,
neither described in any detail its practical use. Would tempo be
effectively communicated just by placing one number from Mälzel's

---

[25]"Mälzels Metronom ist da!—Die Nützlichkeit seiner Erfindung wird sich immer
mehr bewähren; auch haben alle Autoren Deutschlands, Englands, Frankreichs, ihn
angenommen; wir haben aber nicht für unnötig erachtet, ihn zufolge unserer
Überzeugung auch allen Anfängern und Schülern, sey es im Gesange, dem Pianoforte
oder irgend einem andern Instrument, als nützlich, ja unentbehrlich anzuempfehlen.
Sie werden durch den Gebrauch desselben auf die leichteste Weise den Werth der Note
einsehen und ausüben lernen, auch in kürzester Zeit dahin gebracht werden, ohne
Schwierigkeit mit Begleitung ungestört vorzutragen; denn indem der Schüler bey der
gehörigen Vorrichtung und vom *Lehrer gegebenen Anleitung, auch in Abwesenheit desselben nicht außer dem Zeitmaße nach Willkühr singen oder spielen kann,* so wird damit sein
Taktgefühl in kurzem so geleitet und berichtiget, daß es für ihn in dieser Sache bald
keine Schwierigkeit mehr geben wird.—Wir glaubten, diese so gemeinnützige Mälzelsche Erfindung auch von dieser Seite beleuchten zu müssen, da es scheint, daß sie in
dieser Hinsicht noch nicht genug beherziget worden ist. Ludwig van Beethoven.
Anton Salieri" (Beethoven, *Ludwig van Beethovens sämtliche Briefe,* ed. Emerich Kastner
[Tutzing: Hans Schneider, 1975], 465–66).

scale before a given composition or movement? As for the machine's pedagogic use, we read only that it was to serve as a guide to correct pupils who "capriciously . . . play out of tempo." Are we to assume—since there is no elaboration—that to "play in tempo" would henceforth be equivalent to playing with metronomic regularity? As we shall see, both assumptions are highly problematic, for, once introduced, the metronome began to instruct not only the pupils but the pedagogues as well—at least the more sensitive pedagogues—in the limitations of the machine and the nature of musical time.

Beethoven was a quick study: he sensed limitations almost immediately. In 1817—at the earliest stage of his work with the new device—he was so troubled by the notion that a single number on Mälzel's scale might be presumed sufficient to represent tempo that he wrote on the holograph of his song "Nord oder Süd,"

> 100 according to Mälzel, but this can apply only to the first measures, because feeling also has its tempo; this is, however, not completely expressed in this figure (namely, 100).[26]

The objection is sometimes raised that texted music should be discounted when discussing instrumental music because "a vocal text can only complicate an already complex problem with questions of prosody and programme."[27] But given Beethoven's background, we have reason to believe that he, like musicians of his generation and generations before, conceived of instrumental music in terms of prosody. There is even some relatively explicit evidence: for example, the inscriptions found beneath two melodies in C major in Beethoven's "Rolland" sketchbook, which dates from the late summer or fall of 1823: "to create instrumental melodies according to syllabic meter."[28]

---

[26]"100 nach Mälzl, doch kann dieß nur von den ersten Täkten gelten, denn die Empfindung hat auch ihren Takt, dieses ist aber doch nicht ganz in diesem Grade (100 nämlich) auszudrücken" (Beethoven quoted in Thayer, *Beethovens Leben,* vol. 4, 66). The parenthesis is Beethoven's.

[27]William S. Newman, "Tempo in Beethoven's Instrumental Music: Its Choice and Its Flexibility," part 1, *Piano Quarterly* 116 (winter 1981–82): 22.

[28]"[A]uf Sylbenmasse instrumental Melodien (schaffen) machen." Quoted in Rosenblum, *Performance Practices,* 100. The sketchbook is described by Sieghard Bran-

If Schindler is correct in suggesting that Beethoven's struggles with tempo reflected musical content that resisted fixation partly because it "[carried] over the prosody of the language and the rules of verbal and sung declamation into instrumental forms," as Clementi had done, then, text or no text, it is impossible to avoid questions of prosody.[29] With certain works it may be impossible to avoid the question of *program* as well, but at the very least, "feeling" is not something we find only in texted works.

Beethoven's "feeling has its tempo" tells us even more than this: it tells us that feeling's tempo is not metronomic, that it has a shape, a *form,* which, though not simple to describe, is something we *recognize.* Beethoven is not describing a tempo flexibility that "emphasize[s] feeling rather than form"; on the contrary he is suggesting that we pay attention to the *form* of *feeling.* I mention this because some discussions of the classical style describe form as if it were threatened by the projection of its content.[30]

From the evidence it does appear that Beethoven spent his life striving to find ideal tempi for his works, and in assigning metronome settings, he sometimes settled on tempi radically different from those he had earlier imagined. His penciled indication at the opening of the holograph of the Ninth Symphony is a case in point: "[$\downarrow$? =] 108 or 120 Mälzel" was changed to $\downarrow$ = 88 for the printed edition.[31] Furthermore, when he pondered the effect of mechanical styles, he found something in mechanism itself that was distasteful to him, as he

denburg in Douglas Johnson, Alan Tyson, and Robert Winter, *The Beethoven Sketchbooks: History, Reconstruction, Inventory* (Berkeley and Los Angeles: University of California Press, 1985), 401, 403.

[29]See Kenneth Drake's *The Sonatas of Beethoven as He Played and Taught Them* (Bloomington: Indiana University Press, 1981), 106. Despite the suggestion that vocal music ought to be avoided, Newman uses the "Nord oder Süd" quotation to support his position on tempo flexibility in the instrumental music in part 2 of his article in *Piano Quarterly* 117 (spring 1982): 27.

[30]For example, Rosenblum's comment that the tempo flexibilities specified in the first movements of the sonatas Op. 31, Op. 57, and Op. 111 "spring from and emphasize feeling rather than form," and her suggestion that Czerny, in his prescriptions for several early sonatas, "may have been trying to keep sentiment from overcoming reason, which would be detrimental to form and character—certainly a Classicistic approach" (*Performance Practices,* 385 and 390–91).

[31]Czerny, *Proper Performance,* Badura-Skoda's introduction, 3.

revealed in a letter of 16 July 1823 to Ferdinand Ries on the subject of *allegri di bravura:*

> As for the *allegri di bravura* I must look over yours— —To be blunt, I'm no friend of [pieces] like this because they only promote mechanism overmuch; at least those that I know.[32]

For all these reasons Beethoven presented to the world mixed signals. Again and again he put off sending metronome marks he had promised; his Op. 106, the only piano sonata he marked, almost immediately raised questions over its tempi that are debated to this day; and sometimes his patience for the whole exercise wore thin.[33] To his publisher Schott he wrote on 19 August 1826: "The metronome marks (the devil take all machines) will follow—follow—."[34] While he valued the metronome to the end of his life, Beethoven learned from experience: he knew the difference between tempo and what his metronome marks could indicate. But did his followers?

Ries and Czerny on the Question of Tempo

Among Beethoven's followers, a polarization developed that mirrored to some degree the composer's own ambivalence toward the metronome, but as is sometimes true of the followers of great personalities, not one of them seemed able fully to comprehend the para-

---

[32]"Mit den *allegri di bravura* muß ich die Ihrigen nachsehen.— —Ausrichtig zu sagen, ich bin kein Freund von dergleichen, da sie den Mechanism nur gar zu sehr befördern; wenigstens die, welche ich kenne" (Beethoven, *Beethovens sämtliche Briefe,* ed. Alfred C. Kalischer [Berlin: Schuster and Loeffler, 1908], vol. 4, 291).

[33]On the delays, see Fritz Rothschild, *Musical Performance in the Times of Mozart and Beethoven: The Lost Tradition in Music, Part 2* (New York: Oxford University Press, 1961), 109. Rosenblum cites early reservations about the Op. 106 tempi in *Performance Practices,* 328.

[34]"Die Metronomisierungen (hol' der Teufel allen Mechanismus) folgen— folgen—" (Beethoven, *Briefe,* Kastner ed., 816). Since the letter contains a postscript that mentions his nephew Karl's attempt (on 30 July) to take his own life with a pistol, the reference may suggest a deeper concern.

doxes and contradictions. Beethoven's pupil Czerny aligned himself with the proponents of the machine, while his amanuensis in the last years, Schindler, opposed it tirelessly.

Somewhat less polemical than the writings of Czerny or Schindler are the reminiscences of Ferdinand Ries, who studied with Beethoven from the winter of 1801–02 (his seventeenth year) to the autumn of 1805.[35] Ries gradually established a successful concert career, and for years he and Beethoven shared a sincere friendship, despite Beethoven's complaint that Ries imitated him too much.[36] The accusation itself suggests that Ries had a keen ear for style, and Czerny admitted as much: Ries, he said, played "with great facility and had absorbed a lot of his master's off-handed moodiness in performance." But Czerny could not resist adding that "his playing left one cold, and Beethoven was not entirely satisfied with him either."[37] Ries submitted a number of anecdotes to the *Notizen* published with Wegeler; in one of them he relates that

> in general [Beethoven] played his own compositions very much according to his humor, though he usually kept a very steady rhythm and only occasionally, indeed, very rarely, speeded up the tempo somewhat. At times he restrained the tempo in his crescendo with a ritardando, which had a beautiful and most striking effect.
>
> In playing he would give various passages, sometimes in the right hand and sometimes in the left, a lovely, utterly inimitable expression.[38]

---

[35]Forbes, *Thayer's Life of Beethoven,* 296 and 382; and Joseph Kerman and Alan Tyson, *The New Grove Beethoven* (New York: W. W. Norton, 1983), 32.

[36]According to Czerny Beethoven complained: "Er ahmt mich zu sehr nach" (Czerny, *Erinnerungen,* 42).

[37]"Ries spielte mit großer Fertigkeit und hatte sich im Vortrag sehr viel von der humoristisch hingeworfenen Manier seines Meisters angewöhnt, doch ließ sein Spiel kalt und auch Beethoven war mit ihm nicht vollkommen zufrieden" (Czerny, *Über den richtigen Vortrag,* 12; from the *Anekdoten und Notizen über Beethoven,* written ten years after his autobiography for Otto Jahn; the notes follow no fixed order and are dated September, November, and December 1852).

[38]"Im Allgemeinen spielte er selbst seine Compositionen sehr launig, blieb jedoch meistens fest im Tacte, und trieb nur zuweilen, jedoch selten, das Tempo etwas. Mitunter hielt er in seinem *crescendo* mit *ritardando* das Tempo zurück, welches einen sehr schönen und höchst auffallenden Effekt machte.

"Beim Spielen gab er bald in der rechten, bald in der linken Hand irgend einer Stelle

Three characteristics of Beethoven's stance are especially worth noting here: his strongly personal characterizations of his own works, his taste for clear, dependable tempi, and his judiciously used but especially effective ways of modifying those tempi. Ries may be describing unnotated tempo changes since notated changes are less likely to have elicited special comment.

Carl Czerny studied many of Beethoven's works with the composer, with whom he began working during the winter of 1799–1800. He mentioned to Otto Jahn that "as late as the years 1811–1812 I studied things with him and he corrected with great care."[39] Czerny, like Ries, seems on balance a trustworthy source, despite the fact that, compared with Ries, he has more axes to grind, especially when he entertains questions of performance practice. When we consider the extraordinary extent to which he devoted himself to pedagogy, this should come as no surprise: clearly he felt himself entrusted with the preservation of a tradition.[40] Of our three commentators he speaks most often of the need to play "strictly in time" and associates such strictness with the beat of a metronome.[41] But the frequency of his admonitions betrays a didactic purpose: in his discussion of the "by-paths" into which the pianists of his day were wandering, vagaries of tempo hold a place second only to "abuse of the pedal":[42]

---

einen schönen, schlechterdings unnachahmbaren Ausdruck" (Ferdinand Ries, *Biographische Notizen über Ludwig van Beethoven von Wegeler und Ries,* ed. Alfred C. Kalischer, 2d ed. [Berlin: Schuster and Loeffler, 1906], 127; translation adapted from *Beethoven Remembered: The Biographical Notes of Franz Wegeler and Ferdinand Ries,* trans. Frederick Noonan [Arlington, Va.: Great Ocean Publishers, 1987], 94). For a more detailed assessment of Ries and his memoirs see Alan Tyson's "Ferdinand Ries (1784–1838): The History of His Contribution to Beethoven Biography," *19th-Century Music* 7 (1984): 209–21.

[39]Forbes, *Thayer's Life of Beethoven,* 373.

[40]Given his effort in the *Pianoforte-Schule* to describe part of the history of keyboard playing by distinguishing between the styles of the great composer-performers, it is tempting to say that Czerny felt himself entrusted with *traditions;* but his notion of progress in the evolution of style undermines his sensitivity to distinctions to such a degree that I prefer to use the singular. This will be taken up in greater detail presently.

[41]Czerny's favorite expression in this regard is "streng im Tempo." For a sensitive general description of Czerny see Paul Badura-Skoda's introduction to *Proper Performance,* 1–3.

[42]"Der erste Abweg ist der Missbrauch in der Anwendung des Pedals" (Czerny, *Die Kunst des Vortrags,* vol. 4 of his *Vollständige theoretisch-practische Pianoforte-Schule,* Op. 500 [Vienna, 1846], 31).

The proper maintenance of tempo has almost been completely forgotten, as the *tempo rubato* (that is, the arbitrary holding back or
quickening of the tempo) is now often used to the point of caricature.[43]

In recounting the sort of "caricature" he apparently had to endure
all too frequently, Czerny makes it clear that his stylistic ideal is
Hummel, whose playing he describes as very nearly metronomic:

How often have we had to hear in recent time[s], for example, in the
performance of a Hummel Concerto, already in the *first* movement
(which is still only in one tempo), the first line played *allegro,* the
middle melody *andante,* the passage following that *presto,* and then
again individual places stretched out endlessly, and so on,—while
Hummel himself played his compositions in such a constant tempo
that one could almost always have let the metronome beat to it.[44]

Czerny also associates "caricature" with sentimentality, as in his
suggestions for the performance of the first movement of the Trio in
E-flat, Op. 1, no. 1, for which he recommends a metronome setting
of $\downarrow = 84$:

Although the gentler passages must be delivered with expression,
nowhere may a sentimental lingering take place, because the character of the whole is decisive and vigorous.[45]

[43]" . . . [M]an das richtige Tempo-halten fast ganz verlernt, da das *Tempo rubato*
(nämlich das willkürliche Zurückhalten oder Beschleunigen des Zeitmasses) jetzt oft
bis zur *Carricatur* angewendet wird" (ibid., 31).

[44]"Wie oft haben wir in den neueren Zeit hören müssen, dass z. B. beim Vortrage
eines Hummel'schen *Concerts* schon im *ersten* Satze, (der doch nur aus einem Tem-
pobesteht) die ersten Zeilen *Allegro,* die Mittel-Melodie *Andante,* die darauf folgende
Passage *Presto,* und dann wieder einzelne Stellen unendlich gedehnt, u.s.w.
vorgetragen wurden,—während doch Hummel selbst seine *Compositionen* in einem so
festen Zeitmasse vortrug, dass man beinahe immer das *Metronom* dazu hätte schlagen
lassen können" (ibid.; translation from Rosenblum, *Performance Practices,* 383). For
Hummel's description of concerto playing, see n.50.

[45]"Obwohl die sanfteren Stellen mit Ausdruck gespielt werden müssen, so darf
doch nirgends ein sentimentales Dehnen Statt finden, da der *Character* des Ganzen
entschieden und kräftig ist" (Czerny, *Über den richtigen Vortrag,* 85).

Czerny's solution to the problem of unsteady tempo, then, appears on the surface to be founded upon a metronomic ideal, the beats of the machine marking a kind of *tempo giusto* that is to be taken as music's norm. But in his discussion of the Trio in C minor, Op. 1, no. 3, a contradiction emerges. Czerny describes the middle subject as "tranquil, and with melodious expression, but not slower,"[46] and then adds the following parenthetical qualification:

> (Here we must insert the special, generally applicable remark that there is a certain way of playing melodious passages *more tranquilly* and yet *not perceptibly slower,* so that everything appears to proceed at one and the same tempo, and that one would at best only notice the difference if the metronome were beating along. A *noticeable* change of tempo may only be allowed where the Author has expressly indicated it with a *più lento, ritardando,* and so forth.)[47]

The melodious tempo is to be tranquil "but not perceptibly slower," yet the metronome allows us to discover that the tempo is *in fact* slower. Czerny asks for a slowness that is "not perceptible," yet he *demands* that the change be perceived—as tranquility, "melodious expression." Two characters appear "to proceed at one and the same tempo," but a single metronome setting cannot be said to designate both. Whether such a number can, in fact, be said adequately to designate the tempo of even *one* character shall be taken up later in this discussion. For now, let us note that Czerny's ♩. = 60 is an inadequate representation of tempo in this *Allegro con brio* movement, and that in fact no single metronome setting can adequately represent tempo in any movement with such a contrasting theme.[48]

---

[46]"Der Mittelgesang (vom 58*sten* Takt) ruhig und mit melodiösem Ausdruck, aber nicht langsamer" (ibid., 87).

[47]"(Wir müssen hier die besond're, überhaupt geltende Anmerkung einschalten, dass es eine gewisse Art gibt, die melodiösen Stellen *ruhiger,* und doch *nicht merkbar langsamer* vorzutragen, so dass alles in einem und demselben Tempo zu gehen scheint, und dass man den Unterschied höchstens nur dann merken würde, wenn der Metronom mitschlüge. Einen *auffallenden* Tempowechsel darf man sich nur da erlauben, wo der Autor es ausdrücklich durch ein *più lento, ritardando,* u.s.w. angezeigt hat)" (ibid.).

[48]Rosenblum points out that "the intervals on a metronome are between 3.5 and 5.5% of the scale" with an average difference of 4.4%. Given the finding by N.

Since Czerny believed that Hummel "almost always" played met-
ronomically, it seems only fair to let Hummel speak for himself on
this matter. While he deplores those many performers who try "to
substitute for natural inward feeling a pretended [feeling] . . . by introducing constantly and to the point of tedium an arbitrary dragging
(tempo rubato)," Hummel, unlike Czerny, characterizes "singing passages" in an *allegro* without reference to the metronome: these passages

> should of course be delivered with some yielding, in order to give
> them the necessary feeling; but we must not deviate too con-
> spicuously from the predominating tempo, because the unity of the
> whole suffers, and it takes on too rhapsodic a character.[49]

His advice on the use of the machine is also of a different cast; in fact,
he chooses more than once to stress the importance of *not* playing
with the beats of the metronome:

> But there are still many who mistakenly believe that use of the
> metronome requires that its uniform pace be precisely followed

---

Garbuzov (1950) that "tempo change can be distinguished only when it deviates more
than 4% from the given of expected tempo," it would appear that most of the
increments on the metronome scale represent degrees of change that are at least
marginally discernible to the human ear when other factors do not interfere with that
perception. Czerny's statement that only a metronome would be sensitive enough to
detect tempo change in an *allegro* seems to suggest, then, that he imagined confining
variation to one or two increments. Compare the degree of variability in his metronome settings for Beethoven's sonatas below. (See Rosenblum, *Performance Practices*,
476n.164.)

[49]"Es haben in neuern Zeiten Manche versucht, das natürliche innere Gefühl durch
ein scheinbares zu ersetzen; als . . . durch ein, bis zum Langweilen, jeden Augenblick
angebrachtes willkührliches Dehnen *(tempo rubato).* . . . Die darin vorkommenden
sangbaren Stellen können . . . zwar mit etwas Hingebung vorgetragen werden, um
das nöthige Gefühl hineinzulegen; allein zu auffallend darf von dem herrschenden
Zeitmass nicht abgewichen werden, weil die Einheit des Ganzen darunter leidet, und
dieses ein zu rhapsodisches Ansehn bekommt" (Johann Nepomuk Hummel, *Ausführliche theoretisch-practische Anweisung zum Piano-Forte-Spiel* [Vienna: Haslinger,
1828], 417–18).

throughout the whole piece without permitting feeling, let alone freedom. . . . But [they] should by no means slavishly follow its beats and thereby thwart an occasional necessary *ritenuto* or *accelerando.*[50]

Hummel's method of developing a sense of proportion in his students was based on a rhetorical model: "Just as in speaking, emphasis on certain syllables or words is necessary to make the discourse moving and the sense of the words clear to the hearer, so it is in music." He would choose a piece the student knew well and ask that it be played four bars at a time with the student explaining at each passage which of all the notes needed an emphasis, and especially where natural inner feeling would lead one to place the principal expression of the whole period, and "which series of notes in melodic passages were to be delivered with more tautness or slackening."[51]

---

[50]"Nur giebt es noch Viele, die bei der Anwendung des Metronom's irrig meinen, er sei dazu bestimmt, seinem gleichmässigen Gang des ganze Stück hindurch folgen zu müssen, ohne dem Gefühl dabei Freiheit zu lassen. . . . [Sie] sollen aber keinesweges seinen Schlägen knechtisch folgen, und dadurch an einem zuweilen nöthigen Anhalten oder Vorwärtsgehen gehindert werden" (ibid., 439–40). Even for his Piano Concerto in A minor, Op. 85, Hummel describes eight unnotated tempo changes within the first hundred bars of the opening piano solo (much of which is accompanied), though he cautions here that "all yielding in single bars within short singing passages, or within pleasing middle ideas must be done almost imperceptibly, and not be dragged down to an *adagio;* so that the difference between the holding back and the forward motion never seems too conspicuous over against the main tempo [Alles Nachgeben in einzelnen Takten bei kurzen Gesangstellen, bei gefälligen Mittel-Ideen muss fast nur unmerklich geschehen, und nicht bis zum *Adagio* herabgezogen werden; so, dass der Abstand zwischen dem Zurückhalten und dem Vorwärtsgehen nie zu auffallend gegen das Haupttempo erscheint]" (ibid., 423).

[51]"Wie in der Sprache die Betonung gewisser Silben oder Worte nöthig ist, um die Rede dem Hörer eindringlich und den Sinn der Worte deutlicher zu machen, so findet sie auch in der Musik statt. . . . Ich liess sie ein Tonstück, welches sie bereits mit Fertigkeit inne hatten, stellenweise, d. h. von 4 zu 4 Takten spielen, und mir sodann bei jeder Stelle von ihnen erklären, welche Noten gegen andere betont werden müssen, vorzüglich aber, wo ihr natürliches inneres Gefühl den Hauptausdruck der ganzen Periode hinlege; ingleichen, welche Tonfolgen in Gesangstellen mehr angezogen oder nachlassend vorgetragen werden" (ibid., 429).

The Accuracy of Czerny's Memory for Tempo

Czerny insists that unnotated variations in tempo must be extremely subtle in order that they not be associated with "tempo change." But he goes even further, suggesting that a proper absolute tempo is essential to a work's meaning. Given his firmness on this point, we must ask whether his own tempo designations demonstrate the kind of accuracy and subtlety he insists on; whether, for example, his multiple metronome markings for particular movements in works by Beethoven show a high degree of consistency. Of course, consistency alone is no proof that his designations accurately reflect Beethoven's practice, but Czerny obviously believes that they do:

> In these matters there can be only *one* perfectly correct mode of execution, and we have tried, according to the best of our remembrance, to indicate the tempo, as the most important part of proper interpretation, according to Beethoven's own view.[52]

The renowned Beethoven scholar Gustav Nottebohm was much impressed by Czerny's memory for tempo:

> Although not of authentic validity, still these indications can lay claim to a certain confidence, especially for those works of which we know that Czerny either heard them played by Beethoven or studied [them] under his instruction. . . . Anyone who knew Czerny personally, who had the opportunity to observe his nature, which was above all directed toward the practical, will believe him capable of impressing firmly on his memory a tempo that he had heard, and will have noticed the certainty that he had in such outwardly tangible musical matters.[53]

---

[52]"Aber es kann in diesem Punkte doch nur *eine* ganz richtige Art der Ausführung geben, und wir haben uns bestrebt, nach uns'rer bessten Erinnerung das Zeitmaass, als den wichtigsten Theil der richtigen Auffassung, so wie auch den Vortrag nach Beethovens eigener Ansicht anzudeuten" (Czerny, *Über den richtigen Vortrag,* 113).

[53]"Wenn auch nicht auf authentische Gültigkeit, so kann diese Bezeichnung doch Anspruch auf einiges Vertrauen machen, namentlich bei denjenigen Werken, von denen wir wissen, dass Czerny sie entweder von Beethoven spielen hörte oder unter

Indeed, Czerny had provided for Nottebohm a sizeable list of works he had studied with Beethoven, including the Piano Sonatas Opp. 13; 14, nos. 1 and 2; 31, no. 2; and 101; the *Andante* from Op. 28; the First, Third, Fourth, and Fifth Piano Concertos; the Choral Fantasy; the Piano Trio, Op. 97; "and many others." In his memoirs he mentions having played the *Waldstein* Sonata, Op. 53, "at sight" and the *Appassionata* Sonata, Op. 57, "several times" for Beethoven. Schindler mentions Czerny's having studied the *Hammerklavier* Sonata, Op. 106, with Beethoven "several times," and according to Paul Badura-Skoda "a certain internal evidence suggests that Czerny was aware of Beethoven's intentions concerning (at least) the Sonatas Op. 26, Op. 27/2, Op. 31/2 and 3, Op. 81a, the Diabelli Variations Op. 120 and the Kreutzer Sonata; Czerny arranged the [last] for piano, two and four hands, during Beethoven's lifetime."[54]

Nevertheless despite this pedigree, and the confidence and certainty with which Czerny put forth his metronome marks, taken as a whole they suggest something other than "firm impressions." Among the three or perhaps four sets of metronome indications for the Beethoven sonatas attributable to him, no two sets are alike, and the variations in his markings are often significant.[55] While the indications in his *Über den richtigen Vortrag* of 1846 and those he provided for the edition of sonatas published by Simrock between 1856 and 1868 have both long been associated with Czerny, less well known are the two sets that appeared in Haslinger's *Gesamtausgabe,* the publication of which began in 1828. Sandra Rosenblum has ascertained that Czerny was almost certainly responsible for at least one if not both of those sets.[56]

---

seiner Leitung studirte. . . . Wer C. Czerny persönlich gekannt hat, wer seine vorzüglich auf das Praktische gerichtete Natur zu beobachten Gelegenheit hatte, der wird ihm die Fähigkeit, sich ein gehörtes Tempo fest einzuprägen, zugetraut, und die Sicherheit bemerkt haben, die er in derartigen, von aussen fassbaren musikalischen Dingen hatte" (Gustav Nottebohm, *Beethoveniana* [New York: Johnson Reprint Corporation, 1970], 136; translation from Rosenblum, *Performance Practices,* 329).

[54]Badura-Skoda's introduction to Czerny's *Proper Performance,* 3.

[55]I accept Rosenblum's threshold here: "A change of three or more [metronome steps] is significant, since that degree of tempo change is obvious to the listener and may alter the character of a movement" (Rosenblum, *Performance Practices,* 331; see also her discussion of the four sets of metronome indications, 329–48). Note that this threshold is well beyond Czerny's ideal for subtlety.

[56]Ibid., 330, 333.

Of the four sets, the slowest is the one published in *Über den richtigen Vortrag;* Rosenblum's comparisons with Czerny's earliest settings illustrate not only his slowing of tempi but his reassignment of note values for the pulse as well: "In this set . . . he slowed the Grave of Op. 13 from $\flat$ = 58 to $\flat$ = 92, the Andante of Op. 14/2 from $\downarrow$ = 66 to $\downarrow$ = 116, and the Allegro ma non troppo of Op. 78 from $\downarrow$ = 132 to 116. Only the Prestissimo of Op. 109 became significantly faster."[57] Yet by the time Czerny had completed his metronome indications for the Simrock edition eleven years later, he "remembered" many tempi as having been considerably faster. Eighty percent of his markings differ from those in *Über den richtigen Vortrag*, one quarter of those significantly, and of the changed indications 82.5 percent are toward faster tempi, making Simrock faster than all but his earliest set for Haslinger.[58]

And what of those works he had studied with the master, and could recall with the "certainty" of which Nottebohm so approved? Rosenblum notes that, "curiously," these "were changed about as much as the others."[59] All this reinforces the impression that Czerny experienced considerable difficulty in recalling even those tempi he had learned from Beethoven. And yet it is Czerny who insists that "the whole character of the piece is distorted by a false tempo."[60]

Unity of Tempo and the Question of "Accuracy"

Sixty years after Beethoven and his contemporaries began their struggles with the metronome, Johannes Brahms was regarding the machine with less enthusiasm. For a time, having observed the tendency in himself and others to choose a new metronome mark upon each examination of a piece, he felt it wisest to describe choosing a metronome setting as a problem requiring a "best solution." In 1878

---

[57]Ibid., 336.
[58]Ibid., 336, 333, and 332 (chart 3).
[59]Ibid., 336.
[60]" . . . [B]ei einem falschen Zeitmaasse der ganze *Character* des Tonstückes entstellt wird" (Czerny, *Über den richtigen Vortrag*, 112).

he sent some suggestions to Clara Schumann (then in the process of preparing her husband's complete works for publication):

> To give metronome marks immediately for dozens of works, as you wish to do, seems to me impossible. In any case you must definitely allow the work to lie for at least a year, and examine it from time to time. You will then write in new numbers each time and finally have the best solution.[61]

Not long afterward, writing from Vienna in February of 1880 to George Henschel, who wanted to know whether the metronome marks he had placed on his Requiem "should be strictly adhered to," Brahms's opinion was closer to the even more negative evaluations of Mendelssohn and Wagner:

> I think here as well as with all other music the metronome is of no value. As far at least as my experience goes, everybody has, sooner or later, withdrawn his metronome marks. Those which can be found in my works—good friends have talked me into putting them there, for I myself have never believed that my blood and a mechanical instrument go well together. The so-called "elastic tempo" is moreover not a new invention. "Con discrezione" should be added to that as to many other things.[62]

But if we grant for now that the setting of a metronome marking is a problem requiring a "best solution," just what does such a "solution" represent? Let us take a test case in which we assume that unity of tempo is the ideal. Even here the metronome may prove entirely inadequate as a tool for achieving that unity if texture, import, and

---

[61]" . . . [W]ie Du willst, gleich Dutzende von Werken metronomisieren, scheint mir nicht möglich. Jedenfalls läßt Du natürlich die Arbeit mindestens ein Jahr liegen und untersuchst sie von Zeit zu Zeit. Du wirst dann jedesmal neue Zahlen dabei schreiben und schließlich die beste Auswahl haben" (Brahms quoted in Dietrich Kämper, "Zur Frage der Metronombezeichnungen Robert Schumanns," *Archiv für Musikwissenschaft* 21 [1964]: 142; translation adapted from David Fallows, "Tempo and Expression Marks," *New Grove Dictionary of Music and Musicians* 18.681).

[62]George Henschel, *Personal Recollections of Johannes Brahms* (New York: A.M.S. Press, 1978), 78–79.

density vary too greatly. Sir Donald Tovey's illustration of this point is especially compelling. He recommends the following metronome settings in order to create an impression of a unified tempo in the opening movement of Beethoven's Piano Sonata Op. 110 (*Moderato cantabile molto espressivo*):

> Crotchets at 66 will do well for the opening; and the demisemiquavers should then show no tendency to hurry. But when they are well under way they will probably reach a pace a degree or two faster without seeming to have changed. On the other hand, the themes of the Second Group (bars 21–40) will be cramped and hurried by a metronome degree above ♩ = 60, and even this will need a relaxation at bars 24/25–26. The natural swing of the tempo thus needed is not a rubato at all; on the contrary, its object is to humour the ear, which would otherwise feel that the demisemiquavers began, after a while, to drag, while the fine detail was hurried.[63]

We note, of course, that Tovey tacitly defers to the machine: we "humor" our ears with a "natural swing of the tempo." But before there were metronomes, would we have been "humoring our ears," or would we, rather, have been "playing in tempo"? When did we begin to labor under the assumption that our musical speech is best judged by a ticking machine? Surely it was good sense that prevented Beethoven's offering a setting here in the first movement of Op. 110, where texture varies so extremely that any single metronome setting is applicable only briefly.

On the other hand, that Beethoven should have pursued the task of numbering his works is not surprising, given the optimistic views of the early promoters of Mälzel's device. A lot was at stake (the life of the music!), and public allegiances had been proclaimed. From our vantage point we may admire the wisdom of twentieth-century commentators such as Rudolf Kolisch who stress that Beethoven's metronome indications are not to be taken too literally, that they are to be used as a guide, and that "mere nuances within the type" never de-

---

[63]Donald F. Tovey and Harold Craxton, eds., *Beethoven Sonatas for Pianoforte*, 3 vols. (London: Associated Board of the Royal Schools of Music [1931]), vol. 3, 214.

stroy the meaning.[64] But those who insist like Max Rudolf that the indications were "never intended to pinpoint the speed of music,"[65] must remember that, alas, pinpointing the speed is precisely what Beethoven originally envisioned—as we see from his early endorsements—and what Czerny envisioned as well. In the third volume of his *Pianoforte-Schule* Czerny lists the manifold uses of the metronome, and at the very top of his list we find:

> 1st one can know with the utmost certainty the tempo desired by the composer, and preserve it for all futurity.[66]

Schindler's Point of View

The use of this *"loud-beating"* machine, Czerny's "very important modern invention,"[67] is also addressed by Anton Schindler, who is well aware of Beethoven's passionate concern for proper tempi:

> When a work by Beethoven had been performed, his first question was always, "How were the tempos?" Every other consideration seemed to be of secondary importance to him.[68]

[64]Rudolf Kolisch, "Tempo and Character in Beethoven's Music," *Musical Quarterly* 29 (1943): 180.

[65]Rosenblum, *Performance Practices*, 327, quoting Max Rudolf, *The Grammar of Conducting*, 2d ed. (New York: Schirmer Books, 1980), 329.

[66]"1*stens* Kann man das vom Tonsetzer gewünschte *Tempo* auf das Genaueste erfahren, und für alle Zukunft aufbewahren" (Czerny, *Pianoforte-Schule*, vol. 3, 48).

[67]"Das Mälzelsche *Metronom,* (von welchem wir vorzüglich die bessere, *lautschlagende* Gattung hier besprechen,) ist eine sehr wichtige Erfindung der neueren Zeit . . . " (ibid.).

[68]"Wenn ein Werk von Beethoven zur Aufführung gekommen, so war seine erste Frage allzeit: 'Wie waren die Tempi?' Alles Andere schien ihm secondärer Art zu seyn" (Anton Schindler, *Biographie von Ludwig van Beethoven*, 4th ed. [Münster: Ashendorff, 1871], 247; translation from Anton Schindler, *Beethoven as I Knew Him*, ed. Donald W. MacArdle, trans. Constance S. Jolly [London: Faber and Faber, 1966], 423). Rosenblum notes that "although the veracity of Schindler's reporting on performance practices is open to serious doubt . . . there is ample evidence in letters, comments to close friends, and in the Conversation Books that realization of his tempo indications was a primary concern of Beethoven" (Rosenblum, *Performance Practices*, 321n.108).

But Schindler self-consciously places himself in an opposing camp. He argues that Beethoven's tempi cannot be understood as related in any simple way to a metronomic beat:

All the pieces which I have heard Beethoven himself play were, with few exceptions, given without any constraint as to the rate of the time. He adopted a *tempo-rubato* in the proper sense of the term, according as subject and situation might demand, without the slightest approach to caricature. Beethoven's playing was the most *distinct* and *intelligible declamation,* such, perhaps, as in the same high degree can only be studied in his works. His *old* friends, who attentively watched the development of his genius in every direction, declare that he adopted this mode of playing in the first years of the Third Period of his life, and that it was quite a departure from his earlier method, which was less marked by shading and coloring.[69]

Given that Czerny's recollections of Beethoven's playing focus on the earlier years, and that Schindler mentions this freedom of tempo "without the slightest approach to caricature" as a later development, it may be that there is some truth to Schindler's description of a "Third Period" playing style that differed markedly from Beethoven's early playing. Yet when he describes the degree to which

---

[69]"Was ich selbst von Beethoven immer vortragen hörte, war mit wenig Ausnahme stets frei alles Zwanges im Zeitmaasse; ein 'Tempo rubato' im eigentlichsten Sinn des Worts, wie es Inhalt und Situation bedingte, ohne aber nur den leisesten Anklang an eine Carricatur zu haben. Es war die *deutlichste, fasslichste Declamation,* wie sie in dieser hohen Potenz vielleicht nur aus seinen Werken heraus zu studiren seyn dürfte. Seine *älteren* Freunde, die der Entwickelung seines Geistes nach jeder Richtung hin aufmerksam gefolgt sind, versicherten, dass er diese Vortragsweise erst in den ersten Jahren seiner *dritten Lebensperiode* angenommen, und von der früheren weniger nuancirten ganz abgewichen sey" (Anton Schindler, *Biographie von Ludwig van Beethoven,* 1st ed. [Münster: Aschendorff, 1840], 228; translation from Anton Schindler, *The Life of Beethoven* [based on his *Biographie von Ludwig van Beethoven,* 1st ed.], trans. and ed. Ignaz Moscheles [London, 1841; reprint, Boston: Oliver Ditson (1842?)], 156–57; original emphasis restored). Schindler was not alone in using the Italian term *tempo rubato* to describe effects in Beethoven's music, but in his 1860 revision of his Beethoven biography he saw fit, for some reason, to denounce the use of the term in describing Beethoven's music (claiming, of course, that Beethoven had objected to it). Schindler's meaning here is in no way changed by his later retraction of the term. See Rosenblum, *Performance Practices,* 388.

tempo modification is necessary in Beethoven, Schindler quotes Czerny's description of an early work, the *Largo* of the Sonata in D, Op. 10, no. 3, and then adds his own summary:

"To perform music of this nature, it is not enough to put oneself in the appropriate frame of mind. The fingers and hands themselves must affect the keyboard with a different, a heavier weight than is necessary for happy or tender compositions, in order to bring out the more resonant tone of each note and to give life to the slow pace of a serious *adagio* movement. The effectiveness of this Largo will be increased by a well-calculated *ritardando* and *accelerando*. Thus, for instance, the second half [only?] of measure 23 should be played somewhat faster, as well as the second half of measure 27 and of measure 28. Measures 71–75 require an augmentation of intensity and power, until in measure 76 the former tranquility returns."

Beethoven himself said that the pace of this rich movement must be changed fully ten times, though only so as to be perceptible to the most sensitive ear. The principal theme is always to be repeated in the tempo of its first statement; all the rest is subject to variation in the tempo, each phrase according to its own meaning.[70]

[70] "'Beim Vortrage von Tonstücken dieser Art genüzt es nicht sich in die geeignete Stimmung zu versetzen: auch die Finger und Hände müssen mit einem andern, schwereren Gewichte die Tastatur behandeln, als bei muntern, oder zärtlich gefühlvollen Compositionen nöthig ist, um jene bedeutendere Art des Ton's hervorzubringen, die den langsamen Gang eines ernsten Adagio gehörig beleben kann. In diesem Largo muß auch ein wohl berechnetes *Ritardando* und *Accellerando* die Wirkung vergrößern. So z. B. ist die 2. Hälfte [nur?] des 23. Tactes etwas schneller zu spielen. Eben so die 2. Hälfte des 27. und der 28. Tact. Eben so vom 71. Tact bis zum 75. ein Steigern der Lebhaftigkeit und der Kraft, bis beides im 76. Tact wieder zur früheren Ruhe zurückkehrt.' Nach Beethoven ist ein nahezu zehnmaliger Wechsel mit der Bewegung zur Darstellung dieses inhaltreichen Satzes erforderlich, meist nur dem seinen Ohr merkbar. Das Haupt-Motiv behält seine erste Bewegung bei der Wiederkehr, alle andern unterliegen der Veränderung und sind unter einander so vermittelt, wie es von deren Sinn geboten wird" (Schindler, *Biographie*, 4th ed., 243; translation from Schindler and MacArdle, *Beethoven*, 421). Schindler also mentions Beethoven's use of "the rhetorical pause and the caesura, both adopted from Clementi" (Schindler and MacArdle, *Beethoven*, 417), both of which are discussed in more detail presently.

Here Czerny is speaking of unnotated tempo modification, and Schindler's amplification is not at all far-fetched given the episodic nature of the *Largo* and his insistence that Beethoven wanted the principal theme to restore the original tempo at each return. But we cannot seriously evaluate Schindler's arguments without taking into account the controversy over his credibility, which has been disastrously undermined both by the misstatements and falsifications in his Beethoven biographies (exposed years ago by Nottebohm, Thayer, and others) and by over two hundred forgeries in Schindler's hand in the conversation books, including all his entries from 1819 and 1820 and later entries as well.

Schindler's Character

Schindler's forgeries were long suspected, but their extent and significance have been made clear only recently, through the work of Dagmar Beck, Grita Herre, Peter Stadlen, and others. Soon after Beethoven's death Schindler's acquaintances realized that he was using his previous position to bolster his sense of importance. Unfortunately he was in possession of many of the conversation books, and when he began to fear that there was too little documentary evidence of his importance to Beethoven, he began the forgeries expressly to prove that he had worked closely with Beethoven during years when they were simply not in contact, and even to suggest that he had studied the sonatas and symphonies under Beethoven's guidance.[71] Ferdinand Hiller's portrait of Schindler as the almost pitiably servile domestic seems much nearer the truth:

> Schindler . . . had brought us to Beethoven, and from then on we saw him rather frequently. The fact that the great master was able to

[71]For further information on Schindler and his forgeries see Peter Stadlen's "Schindler's Beethoven Forgeries," *Musical Times* 118 (1977): 549–52, and also his "Schindler and the Conversation Books," *Soundings* 7 (1978): esp. 5 and 8–9. See also Donald W. MacArdle's "Anton Felix Schindler, Friend of Beethoven," *Music Review* 24 (1963): 50–74, esp. 70–71, and Czerny, *Proper Performance*, Badura-Skoda's introduction, 3.

associate with this knight of the most woeful countenance day after day for a number of years, that he did not turn him out, can only be due to the fact that at that time contact with the outside world had become a matter of indifference to him and that he had need of an intelligent servant. I do not by any means deny that Schindler had a knowledge of music and certain intellectual abilities—but his personality was as spare as his figure and as dry as his facial features. It is certain that he was of service to Beethoven in many ways—but it is just as certain that no friendship in the world was ever exploited more cleverly and to greater advantage. In later years, on occasions when Schindler was visited by a music lover whom he wanted to honor or please particularly, he would appear wearing an unattractive dressing gown which Beethoven had once worn threadbare, thus presenting, without realizing it, a most accurate picture of his relation to the great man who had merely tolerated him.[72]

This was Schindler, who shared with Ries and Czerny, whom he saw as rivals, neither renown as a virtuoso nor the kind of sensitivity to proportion that long and successful experience in solo performance at the keyboard can bring. His defensiveness gave rise to writing that, at its worst, combines fawning deference and ill-informed zeal. For example, in his discussion of tempo, Schindler cites Czerny's tendency to play with "metronome-like rhythmic regularity," and makes it clear that he finds it intolerable, a falsification of Beethoven's intentions.[73] But then he contends that Beethoven renounced use of the metronome after his early enthusiasm, and in marshaling evidence gets himself in hot water:

Actually, he himself assigned metronome marks to only two of his works: the great sonata opus 106, at the explicit request of Ries for the London edition, and the ninth symphony at the request of the publishing house of Schott in Mainz and the Philharmonic Society of London. In connection with the latter transaction, there occurred

[72]Quoted by Eva Badura-Skoda in her introduction to *Beethoven Remembered*, xvi–xvii.

[73]Schindler and MacArdle, *Beethoven*, 415. Schindler's expression is "der Metronomisirung," but in this case the expression does seem to refer to Czerny's performance, as MacArdle translates it. (Schindler, *Biographie*, 4th ed., 235.)

an event that illustrates the master's low opinion of the metronome. He asked me to make a copy for London of the metronome notations he had a few days before made for Mainz, but the list had been mislaid and we could not find it. London was waiting and there was no time to lose, so the master had to undertake the unpleasant task all over again. But lo! no sooner had he finished than I found the first version. A comparison between the two showed a difference in all the movements. Then the master, losing patience, exclaimed: *"No more metronome! Anyone who can feel the music right does not need it, and for anyone who can't, nothing is of any use; he runs away with the whole orchestra anyway!"*[74]

Schindler's insistence that Beethoven gave metronome settings for only two of his works is, of course, false. As for the "No more metronome!"—if Beethoven said it—it was simply another rash overstatement, like his 1817 promise never again to use Italian tempo designations, for documentary evidence proves that, quite the contrary, he used it to the last. We have, for example, a letter from mid-December of 1826 in which Beethoven declares to Schott that the success of the Berlin performance of his Ninth Symphony on the twenty-seventh of November has convinced him more than ever of the machine's value:

> The metronome markings [of the *Missa Solemnis*] will be sent to you very soon. Do wait for them. In our century such indications are

---

[74]"In der That finden sich nur zwei Werke von ihm selber metronomisirt, und zwar die große Sonate, Op. 106, auf ausdrücklichen Wunsch von Ries für die Londoner Ausgabe, dann noch die 9. Sinfonie zufolge Wunsches der Verlagshandlung Schott in Mainz und der Philharmonischen Gesellschaft in London. An letzteres Geschäft knüpft sich ein Vorfall, der des Meisters geringe Werthschätzung des Metronoms klar und deutlich zeigt. Er ersuchte mich, die einige Tage vorher für Mainz gemachte Notirung für London zu copiren, allein diese war verlegt und ließ sich nicht auffinden. Die Absendung drängte, er mußte sich demnach zu abermaliger Vornahme dieses unangenehmen Geschäfts bequemen. Aber siehe, kaum war die Arbeit gethan, als ich die frühere Notirung auffand. Ein Vergleich zeigte die Abweichung des Zeitmaßes bei allen Sätzen. Da rief der Meister voll Unwillen aus: *"Gar kein Metronom! Wer richtiges Gefühl hat, braucht ihn nicht, und wer das nicht hat, dem nützt er doch nichts, der lauft doch mit dem ganzen Orchester davon!"* (Schindler, *Biographie*, 4th ed., 250; translation from Schindler and MacArdle, *Beethoven*, 425–26; original emphasis restored).

certainly necessary. Moreover, I have received letters from Berlin
informing me that the first performance of the [ninth] symphony
was received with enthusiastic applause, which I ascribe largely to
the metronome markings. We can scarcely have *tempi ordinari* any
longer, since one must fall into line with the ideas of unfettered
genius.[75]

The Viennese musicologist and performer Peter Stadlen, one of the
most articulate critics of Schindler, suggests that the latter's claims
about Beethoven's tempi are suspect at best:

The qualms imputed to Beethoven about the difficulties of notating
continual tempo fluctuations are of course intended to reinforce the
claim that he was in fact so inclined; for did he not talk to Schindler
about the need for musical declamation to observe the incisions and
points of repose which the composer, like the poet, is unable to
indicate. Hence his alleged intention to print in the proposed Collected Edition the poetic programme of each movement, for example in either of the two Sonatas op. 14 the dialogue between man
and woman, the contrast between imploring and resisting elements.[76]

Rosenblum is also critical. Disturbed by Schindler's removal of one
of the composer's slurs "in order to create 'space' for [a] caesura" in
the first movement of the Piano Sonata Op. 10, no. 1, she declares

[75]"Die Metronomisierung folgt nächstens. Warten Sie ja darauf. In unserem Jahr-
hundert ist dergleichen sicher nöthig; auch habe ich Briefe von Berlin, daß die erste
Aufführung der Symphonie mit enthusiastischem Beifall vor sich gegangen ist, welches ich großenteils der Metronomisierung zuschreibe. Wir können beinahe keine
tempi ordinari mehr haben, indem man sich nach den Ideen des freien Genius richten
muß" (Beethoven, *Briefe,* Kastner ed., 832–33; translation from Rosenblum, *Performance Practices,* 322; the source is Anderson, *Letters of Beethoven,* vol. 3, 1325 [letter
1545]).

[76]Stadlen, "Conversation Books," 8. See also Anton Schindler, *Biographie von Ludwig van Beethoven,* 1st ed., 195–96; and Schindler and MacArdle, *Beethoven,* 406–27.
Like Schindler, Czerny insists it was "certain" that Beethoven was often inspired by
poetic images and visions. He goes so far as to identify some specifically, but notes
that Beethoven was reluctant to discuss them (*Über den richtigen Vortrag,* 16, 19, 48n,
and 54n).

that his "'rhetorical pauses' (i.e., lengthened rests), *fermatas,* and caesurae destroy the propulsion of the movement and create a caricature of those means of agogic expression." As she sees it, "no corroboration for Schindler's excesses has come to light," although she does grant that "sometimes, as in Op. 10/1/i, his suggestions demonstrate misguided use of *bona fide* aspects of interpretation."[77]

While it must be granted that Schindler seems immature as a musician and must be considered untrustworthy as a scholar, the principles he claims to have learned from Beethoven need to be explored more deeply, since it is entirely possible that Schindler captured in some of his forgeries things he knew to be true.[78] Beethoven—like many composers before and after him—may have been close-mouthed about nuances in his own performances; nevertheless Schindler's descriptions are sometimes convincing precisely because they *can* make musical sense. What is more, as he recognized, many of them were substantiated by the best minds of his day. It seems especially significant that his insistence on flexibility owes something to Czerny, a fact of which Schindler seems well aware. Let us observe the course of his argument.

Schindler's Defense of the Rhetorical Tradition

To support his contention that perceptible tempo flexibility is essential to Beethoven's meaning, Schindler turns to Carl Maria von Weber's description of tempo, which, based as it is on a vocabulary drawn from rhetorical theory, points up the extremely limited value

[77]Rosenblum, *Performance Practices,* 389–90.

[78]Stadlen carefully acknowledges this and even finds evidence for it, but other commentators have simply shunned Schindler's writings since the wide publicity given to the forgeries. William Newman responds with a lament about the gullibility of historians: "All of these peevish forgeries by the middle-aged Schindler strike us today as not only preposterous but naive. As with other major hoaxes in music history, they leave us wondering how we ever could have been taken in so generally and for so long. But, of course, historians need to remind themselves regularly how much easier hindsight comes than foresight" (William S. Newman, "Yet Another Major Beethoven Forgery by Schindler?" *Journal of Musicology* 3 [1984]: 404). As I suggest below, Schindler's forgeries "take us in" partly by virtue of their strengths.

of the metronome. Weber speaks of human pulse as a model, and of tempo as informed by an apprehension of periodicity in declamation:

> The beat, the tempo, must not be a controlling tyrant nor a mechanical driving hammer; it *should* be to a piece of music what the pulse beat is to the life of a man. There is *no slow movement* without places that demand a quicker motion in order to avoid a sense of *dragging*. In the same way, there is *no Presto* that does not require a contrasting, *more tranquil*, execution of many passages, for otherwise the expressiveness would be lost in *excessive speed.* . . . A *quickening* of the tempo or a *holding back* must never produce a sense of *pushing* or *forcing*. It can occur, then, only in *periods* or *phrases* (in the musical and poetic sense of the words) as the emotional content of the performance demands. . . . In music we have no way of indicating all this. It resides only in the *feelings of the human heart*, and if the feelings are not *there*, nothing is of any avail, neither the metronome, which serves only to prevent the grossest misunderstandings, nor the expression marks, which are so unsatisfactory but which I might be tempted to use in great abundance if the warning of repeated experience did not remind me that such indications are *superfluous, useless*, and *generally misinterpreted*. When I give any performing indications, *it is only because a good friend asks me directly.*[79]

[79]"Der Tact, das Tempo, soll nicht ein tyrannisch hemmend—oder treibender Mühlenhammer seyn, sondern dem Musikstücke *das,* was der Pulsschlag dem Leben des Menschen ist. Es gibt *kein langsames Tempo,* in dem nicht Stellen vorkämen, die eine raschere Bewegung forderten, um das Gefühl des *Schleppenden* zu verhindern. Es gibt *kein Presto,* das nicht eben so, im Gegensatze, den *ruhigen* Vortrag mancher Stelle verlangt, um nicht durch *Uebereilen* die Mittel zum Ausdruck zu benehmen. . . . Das *Vorwärtsgehen* im Tempo, wie das *Zurückhalten,* darf nie das Gefühl des *Rückenden* oder *Gewaltsamen* erzeugen. Es kann also—in musikalisch und poetischer Bedeutung—nur *Perioden-* und *Phrasenweise* geschehen: bedingt durch die Leidenschaftlichkeit des Ausdrucks. . . . Für alles dieses haben wir in der Musik keine Bezeichnungsmittel. Diese liegen allein in der *fühlenden Menschenbrust,* und finden sie sich *da* nicht, so hilft weder der grobe Mißgriffe verhütende Metronom, noch die so höchst unvollkommenen Andeutungen, die ich in der Reichhaltigkeit des Stoffes um vieles weiter auszuführen versucht seyn möchte, warnten mich nicht aufgedrungene Erfahrungen, in deren Folge ich sie jetzt schon als *überflüssig* und *nutzlos* betrachte, und *gemißdeutet* hoffe. Mögen sie nun aber dastehen: *einzig veranlaßt durch freundliche Anfrage*" (Carl Maria von Weber quoted in Schindler, *Biographie,* 4th ed., 227–28; translation from Schindler and MacArdle, *Beethoven,* 410–11; original emphasis restored). Schindler indicates that Weber's comments appeared in no. 28 of the *Berliner Musik-Zeitung* for 1827.

Schindler follows with observations by the aestheticians Hand and Schilling on the limits of tempo flexibility, and a description of musical character by A. B. Marx, the critic who had vehemently protested some of Schindler's suggestions for performance in the Beethoven biography of 1840. Proving points with the arguments of his detractors is a technique Schindler obviously enjoys, for he sums up his argument with support from Czerny himself:

> If Hummel's text [his *Klavierschule*] fails to devote a chapter to free, declamatory performance, but instead deals almost exclusively with the matter at hand and only fleetingly mentions specific works, we are all the more grateful to Carl Czerny. The chapter "On Modifications in Rhythm" in the third part of his textbook presents a clear lesson. In the very first paragraph he quite rightly calls this modification "the most important consideration in performance." Czerny himself says in the second chapter of the fourth part that everything he says here is still insufficient for playing Beethoven's music.[80]

We are now in a position to draw a surprising conclusion: the myriad factors that constantly influence tempo are *by no means unknown to Czerny*. In the very chapter Schindler cites from the *Vollständige theoretisch-practische Pianoforte-Schule,* Czerny includes seven examples in which tempo variation occurs in nearly every measure. What is more, these examples (like so much of Czerny's music) are designed to represent not anomalies but rather the *ordinary* course of music. *Allegros* predominate, and these are (according to Czerny's appended descriptions) replete with unnotated tempo fluctuations, but his explication of the *Andantino espressivo* as given in Example 1 is more relevant to the Beethoven examples explored later.

---

[80]"Wenn Hummel in seiner Schule der freien, declamatorischen Vortragsweise kein besonderes Capitel widmet, sich vielmehr ausschließlich nur auf seine Sache beschränkt und dabei noch sehr oberflächlich zu Werke geht, so haben wir desto mehr Carl Czerny zu verdanken. Das Capitel 'von den Veränderungen des Zeitmaßes' im 3. Theil seiner Schule stellt eine anschauliche Lehre hin. Gleich §. 1 nennt er diese Veränderung mit Recht 'das wichtigste Mittel des Vortrages.' Daß jedoch alles dort Gegebene bei Beethoven's Musik noch unzulänglich ist, zeigt Czerny im 2. Capitel des 4. Theils" (Schindler, *Biographie,* 4th ed., 231; translation from Schindler and MacArdle, *Beethoven,* 411–12).

Example 1. Andantino espressivo from Czerny's *Vollständige theoretisch-practische Pianoforte-Schule,* Op. 500, vol. 3, 26

Remarks on the Above Example

1.) The 1st measure is to be played strictly in *tempo*.

2.) The last 3 eighths of the 2nd measure are to *ritard* a little bit, hardly noticeable, because the following 3rd measure is a return of the first measure (also of the main idea), although [built] on the next interval.

3.) The last, slightly arpeggiated chord in the 3rd measure is to be expressed [with] a little bit [of a] *ritenuto*.

4.) The last 3 eighths of the 4th measure are to be expressed with somewhat more warmth (thus *almost accelerando*), which is not to be taken away again until the 3 last eighths of the 5th measure.

5.) In the 6th measure is one of those ornaments consisting of many notes, which creates a *ritarding* in both hands to such a degree

that the quick notes don't pour forth too hurriedly, but rather
very tenderly and gracefully blend into one another little by
little; the last 9 notes of this ornament are to *ritard* more
markedly, and on the penultimate note (the G) a small pause is
to be made.

More will be said later about the division of this long ornament.

6.)   The 7th and 8th measures remain strictly in *tempo*.

7.)   The 9th measure with vigor and warmth (thus *almost* a little
accelerando).

8.)   The 2nd half of the 10th measure somewhat more peacefully.

9.)   The 11th measure a little *ritardando*, and the last *dissonant chord*
very soft, even somewhat more held back, because in this way
each *dissonant chord* (when it is *piano*) produces more of an
effect.

10.)   The 3 first eighths of the 12th measure in *tempo*; however the
last 5 eighths significantly *ritardando*, because they form the
transition to the theme.

11.)   The 13th measure in *tempo*.

12.)   The first quarter of the 14th measure already [a] considerable
ritardando, which in the 2nd quarter is noticeably increased, and
through which the above 8 notes must be marked strongly and
crescendo. The fermata must last roughly 5 eighths, and the
following run must be moderately fast, tender, and *diminuendo*,
until finally the 8 last notes of it become markedly *ritardando*.

13.)   The 1st half of the 15th measure in *tempo*, the 2nd half *ritardando*,
through which the end of the ornament must be suspended
exceedingly tenderly. Here the *ritarding* is most noticeable because this measure contains a softly uttered closing cadence.

14.)   The last measure in a peaceful *tempo*.

The following two remarks are to be heeded well.

I.)   Although in this theme a *ritardando* is brought to bear in almost
every measure, still the whole must (especially in the accom-
panying left hand) be declaimed so naturally, logically, entirely
without distortion, that the hearer does not remain in doubt
over the actual tempo or become bored.

II.) Since each part is to be played a 2nd time, each expression and consequently also each *ritardando* can upon repetition be brought out by marking them a little more strongly, whereby the whole acquires more interest.[81]

Czerny and Schindler inflect our impression of Beethoven's playing in almost opposite ways, but in the end their differences seem to be based more on dissimilar personalities than on fundamental disagreement about the nature of musical discourse. Czerny is far more con-

[81]Anmerkungen zum vorstehenden Beispiel: 1.) Der 1ste Takt ist streng im *Tempo* zu spielen. 2.) Die letzten 3 Achteln des 2ten Takts sind ein klein wenig, kaum merkbar, zu *ritardiren*, da der nachfolgende 3te Takt wieder eine Wiederhohlung des ersten Takts, (also des Hauptgedankens) wiewohl auf einer andern Stufe, ist. 3.) Der letzte, etwas arpeggirte *Accord* im 3ten Takte wird ein klein wenig *ritenuto* ausgedrückt. 4.) Die letzten 3 Achteln des 4ten Takts werden mit etwas mehr Wärme, (folglich *beinahe accelerando*) vorgetragen, welche erst in den 3 letzten Achteln des 5ten Takts wieder abnimmt. 5.) Jm 6ten Takte ist eine von jenen, aus vielen Noten bestehenden Verzierungen, welche ein *ritardiren* in beiden Händen in soweit nöthig macht, dass die geschwinden Noten nicht übereilt herausgesprudelt werden, sondern sehr zart und graziös nach und nach verschwimmen; erst die letzten 9 Noten dieser Verzierung sind mehr merkbar zu *ritardiren*, und auf der vorletzten Note (dem *Gis*) eine kleine Haltung anzubringen. Über die Eintheilung dieser längeren Verzierungen wird später gesprochen werden. 6.) Der 7te und 8te Takt bleiben streng im *Tempo*. 7.) Der 9te Takt mit Kraft und Wärme, (folglich *beinahe* etwas *accelerando*.) 8.) Die 2te Hälfte des 10ten Takts etwas ruhiger. 9.) Der 11te Takt etwas *ritardando*, und der letzte *dissonirende Accord* sehr sanft, noch etwas mehr zurückgehalten, weil jeder *dissonirende Accord*, (wenn er *piano* ist) auf diese Art mehr Wirkung macht. 10.) Die 3 ersten Achteln des 12ten Takts im *Tempo;* dagegen die 5 letzten Achteln bedeutend *ritardando*, da sie den Übergang in das *Thema* bilden. 11.) Der 13te Takt im *Tempo*. 12.) Das erste Viertel des 14ten Takts schon ziemlich *ritard.* welches sich in der 2ten Viertel bedeutend vermehrt, und wobei die 8 obern Noten stark und *cresc.* markirt werden müssen. Die Haltung muss ungefähr durch 5 Achteln dauern, und der nachfolgende Lauf mässig schnell, gleich, zart, und *diminuendo* sein, bis endlich die 8 letzten Noten desselben merkbar *ritardando* werden. 13.) Die 1ste Hälfte des 15ten Takts im *Tempo*, die 2te Hälfte *ritard.* wobei der Schluss der Verzierung äusserst zart verschweben muss. Hier ist das *ritardiren* am nöthigsten, da dieser Takt eine sanft vorzutragende Schluss-*Cadenz* enthält. 14.) Der letzte Takt im ruhigen *Tempo*. Folgende zwei Bemerkungen sind wohl zu beachten. I.) Obwohl in diesem Thema fast in jedem Takt ein *ritard.* angebracht wird, so muss das Ganze, (besonders in der begleitenden linken Hand,) so natürlich, folgerecht, ohne alle Verzerrung, vorgetragen werden, dass der Zuhörer nie über das eigentliche Zeitmass in Zweifel gelassen oder gelangweilt wird. II.) Da jeder Theil 2^{mal} gespielt wird, so kann beim zweitenmale jeder Ausdruck und folglich auch jedes *ritard.* um ein Weniges merkbarer angebracht werden, wodurch das Ganze an Jnteresse gewinnt" (Czerny, *Pianoforte-Schule*, vol. 3, 27).

cerned with the dangers of sentimentality and loss of cohesion, while Schindler argues that without a deep understanding of content and the drama of individual gestures, attempts at cohesion are merely superficial, and not surprisingly he deliberately avoids using Czerny's mechanical solution. Granted, he lacks good judgment and restraint at times, but his view of tempo may well be one with which Beethoven sympathized, for, as we have seen, the composer was put off by the sound of "mechanism," did find that certain works resisted summation of tempo in any simple way, and was—just as was Czerny—vexed by changing perceptions of proper tempo.

While many of Schindler's stories have proved apocryphal, his assertion that Czerny's performance suggestions are inadequate in representing Beethoven's tempi and at times "ambiguous and misleading" must be seriously considered.[82] Schindler's "qualms" about mechanical tempi—imputed to Beethoven, but not without some grounds for doing so—led him to conclude that the best vocabulary for discussing character and tempo in Beethoven's works is to be found in the theories of rhetoric and poetry, which, when applied to music in the traditional way, articulate both a hierarchy of relationships and an array of distinctions in meaning and gesture. Given Beethoven's background, that is good advice.

Interpreting a Metronome Marking

From the point of view of rhetorical theory, then, the metronome provides no simple answer to the question of Beethoven's tempi, which cannot be summarized in a number, in a word, or in those carefully wrought German descriptive phrases Beethoven fashioned for some of his later works, although any or all of these can provide clues. But how did Beethoven or Czerny—how shall *we*—set about determining tempo?

Apparently we should expect to enter into a process similar to the one that Brahms later described and that Beethoven and Czerny expe-

[82]Schindler and MacArdle, *Beethoven*, 420.

rienced, arriving again and again at different metronome settings as we attempt to account for all the musical parameters. Both the creator and the performer had to balance detail with large-scale form; they had to account for every level from the most *innig* aspects of the smallest details to the broadest frames of reference in the public realms of genre and general character. But the question remains as to why, when they had come to grips with this problem of differentiation and relationship, they persisted in summarizing a movement or a whole work with a single number. Given their avowed interest in accurately communicating tempo, they could easily have affixed new settings to themes whose character demanded subtle alteration, or at least specified a range at the beginning of the piece.

I suspect that Beethoven's reasons for maintaining this practice were in some important ways different from Czerny's. Like Czerny, Beethoven was passionate about coherence and experienced the wholeness of his works very strongly; he believed in a "proper tempo," and his choice of metronome setting represented something perceived as essential to the piece. But in "Nord oder Süd" it was "the first measures," and in certain unmarked works in which texture varied extremely (like the Piano Sonata Op. 110) one can imagine his conceiving a tempo that remained unstated by any part but was referred to by all, a sort of fixed point from which character emerged. In the works for larger ensembles we might expect to find the greatest limitation on flexibility, the limit being whatever can be effectively communicated to an orchestra through the gestures of a conductor, but even here it is wise to remember Beethoven's determination to wring the most intense expression from his players. Ignaz von Seyfried reminds us that even in the early years (1800–05) he

was ceaselessly engaged in calling attention to . . . authentic expression by means of the most manifold gesticulations. Thus he often struck *down* with his baton at a strong dynamic point, though it might occur on the weak beat of the measure. He was accustomed to indicate a *diminuendo* by trying to make himself smaller and smaller, and at the *pianissimo* slipped under the conductor's desk, so to say. As the tonal masses increased in volume, he too seemed to swell, as though out of a contraction, and with the entrance of the entire body of instrumental tone he rose on the tips of his toes, grew to well-nigh giant size, and swaying in the air with his arms, seemed to be trying to float up into the clouds. . . . He was very meticulous with regard to expression, the more delicate shadings, an equalized distribution of light and shade, and an effective *tempo rubato,* and without betraying the slightest impatience always took pleasure in discussing them individually with the various musicians.[83]

For Czerny, on the other hand, I sense that concerns no less important but somewhat less elevated mitigated against his ever specifying tempo range. As a pedagogue he felt it incumbent upon himself to take a firm stand against "caricature," and he remained convinced that the single number was the most effective weapon with which he could arm the amateur, who faced the crisis of loss of cohesion with the appearance of each new musical character that Beethoven sent his way.[84]

As for the problem of indecision, both Czerny and Beethoven were balancing whatever aspects of content seemed important during a reading with those other variables of which good musicians are aware: variations in instruments, and in the acoustic and symbolic spaces that the compositions occupy. All these variables are "alive," and taken together they may lead us away from the arbitrary norm of metronomic time far more radically than Czerny could ever admit.

---

[83]Oscar Sonneck, ed., *Beethoven: Impressions by His Contemporaries* (New York: G. Schirmer, 1926), 40–41; and Forbes, *Thayer's Life of Beethoven,* 371; see also 565–66 (a corroboration by Spohr), 570 (a corroboration by the singer Franz Wild), and 811 (a corroboration by the dramatic singer Wilhelmine Schröder-Devrient).

[84]Had Schindler been less fanatical in rejecting the metronome, he might have left us metronome indications for his "recollection" of Beethoven's playing of the Sonata Op. 14, no. 2 (one of several descriptions in his early *Biographie* that A. B. Marx criticized and Schindler eventually withdrew in part). As it is we are left with his characterizations for the themes of the first movement *Allegro,* which range from an *allegro* proper, commenced "with vigor and passion," to an *andantino* and even an *andante.* The range is typically exaggerated but, taken purely in Beethoven's preferred sense, as character terms, his choices seem thematically descriptive in every case (Schindler and Moscheles, *Life of Beethoven,* 157–60; Marx's response to Schindler appears in Adolf Bernhard Marx, *Ludwig van Beethoven, Leben und Schaffen* [Berlin, 1859], 5th ed., 3 books in 2 vols. [Leipzig: Adolph Schumann, 1902], vol. 1, 128–32 and 134–35).

Beethoven, though reluctant to admit this, faced it at the earliest opportunity and gave voice to it in a positive way: "Feeling also has its tempo." Czerny, on the other hand, remained adamantly defensive about it, even in the face of his own history of significantly revising metronome settings. This is a crucial temperamental difference between master and disciple. But there is yet another reason why Czerny cannot simply be taken at his word when he claims to be an authoritative spokesman for Beethoven. There is evidence that his principles for conceiving the very substance of musical utterance differed from Beethoven's in ways that gradually led him away from Beethoven's aesthetic.

Czerny on "Proper Performance"

In his "Recollections" Czerny writes, "I was about ten years old when Krumpholz introduced me to Beethoven."[85] Joseph Kerman describes the period as one in which the composer "appeared much concerned with being original." In the eyes of Czerny, who viewed even the early Trio in C minor, Op. 1, no. 3 as an indication of "how soon Beethoven strove to release himself from the *old-fashioned style*,"[86] Beethoven was about to succeed. For after 1803 he no longer "remained faithful . . . to the Mozart-Haydn style."[87]

[85]"10 Jahre war ich ungefähr alt, als ich durch Krumpholz zum Beethoven geführt wurde" (Czerny, *Erinnerungen*, 13).

[86]" . . . [W]ie frühzeitig sich Beethoven von dem *ältern Style* loszuringen strebte" (Czerny, *Über den richtigen Vortrag*, 87).

[87]Kerman and Tyson, *New Grove Beethoven*, 103; and Czerny, *Über den richtigen Vortrag*, 26. Czerny states that "up to his 28*th* work (about 1803) he remained faithful to a certain degree to the *Mozart-Haydn* style; but from then until about his 90*th* work (from 1803 to 1815) he fully displayed his truly characteristic [style], and from this point (until his death in 1827) he once again took a new direction, which is no less grand, but differs considerably from both earlier [styles]" [er bis zu seinem 28*sten* Werke (um 1803) dem *Mozart-Haydn*-schen Style in einem gewissen Grade treu blieb, hierauf aber bis ungefähr zu seinem 90*sten* Werke (von 1803 bis 1815) seine ganze wahre Eigenthümlichkeit entfaltete und hierauf (bis an sein Ende 1827) noch einmal eine neue Richtung einschlug, die nicht minder grossartig ist, sich aber bedeutend von den beiden frühern unterscheidet] (Czerny, *Über den richtigen Vortrag*, 26).

We need to determine just how Czerny distinguishes Beethoven's style from "the old-fashioned style," and in particular how he distinguishes Beethoven's syntax from that of Mozart and Haydn. In his *Pianoforte-Schule* he likens Mozart's style to "the modern clear and brilliantly piquant manner of playing" that Hummel perfected, especially effective with German instruments, which were "more suited for public dissemination, as well as for the use of youth" because they "combined light and shallow touch with greater clarity [of tone]." Mozart's was a school "based more on the *staccato* than on the *legato;* a more witty and spirited execution" for which the pedals were "seldom used, and . . . never essential."

In stark contrast is the playing of Beethoven,

> who elicited from the *fortepiano* through entirely new and daring runs, through the use of the pedals, through an extraordinarily *characteristic* manner of playing that was distinguished particularly by the strict *legato* of its *chords,* and which therefore brought about a new kind of singing—many effects never before imagined. His execution did not possess the pure and brilliant elegance of many other *keyboardists,* but on the other hand it was witty, grand, and especially in the *Adagio,* replete with feeling in the highest degree and romantic. His performance was, like his *composition,* musical painting of the highest sort, aimed solely for the total effect. . . .
>
> Predominant [in his style] is characteristic and passionate vigor, alternating with all the charms of the bound *cantabile.*
>
> The means of expression is often heightened to extremes, especially in reference to [his] more capricious mood. The piquant, brilliantly showy manner is only rarely applicable. Rather, total effects are much more often applied, partly through a full-voiced *legato,* and partly through skillful use of the *loud pedal,* etc.
>
> Great fluency without brilliant pretension. In the *Adagio* more rapturous expression and more tender singing.[88]

[88]"*Mozarts* Manier, welche sich mehr [die neuere klare und brilliant-pikante Manier] näherte, und vorzüglich durch *Hummel* so trefflich vervollkommt wurde, eignete sich mehr für die deutschen *Fortepiano,* welche leichten und seichten Anschlag mit grosser Deutlichkeit vereinten, und sich demnach mehr für die allgemeine Verbreitung, so wie für den Gebrauch der Jugend eigneten. . . .

For Czerny the "schools" are defined by the instruments, touches, and effects of their practitioners: Mozart's spirited wit he associates with unpedaled staccato, Beethoven's "new kind of singing" with pedaled legato. But because he was apparently vexed by aspects of Beethoven's practice that were not sufficiently distinguishable from "the old-fashioned style" to suit his taste, the distinction is a dangerous one for Czerny. This is revealed in part when we compare two of his axioms for performance. The first is his oft-mentioned warning to performers given in *Über den richtigen Vortrag:*

> Before we deal with Beethoven's *compositions* singly, it is necessary to establish a general rule.
>
> *In the performance of his works, (and actually with all classical authors) the player may permit himself throughout no alteration of the composition, no addition, no abridgement.*[89]

"*Mozart's* Schule: Ein klares, schon bedeutend brillantes Spiel, mehr auf das *Staccato*, als auf das *Legato* berechnet; geistreicher und lebhafter Vortrag. Das *Pedal* selten benützt und niemals nothwendig.

"Jnzwischen erschien (um 1790) *Beethoven*, und entlockte dem *Fortepiano* durch ganz neue kühne Passagen, durch den Gebrauch des *Pedals*, durch ein ausserordentlich *charakteristisches* Spiel, welches sich besonders im strengen *Legato* der *Accorde* auszeichnete, und daher eine neue Art von Gesang bildete,—viele bis dahin nicht geahneten Effekte. Sein Spiel besass nicht jene reine und brillante Eleganz mancher andern *Claviristen*, was aber dagegen geistreich, grossartig, und besonders im *Adagio* höchst gefühlvoll und romantisch. Sein Vortrag war, so wie seine *Compositionen*, ein Tongemälde höherer Art, nur für die Gesammtwirkung berechnet. . . .

"*Beethoven's* Manier: Characteristische und leidenschaftliche Kraft, abwechselnd mit allen Reizen des gebundenen *Cantabile* ist hier vorherrschend.

"Die Mittel des Ausdrucks werden hier oft bis zum Extremen gesteigert, besonders in Rücksicht humoristischer Laune. Die pikante, brillant hervorstehende Manier ist da nur selten anwendbar. Desto öfter sind da aber die Totaleffekte, theils durch ein vollstimmiges *Legato*, theils durch geschickte Anwendung des *Fortepedals*, u.s.w. anzuwenden.

"Grosse Geläufigkeit ohne brillante Prätension. Jm *Adagio* schwärmerischer Ausdruck und gefühlvoller Gesang" (idem, *Pianoforte-Schule*, vol. 3, 72).

[89]"Ehe wir Beethovens *Compositionen* einzeln vornehmen, ist es nöthig eine allgemeine Regel festzusetzen.

"*Beim Vortrage seiner Werke, (und überhaupt bei allen klassischen Autoren) darf der Spieler sich durchaus keine Änderung der Composition, keinen Zusatz, keine Abkürzung erlauben*" (idem, *Über den richtigen Vortrag*, 26).

Seldom quoted is the far more discreet suggestion that immediately precedes it:

> However [the effectiveness of his performance] depended at the same time on his continually changing frame of mind, and even if it were possible to reproduce his style of playing quite exactly, it could not always serve us as a model, (with respect to the altogether different purity and clearness in managing difficulties that is cultivated nowadays); and even the spiritual conception takes on a different value because of changed prevailing taste, and must at times be expressed by other means than were necessary in that time.[90]

This is more than a subtle assessment of Beethoven's—impure and unclear?—keyboard technique. With the claim that changing taste necessitates "other means" for the realization of Beethoven's ideas, Czerny opens the way for "modernization." Now we must discover what "other means" he imagines employing. What is it that he intends to modernize?

Several possibilities can be readily eliminated. In the *Wiener Musik-Zeitung* of 20 September 1845, Czerny recounts his having "[taken] the liberty of complicating the passage work, of using the higher octaves, etc." in a performance of Beethoven's Quintet for Piano and Winds. Beethoven was furious with him, and burst out with such violence that Czerny came away convinced that pitches, ornaments, and registers were to be left unchanged.[91]

We might assume that the "other means" involve liberties with

---

[90]"Jndessen hing er dabei von seinen stets wechselnden Launen ab, und wenn es auch möglich wäre, seine Spielweise ganz genau wiederzugeben, so könnte sie, (in Bezug auf die jetzt ganz anders ausgebildete Reinheit und Deutlichkeit bei Schwierigkeiten) uns nicht immer als Muster dienen; und selbst die geistige Auffassung erhält durch den veränderten Zeitgeschmack eine and're Geltung, und muss bisweilen durch and're Mittel ausgedrückt werden, als damals erforderlich waren" (ibid.).

[91]"Als ich z. B. einst (um 1812) in Schuppanzighs Musik das Quintett mit Blasinstrumenten [Op. 16] vortrug, erlaubte ich mir im jugendlichen Leichtsinn manche Änderungen,—Erschwerung der Passagen, Benützung der höheren Oktave etc.—Beethoven warf es mir mit Recht in Gegenwart des Schuppanzigh, Linke und der anderen Begleitenden mit Strenge vor" (idem, *Erinnerungen,* 34); see also Badura-Skoda's commentary to Czerny's *Proper Performance,* 1.

tempo, since on the page following his warning not to alter the composition, he suggests several tempo modifications that are not to be found in the score.[92] Yet as we have seen these do not qualify as "modernizations" either; rather they are among the sorts of unwritten modifications Czerny assumes to be part of interpretation. Earlier in his *Pianoforte-Schule* he attempted to describe and systematize them—another example of his admirable ability to perceive patterns and commonplaces in music:

A *ritardando* may be made to advantage
   a) In passages [that] form a return to the main subject.
   b) On notes [that] lead up to a single small part of a *cantabile* line.
   c) On sustained notes that are to be struck with particular emphasis, and which are followed by shorter notes.
   d) During the transition to a new tempo, or to a movement wholly different from the preceding one.
   e) Immediately before a fermata.
   f) When a very lively passage, or some brilliant figure-work, gives way to a *diminuendo* introducing a short, delicate run.
   g) On ornaments consisting of a large number of quick notes which cannot be squeezed into the correct tempo.
   h) Occasionally in heavily marked passages, where a strong *crescendo* leads to a new movement or to the end of the piece.
   i) In very whimsical, capricious or fanciful movements, in order to highlight their character better.
   k) Finally, in almost every case where the composer has put *espressivo;* and
   l) At the end of every long trill forming a halt and a cadence in *diminuendo*, as well as on gentle cadences in general.

---

[92]These apply to the first movement of Op. 2, no. 1, and include a *ritardando* and a *crescendo* from the fourth bar to the fermata in the eighth bar, and a tempo modification for the *con espressione* written in the second half of bar 41 (through the first half of bar 42), the tempo reentering decidedly in bar 45: "Vom 4ten Takte dieses Satzes fangt ein kleines *Ritardando* und *crescendo* an, welches bis zur Haltung zunimmt. Die Takte 41 bis 44 des ersten Theils sind ebenfalls mit zunehmendem *Ritard.* vorzutragen, und erst in der 2ten Hälfte des 45sten Taktes tritt das *Tempo* wieder entschieden ein" (Czerny, *Über den richtigen Vortrag*, 27).

NB: It is understood that the word *ritardando* as used above includes all other terms [that] indicate a greater or lesser slowing of the tempo.[93]

Tempo flexibility, then, is governed by a set of principles, and there is every indication that his summary of those principles represents to Czerny a guide to what Beethoven would have done.

But then what is it in Beethoven's works that remains in need of "other means" for realization? The examples in Czerny's *Über den richtigen Vortrag* and his editorial revisions to some of the Beethoven piano sonatas suggest an answer: he was in fact referring to one of his chiefest concerns, that of articulation and touch. Throughout those parts of his *Pianoforte-Schule* in which he deals with Beethoven's works, Czerny again and again presents excerpts with altered slurs, dots, strokes, hairpins, dynamic markings, and note values. For example, of his 139 incipits for the sonatas, only seven of the simplest accurately represent Beethoven's text from first edition or autograph. Were these incipits intended merely for the purpose of identifying works, such alterations might seem somewhat less important, but they are generally employed as references in discussions of character, and often two or more excerpts from a single movement or work are used to illustrate especially important points. Although he was much

---

[93]"Am schicklichsten wird *ritardirt: a)* Jn jenen Stellen, welche die Rückkehr in das Hauptthema bilden. *b)* Jn jenen Noten, welche zu einem einzelnen Theilchen eines Gesangs führen. *c)* Bei jenen gehaltenen Noten, welche mit besonderem Nachdruck angeschlagen werden müssen, und nach welchen kurze Noten folgen. *d)* Bei dem Übergang in ein anderes Zeitmass, oder in einen, vom Vorigen ganz verschiedenen Satz. *e)* Unmittelbar vor einer Haltung. *f)* Beim *Diminuendo* einer früher sehr lebhaften Stelle, so wie bei brillanten Passagen, wenn plötzlich ein *piano* und *delicat* vorzutragender Lauf eintritt. *g)* Bei Verzierungen, welche aus sehr vielen geschwinden Noten bestehen, die man nicht in das rechte Zeitmass hineinzwängen könnte. *h)* Bisweilen auch in dem starken *crescendo* einer besonders markirten Stelle, die zu einem bedeutenden Satze oder zum Schluss führt. *i)* Bei sehr launigen, *capriziösen*, und fantastischen Sätzen, um deren *Charakter* desto mehr zu heben. *k)* Endlich fast stets da, wo der Tonsetzer ein *espressivo* gesetzt hat; so wie *l)* Das Ende eines jeden langen Trillers, welcher eine Haltung und *Cadenz* bildet, und *diminuendo* ist, wie auch jede sanfte *Cadenz* überhaupt. NB. Es versteht sich, dass hier unter dem Wort *ritardando* auch alle übrigen Benennungen mit verstanden werden, welche eine mehr oder minder langsame Bewegung des *Tempo* anzeigen" (Czerny, *Pianoforte-Schule,* vol. 3, 26; translation adapted from Alfred Brendel's *Musical Thoughts and Afterthoughts* [Princeton: Princeton University Press, 1976], 34).

more restrained in altering slurs and dynamics in his editions of the
sonatas, his revisions there also often reveal the gulf between his
language and his teacher's.[94] Czerny alters Beethoven's texts both by
omission and by addition. This would seem to be a blatant contradiction of his edict concerning respect for the texts of the masters: "*no
alteration . . . , no addition, no abridgement.*" Unless, of course, this
aspect of notation is exempt, having been altered so much by changing taste that it requires "other means" for its expression.

In most cases Czerny falsifies Beethoven's slurs by lengthening
them, as, for example, in the Piano Sonata in A-flat, Op. 26, composed in 1800–1801 and published in Vienna in 1802.[95] Recalling that
Czerny sees Beethoven at this time working within the "Mozart-
Haydn style," let us compare the first eight measures of the *Andante
con Variazioni* as it appears in *Über den richtigen Vortrag* (Example 4)
with the autograph (Example 2) and first edition (Example 3).

To my ears Czerny's expansive ligature in Example 4 deprives the
opening melody of both the grace and the internal direction afforded
by Beethoven's shorter slurs.[96] And Czerny's description of the work
seems in keeping with his concept of its slurring: "In the performance
of this theme, the whole art of sustained, harmonious *legato,* and
beautiful touch, must be brought to bear in order to display worthily
the noble, almost religious character of the same."[97] But surely this
"modernization" affects tempo. Having removed the lilt of the slurs,

[94]For just a few of many examples from the early sonatas edited for Simrock in
Bonn (published in 1856): he changes trochaic slurs to iambic in bars 17–18 of the
Largo, con gran espressione of Op. 7, and adds slurs to the *grazioso* bass texture with
octave leaps in bars 15–16 in the *Poco Allegretto e grazioso* of the same sonata; he
supplies bars in dotted rhythms with one overarching slur in bars 50–51 of the *Adagio
molto* movement of Op. 10, no. 1; he extends slurs in both left and right hands to
subsume Beethoven's unslurred quarters and two-note slurs in the opening *Allegro* of
Op. 10, no. 2 from bar 5; and he replaces beat slurs with two-bar slurs beginning at
bar 8 in the opening *Allegro* of Op. 14, no. 2.

[95]Kerman and Tyson, *New Grove Beethoven*, 168.

[96]I use the term "ligature" here in its most generic sense as a sign of binding because
Czerny, in lengthening Beethoven's slurs, began to blur distinctions between slurs and
what came to be called "phrases" or "phrasing slurs" in the nineteenth century. This is
discussed in more detail presently.

[97]"Beim Vortrage dieses Thema muss die ganze Kunst des gehaltenen harmoniösen
Legato und des schönen Anschlags aufgebothen werden, um den edlen, beinahe re-
ligiösen *Character* desselben würdig darzustellen" (Czerny, *Über den richtigen Vortrag,*
41).

Example 2. Beethoven Sonata in A-flat, Op. 26, first movement, measures 1–8 (holograph)

Example 3. Beethoven Sonata in A-flat, Op. 26, first movement, measures 1–8 (first edition, Vienna: Cappi, 1802)

Example 4. Beethoven Sonata in A-flat, Op. 26, first movement, measures 1–8 (Czerny, *Über den richtigen Vortrag,* 41)

Czerny imagines the theme at a surprisingly broad ♪ = 76. Worth noting is the marking in his edition for Simrock (Example 5), which retains more authentic slurring, though some of Beethoven's staccato marks are missing: still very broad, it is somewhat faster at ♪ = 80.[98]

---

[98]The tempo still seems too slow. In his commentary on *Proper Performance* Badura-Skoda recommends "a basic tempo of ♩ = 88–92" which "ought to be maintained throughout the whole movement with but slight differences" (Czerny, *Proper Performance,* commentary, 2).

Example 5. Beethoven Sonata in A-flat, Op. 26, first movement, measures 1–8 (Czerny edition, Bonn: Simrock, 1856)

In the first eight measures of the Scherzo of the same sonata, an *Allegro molto* for which Czerny gives ♩. = 88 in the Simrock edition, the slurring in Simrock (Example 8) crosses measures like 1–2 consistently, whereas the first edition (Example 7) does so less often and the holograph (Example 6) even less.[99] But when in *Über den richtigen*

Example 6. Beethoven Sonata in A-flat, Op. 26, second movement, measures 1–8 (holograph)

[99]The slur missing from the first upbeat in the holograph and first edition is supplied in subsequent cases. On the other hand, this holograph does offer the reader a vivid experience of the way Beethoven's apparent concern for precision combines with a certain seeming illogicality (or at least a playful approach to variation) and a desire to stretch notation beyond conventional limits (as when he makes dips in his

Example 7. Beethoven Sonata in A-flat, Op. 26, second movement, measures 1–8 (first edition, Vienna: Cappi, 1802)

Example 8. Beethoven Sonata in A-flat, Op. 26, second movement, measures 1–8 (Czerny edition, Bonn: Simrock, 1856)

Vortrag Czerny dispenses with the opening two–note slur and binds the pair of eighths into a long slur, some of the power of freshness on the downbeat sforzato is lost along with a number of Beethoven's staccato marks. Czerny senses that the removal of the slur in bar 1 is denying the first beat of bar 2 its due stress, so he inserts a hairpin over the right-hand E-flat (Example 9). The tempo quickens with this loss of detail to ♩. = 92.

Czerny no less than Schindler would have had to face Beethoven's ire for such emendations, given the August 1825 letter to Karl Holz in

---

slurs that have the effect of further segmenting them). Nevertheless we ought not to approach all this by removing the evidence, as Czerny does. Better to live with the strangeness until something comes of it: either an understanding of it as it stands, a decision to pattern the variation, or an ability to improvise in the spirit of it.

Example 9. Beethoven Sonata in A-flat, Op. 26, second movement, measures 1–8 (Czerny, *Über den richtigen Vortrag,* 41)

which he discusses copyist errors in his String Quartet in A minor, Op. 132. In one of his corrections Beethoven associates the articulation of a two-note slur with a slower tempo:[100]

The slurs exactly as they stand now! It is not all the same whether it is like this

or like this!

In the Adagio more often like this

A third example from Op. 26 provides evidence that Czerny's use of the ligature can differ from Beethoven's in an even more visually

[100]"Die Bindungen gerade so wie sie jetzt stehen! es ist nicht gleichgiltig ob so . . . oder so . . . ! —Im Adagio viel mehr so . . . " (Beethoven, *Ludwig van Beethovens sämtliche Briefe,* ed. Fritz Prelinger [Vienna: C. W. Stern, 1907], vol. 3, 212). Beethoven's use of an articulated final note is by no means limited to slow tempi. My point here is that the removal of articulation in a fast tempo often has the effect of lessening the rhythmic verve; once the articulation has been removed, a performer will often attempt to compensate by further increasing tempo. This is discussed in more detail presently.

Example 10. Beethoven Sonata in A-flat, Op. 26, third movement, measures 1–2 (holograph)

Example 11. Beethoven Sonata in A-flat, Op. 26, third movement, measures 1–2 (first edition, Vienna: Cappi, 1802)

Example 12. Beethoven Sonata in A-flat, Op. 26, third movement, measures 1–2 (Czerny edition, Bonn: Simrock, 1856)

Example 13. Beethoven Sonata in A-flat, Op. 26, third movement, measures 1–2 (Czerny, *Über den richtigen Vortrag,* 41)

striking way. In the first two measures of the *Marcia funebre* Czerny is concerned with projecting "a certain earnest grandeur" not only by "the slow stepping tempo but also by a weighty striking of the chords in the strictest *tenuto*."[101] Most likely the notion of tenuto chords is what prompts him to use what will later be called a "phrasing slur" in his incipit for *Über den richtigen Vortrag,* shown in Example 13. In the edition for Simrock (Example 12), the articulation is identical to the holograph and first edition (Examples 10 and 11, respectively), the strange ligature is absent, and the tempo is slower at ♩ = 66.

The extent to which Czerny removes slurs that have an *essential* role in defining character is remarkable. Two more examples from works Czerny identified with Beethoven's more classical period are worth noting here. The first is the opening three measures of the *Adagio con molto espressione* from the Piano Sonata Op. 22. The "molto espressione" comes to the fore at once with the fresh A-natural in the second measure (Example 14). But Czerny seems not to notice the effect (Example 15).

Example 14. Beethoven Sonata in B-flat, Op. 22, second movement, measures 1–3 (first edition, Vienna: Hoffmeister, 1802)

Example 15. Beethoven Sonata in B-flat, Op. 22, second movement, measures 1–3 (Czerny, *Über den richtigen Vortrag,* 40)

[101]"Als Trauermarsch auf den Tod eines Helden muss dieser Satz vom Spieler mit einer gewissen ernsten Grösse gespielt werden, welche sich nicht nur durch das langsam schreitende Tempo, sondern auch durch einen gewichtigen Anschlag der Accorde im strengsten *Tenuto* ausspricht" (Czerny, *Über den richtigen Vortrag,* 41–42).

Example 16. Beethoven Sonata in C Minor, Op. 13 (*Pathétique*), first movement, measure 1 (first edition, Vienna: Hoffmeister, 1799)

Example 17. Beethoven Sonata in C Minor, Op. 13 (*Pathétique*), first movement, measure 1 (Czerny, *Über den richtigen Vortrag,* 37)

In the first measure of the *Pathétique* Sonata, Op. 13, after the first shocking forte, soft unbound chords in dotted rhythm lead to the signature pathetic slur (Example 16). But here Czerny omits the inner ligature and extends the outer ligatures backward to include the soft chords (Example 17). What is more, his tendency to bind the dotted-style chords and to suppress the pathetic slur appears as early as the Haslinger edition, as we see in Example 18 (bars 7–8 especially).

Apparently these changes seemed to Czerny not even minor infractions. But for us they pose a significant problem, making it even more difficult for us to judge the implications of his suggestions about character and tempo. For surely, with the subsuming of arrival notes that Beethoven had *not* subsumed, and the lengthening of slurs that Beethoven had *not* lengthened, character and tempo can be significantly altered. I suspect that this is one reason why Czerny vacillated so much in choosing metronome settings for the Beethoven sonatas. Despite the fact that he had studied the *Pathétique* Sonata with Beethoven, the *Grave* was especially problematic for him. From

Example 18. Beethoven Sonata in C Minor, Op. 13 (*Pathétique*), first movement, measures 1–8 (Vienna: Haslinger [ca. 1830])

the early tempo of ♪ = 58 for both states of the Haslinger edition,
Czerny dropped the tempo to ♪ = 92 (♩ = 46) for *Proper Performance,*
and presented it with the following gloss:

> The introduction is played so slowly and solemnly that we could
> only indicate the metronome mark with sixteenths. The chords all
> very weighty, and in the 5th to the 8th measure the left hand accom-

paniment very *legato*. The closing chromatic run very fast and light until the hold. [102]

But by 1857 he had raised the tempo to ♪ = 63 for the Simrock edition, seventeen points faster on the metronome scale!

Both his uncertainty about tempo and his alterations of articulation bring to mind an incident from Czerny's youth that, once again, aroused Beethoven's anger:

> My musical memory allowed me to play *all* of Beethoven's works, without exception, by memory, and during 1804 to 1805 I had to play them in this way once or twice a week before Prince Lichnowsky, who would give only the Opus number of the piece he wished to hear. Beethoven, who was present on one occasion, was not pleased with this. "Even though he plays correctly for the most part," he said, "this sort of thing will make him lose the quick grasp, the sight reading, and now and then even the proper emphasis." [103]

It is conceivable that Czerny, who took great pride in his memory, relied on it to some degree in preparing his examples for *Über den richtigen Vortrag*. That could explain why Beethoven's sforzati appear in his excerpts as accents, the forte-pianos as sforzati, the bass figurations with additional stems affixed to their lowest notes to create

[102]"Die Jntroduction wird so langsam und pathetisch vorgetragen, dass wir das Metronom nur durch Sechzehnteln bezeichnen konnten. Die Accorde sämmtlich sehr gewichtig, und im 5ten bis 8ten Takte die Begleitung der linken Hand sehr *legato*. Den chromatischen Schlusslauf sehr schnell und leicht, bis zur Haltung" (ibid., 37). Czerny says nothing of the silences after the pathetic slurs, or of the awkwardness of the ornament that appears to accelerate at the end of bar 4; both of these at least merit consideration in Schindler's description.

[103]"Mein musikalisches Gedächtniß gestattete mir, *alle* Beethovenschen Werke, ohne Ausnahme, auswendig zu spielen, und in den Jahren 1804 bis 1805 mußte ich wöchentlich ein bis 2 mal beym Fürsten *Lichnowsky* diese Werke auf die Art vorspielen, indem er nach Belieben nur die Opuszahl bezeichnete. Beethoven, der einigemal dabey zugegen war, war damit nicht zufrieden. 'Wenn er auch im Ganzen richtig spielt,' sagte er, 'so verlernt er auf diese Weise den schnellen Überblick, das Avistaspielen, und hie und da doch auch die richtige Betonung'" (ibid., excerpts from Czerny's "Anekdoten und Notizen über Beethoven," 14).

linear effects, and the dynamic markings with only approximate correctness, with piano for pianissimo, fortissimo for forte, and crescendo and diminuendo hairpins with inaccurate destinations. If this is in fact what Czerny did, then Beethoven's worst fears were realized.

Czerny and the Declamatory Style

While Czerny does occasionally mention the importance of "proper emphasis" in musical declamation, he parts company with Mattheson, Quantz, Emanuel Bach, Kirnberger, and, of course, Schindler, in not giving the idea of musical rhetoric a prominent place in his writing.[104] He is apparently well aware of the declamatory style, yet he mentions it seldom, and when he does, he generally refers to it in its more specialized sense. For example, in describing the first movement *Allegro* of the Sonata in A for Piano and Violin, Op. 30, no. 1 (Example 19), he contrasts the declamatory style with sentimentality, perhaps as another defense against "caricature": "Of a peaceful, gently earnest *character*. More declamatory than sentimental."[105]

One of his most perceptive descriptions of the style appears in his advice on the performance of the last movement of the *Archduke* Trio, Op. 97 (which, as we recall, he studied with Beethoven):

[104]In a description of the importance of *Vortrag* reminiscent of Quantz, Czerny lamented the effects of unexpressive performance: "Many of Beethoven's admirers are frequently quite astonished and distressed when these works do not always elicit those effects which lie in them. Then one routinely ascribes it to corrupt taste and other causes, without reflecting on the fact that one who speaks to others must also express himself clearly, forcefully, correctly and worthily" [Oft manche Bewund'rer Beethovens ganz erstaunt und betrübt sind, wenn diese Werke nicht immer diejenige Wirkung hervorbringen, die in ihnen liegt. Man streibt es dann gewöhnlich dem verdorbenen Geschmack und andern Ursachen zu, ohne daran zu denken, dass derjenige, der zu andern spricht, sich auch deutlich, eindringend, korrekt, und würdig ausdrücken muss] (ibid., 24).

[105]"Von ruhigem, sanft ernsten *Character*. Mehr sprechend als sentimental" (ibid., 73). Czerny's slurring differs markedly from that of the first edition (Vienna: Bureau, 1803).

Example 19. Beethoven Sonata in A, Op. 30, no. 1, first movement, measures 1–7 (Czerny, *Über den richtigen Vortrag,* 73)

The first two bars forceful and abrupt, like an unexpected question. The following lovely melody with tender, declamatory expression; more speech than song.[106]

He describes the Piano Sonata in E-flat, Op. 31, no. 3 (Example 20) in a similar way, calling attention in the first eight measures to the way question and answer can suspend a *tempo giusto:*[107]

This *sonata* is more declamatory than pictorial, and distinguishes itself from the elegiac, romantic *character* of the foregoing through its clever cheerfulness. The opening resembles a question to which the answer follows in the 7th measure, and must therefore possess a certain indecisive cast in tempo and expression.[108]

But here Czerny is too quick to give over the responsibility of discerning the nature of the *tempo giusto* to the metronome:

---

[106]"Die ersten 2 Takte kräftig und kurz, gleich einer unerwarteten Frage. Die folgende schöne Melodie mit zartem, deklamatorischen Ausdruck: mehr Sprache als Gesang" (Czerny, *Über den richtigen Vortrag,* 95).

[107]Note that the "question" that opens Op. 31, no. 3 is *not* a rising gesture. Mattheson would have seen this as evidence of sophistication: he insists that while "in everyday speech and pronunciation the voice is always raised more or less with a question; . . . in melody there are many circumstances which not only permit an exception to this but often require it" (Ernest C. Harriss, *Johann Mattheson's "Der volkommene Capellmeister": A Revised Translation with Critical Commentary* [Ann Arbor, Mich.: UMI Research Press, 1981], 398 [192 in original]).

[108]"Diese *Sonate* ist mehr sprechend als malend, und unterscheidet sich durch ihre geistreiche Heiterkeit völlig von dem elegisch-romantischen *Character* der Vorhergehenden. Der Anfang gleicht einer Frage, auf welche im 7ten Takte die Antwort

Example 20. Beethoven Sonata in E-flat, Op. 31, no. 3, first movement, measures 1–8 (Czerny, *Über den richtigen Vortrag,* 49)

Example 21. Beethoven Sonata in E-flat, Op. 31, no. 3, first movement, measures 41–45 (first edition, Zurich: Nägeli, 1804)

After the fermata, and particularly in the 16th measure and its continuation, [the indecisive cast] yields to a decisive style of performance, and starting from this point the beats of the metronome can be properly adhered to.[109]

Czerny describes both the musical question and the establishment of the "real tempo" in bar 16 very sensitively. But his suggestion that one observe metronomic beats beginning at the *tempo giusto* is dangerous if taken at all literally, since it fails adequately to recognize the subtle inflections due some of the reappearances of the "calling motive," the gesture that opened the sonata and preceded the "questions" of bars 3 to 6. I refer in particular to the reappearance of this motive in bar 43 (Example 21), and to its two lengthened versions at the close of

---

folgt, und muss daher im Tempo und Ausdruck eine gewisse Unbestimmtheit haben" (Czerny, *Über den richtigen Vortrag,* 49). In Czerny's incipit the ritardando begins a beat and a half late, bar 6 is lacking a sforzato between staves, the last two beats of bar 7 should have separate slurs, and the slur over the first beat of bar 8 is editorial.

[109]"Nach der Haltung, und vorzüglich im 16ten Takt und seiner Folge dem entschiedenen Vortrage weicht, daher auch erst von da der Metronom gehörig beobachtet werden kann" (Czerny, *Über den richtigen Vortrag,* 49).

the exposition, bars 83–84 and 87–88 (Example 22).[110] These subtleties in timing are brought into play by a change in texture that Janet
Levy identifies as a common "sign" of classical rhetoric: "the halting
or removal of a palpable pulse from a gesture that previously had
one."[111] The calling motive, which initially appeared without an
eighth-note pulse, is provided with one for the first time in bar 18
after the "real tempo" has appeared, only to have that pulse removed
again at its next appearance in bar 33. The air of uncertainty thus
achieved is intensified by the echoing questions that begin in bar 35.
By bar 43 the calling motive sounds so timid with its sixteenth removed that it has become the perfect setup for the joke that follows in
bar 44. Shall we, during these measures of suspended pulse and growing uncertainty, occupy ourselves with the beats of a metronome?

One work that fares even worse for Czerny's lack of concern for
declamation is the Sonata in F for Piano and Violoncello, Op. 5, no.
1. Not only is his description of the work disconcertingly brief for a
piece of such significance but his incipits reveal a conception of slurring far less articulate than Beethoven's. Compare Czerny's incipit
(Example 23) for the *Adagio sostenuto* (in which the cello part is not
shown) with the text of the first edition (Example 24). Czerny appears unmindful of the fact that the *Adagio sostenuto,* like the last

Example 22. Beethoven Sonata in E-flat, Op. 31, no. 3, first movement,
measures 81–88 (first edition, Zurich: Nägeli, 1804)

---

[110]The image of "someone calling a name" (as if at the beginning of a scene in an
opera) was suggested to me by Neal Zaslaw.

[111]Levy, "Texture as a Sign," 484n.5. Levy discusses "true beginning" and musical
question and answer from the point of view of texture, which, as mentioned above,
she sees as "analogous to that of tone of voice or inflection in ordinary
speech . . . necessary but never sufficient for conveying meaning" (ibid., 483–84 and
491n.12).

Example 23. Beethoven Sonata in F for Piano and Violoncello, Op. 5, no. 1, first movement, measures 1–3 (Czerny, *Über den richtigen Vortrag,* 80)

Example 24. Beethoven Sonata in F for Piano and Violoncello, Op. 5, no. 1, first movement, measures 1–3 (after the first edition, Vienna: Artaria, 1797)

movement of the *Archduke* Trio and the introduction of the E-flat Sonata, Op. 31, no. 3, is based on a musical question. Apart from his suggestion that the metronome be set to ♪ = 88, he says only, "The *Adagio* with earnest expression and strict tempo, but not dragging."[112] Two of his favorite expressions of warning are present here: "in strict time" and "not dragging." It is fairly obvious that "earnest expression" should not give rise to sentimentality or caricature in a movement like this, but something essential about the relationship of

---

[112]"Das *Adagio* mit ernstem Ausdruck und festem Tempo, aber nicht gedehnt." The rest of the first movement fares little better, receiving only a brief paragraph suggesting that, since the piece is long, it is best to play brilliantly and keep the tempo up to "sustain the interest" [das Jnteresse . . . festzuhalten]. The second movement is summarized in one sentence: "The same fiery, very lively and brilliant delivery as in the first movement" [Derselbe feurige, sehr lebhafte und brillante Vortrag, wie im ersten Satze] (Czerny, *Über den richtigen Vortrag,* 80).

content to tempo in the first movement of Op. 5 is missing in Czerny's characterization. We shall speak of it in detail in Chapter 4.

Czerny's Flaw as an Advisor to Performers of Beethoven

Czerny complains about caricature in tempo variation and warns us often about sentimentality, lack of cohesion, and the specter of boredom. The problem with his complaints and warnings is that, couched as they are in negative terms, they offer little insight into what makes the music cohere. Because Czerny's approach is not analytical in any thoroughgoing sense, he rarely describes the character of a gesture, and makes no attempt to elucidate the way in which Beethoven so frequently uses a single gesture as the basis for his far-reaching and eloquent melodic discourse. That is precisely what makes it difficult for him to discuss large-scale connections, despite the fact that he is clearly aware of them. We have seen how much he admires the way Beethoven achieves unity through his play with melodic gesture. In another description of the trios from Op. 70 on, Czerny even speaks of that unity as a special strength of the works of what he calls Beethoven's second period:

> The vast difference in style, spirit, ideas and development that divides Beethoven's second period from [his] first, is nowhere more strikingly evident than when one compares the following *trios*, written about ten years later, with the earlier [ones].
> The originality of the ideas reveals a new world, and the player is obliged to consider these later works different inasmuch as he must concentrate more on the total effect, in order to represent each piece as a characteristic picture in which only *one grand idea* predominates, without being dissipated by episodic ideas or cadences.[113]

[113]"Der gewaltige Unterschied in Styl, Geist, Jdeen, und Durchführung, der Beethovens zweite Periode von der ersten trennt, zeigt sich nirgends auffallender, als wenn man die nun folgenden, um 10 Jahre später geschriebenen *Trio's* mit den frühern vergleicht.

But the "one grand idea" must be made explicit if one wishes to impart something meaningful about unity. For if a tempo fluctuation is unduly extravagant, that is because it obscures something more important, something "grander" that begs to be made palpable on the larger scale. The application of a metronomic tempo may reveal nothing about content and in itself can never solve a problem of large-scale integration. We must try in the end to name the deepest configurations in the work, difficult as that may be. Czerny's tendency to delete Beethoven's details takes him further than ever from being able to impart this kind of advice.

I can think of no better exercise for hearing something of what *Czerny* heard in Beethoven than playing through all his examples from *Über den richtigen Vortrag* as they stand. Why was he inclined to modernize Beethoven's notation of articulation? Because short slurs were, for him, not a means of furthering eloquent expression but something of a threat to the "long line," as we shall see in his theoretical writing. In this sense he was—far more than Beethoven—a nineteenth-century musician.

Beethoven's Use of the Slur According to Czerny and His Successors

Czerny was perhaps the first editor to use the "phrasing slur" as a replacement for local articulation. Something of the basis for his approach is revealed in the *Pianoforte-Schule,* where his concern with continuity results in inattention to the way ligatures express note grouping:

"Die Originalität der Gedanken biethet eine neue Welt, und auch der Spieler hat diese spätern Werke insofern anders aufzufassen, als er mehr auf die Gesammtwirkung denken muss, um jedes Tonstück als ein charakteristiches Gemälde darzustellen, in dem nur *eine grosse Jdee* vorherrscht, ohne durch episodische Gedanken, oder Cadenzen zu zerstreuen" (ibid., 90). Czerny defines the "second period" as extending from what he identifies as Beethoven's twenty-ninth work (the three Op. 31 sonatas of 1803–4) to about his ninetieth (the Op. 90 sonata of 1814; Czerny gives the publication date of 1815) (ibid., 26).

The *bound* touch is that in which one key is held precisely until the moment in which the following key will be struck. For example:

This type of touch is actually that which is indicated by the word legato (bound), and one uses the rounded line ⌒ or ⌣ , which is placed over or under the notes which are to be performed in this manner in order to indicate this legato; these are called *slurs*. . . .

Whenever smaller slurs are written over 2 or 3 note groups, then the second or third note will be somewhat clipped. For example:

. . . But whenever slurs are written over more notes, even though they appear to be separated, they are to be understood as if there were only one [slur], and no noticeable break may be made. For example:

Here the last note of each measure is not to be broken off, rather it will be bound to the one following. If the composer wishes such notes to be broken off, he must place a dot over them.

Often one will come across signs for ties and slurs that meet. For example:

Here the whole must be played *legato,* and in addition each individual tie must be observed for its [full] value.[114]

Although Czerny was fairly straightforward about *his* reasons for altering Beethoven's articulation (it was a matter of current taste), after Czerny a slightly different point of view emerged as editors began to voice the opinion that Beethoven's notation was misleading as an indicator of his *own* practice of articulation, in some way at odds with what he actually did in performance. In more recent years Carl Krebs, Donald Francis Tovey, and Eva Badura-Skoda are among those who have espoused this view, taking up where Czerny left off.

Krebs, in his preface to the Berlin Urtext of 1898, insists that "the slur in Beethoven's piano compositions serves to indicate the phrasing in only a limited way; the end of a slur is by no means always the end of a musical sentence."[115] His language reveals that he is using the term "phrase" in its later nineteenth-century sense: a slur should mark "the phrasing," that is, the entirety of "a musical sentence." In the

---

[114]"Der *gebundene* Anschlag ist derjenige, wo man eine Taste genau bis zu dem Augeblicke hält, in welchem die nächstfolgende angeschlagen wird. Z. B. . . . Diese Art ist es eigentlich, welche man durch das Word *legato* (gebunden) bezeichnet, und man bedient sich der gerundeten Linien . . . oder . . . , welche man über oder unter die, also vorzutragenden Noten setzt, um dieses *legato* anzuzeigen, und welche man *Schleifungsbogen* nennt. . . . Wenn kleinere Schleifbogen über 2 oder 3 Noten abgetheilt stehen, so wird die zweite oder dritte Note etwas abgestossen. Z. B. . . . Wenn aber Schleifbögen über mehreren Noten, obgleich abgetheilt, stehen, so wird angenommen, als ob es nur ein einziger wäre, und es darf kein Absetzen merkbar werden. Z. B. . . . Hier darf die letzte Note jedes Takts nicht abgerissen werden, sondern sie wird zur nächstfolgenden gebunden. Würde der Tonsetzer dieselbe abgerissen haben wollen, so müsste er einen Punkt darüber setzen.

"Oft werden die Bindungs- und Schleifzeichen vereinigt gefunden. Z. B. . . . Hier muss das Ganze *legato* gespielt, und dabei jedes einzelne Bindungszeichen nach seiner Geltung beachtet werden" (Czerny, *Pianoforte-Schule,* vol. 1, 142–43).

[115]Translated by Paul Aron in *Beethoven Sonatas for the Piano,* 2 vols. (New York: Schirmer Books, 1953), vol. 1, i.

eighteenth century, when analogies to grammar still seemed useful, "phrases" were carefully distinguished from "sentences." Krebs's view of the function of notation is anachronistic because in Beethoven's day the larger period structures—both "phrases" and "sentences"—were seldom marked with ligatures, which were generally reserved for indications of binding on a more local level. Even Beethoven's longest ligatures often leave unbound one or more elements that are clearly part of the "sentence."

Krebs showed what Beethoven "really meant" with a few examples in his preface, and kept his ideas out of the text, but nineteenth- and early twentieth-century editors with fewer misgivings about "clarifying" Beethoven's intent followed Czerny's example and added a layer of ligatures over Beethoven's original slurs to indicate "the phrasing."

Example 25. Beethoven Sonata in C Minor, Op. 10, no. 1, first movement, measures 1–57 (first edition, Vienna: Eder, 1798)

Example 26. Beethoven Sonata in C Minor, Op. 10, no. 1, first movement, measures 27–57 (Henle, *Beethoven Werke: Klaviersonaten I*)

Not uncommonly the original slurs disappeared at this point or in subsequent editions that used these layered editions as a basis. The whole practice so enraged Heinrich Schenker that in 1925 he published his "Weg mit dem Phrasierungsbogen!" [Away with the phrasing slur!] in the first volume of his *Das Meisterwerk in der Musik*.[116] Schenker remained in the minority, however. Even editors who were concerned with reproducing Beethoven's original slurs found his chains of short slurs alternating with ties so peculiar that they removed the short slurs and replaced them with a single "summarizing" ligature. This practice continues to the present day in some of the best-known publishing houses. The Henle edition (Example 26) of the *Allegro molto e con brio* of Op. 10, no. 1 offers a case in point, as we see when we compare a few of its measures with the first page of the first edition (Example 25).[117] The short slurs with ties may seem at first a mere impediment of notation, but here they serve an expressive

[116]For a translation of Schenker's article see Sylvan Kalib's *Thirteen Essays from the Three Yearbooks: "Das Meisterwerk in der Musik" by Heinrich Schenker: An Annotated Translation*, 3 vols. (Ann Arbor, Mich.: University Microfilms, 1981), 52–83. See also William Rothstein's "Heinrich Schenker as an Interpreter of Beethoven's Piano Sonatas," *19th-Century Music* 8 (1984): 3–28.

[117]Beethoven, *Sonatas*, Tovey and Craxton ed., vol. 1, 116.

purpose. The discourse centers around the dialectic between the forte chord with its arpeggiation to a reiterated E-flat in bars 1 through 3, and the soft consonance-dissonance pairing that follows in bar 4. Bars 5–8 reverse the polarity: we move from dissonance to consonance with the soft pair of chords in bar 8. This pair is then intensified by reiteration in bars 9–10 and 11–12, and is finally reinforced with dissonant suspensions in bars 14–16 before we close into the return of the first motive at bar 22. Quite unexpectedly bars 32–36 unite the two opening gestures into one: in the upper voice the reiterated E-flat now gently introduces the slur, which is in turn beautifully elaborated both before and after its tied D-flat, the visual and aural focus. (All this has been warmly anticipated in the bass line.) This new *cantabile* unfolds gradually in four-bar phrases, the final tied pitches always introducing a new four-bar group. Far from being an impediment, then, the shorter slurs and ties for bars 41 through 47 in the first edition express the effect of "adding on." Only in bar 48 is the line released into longer slurs. (These the Henle text joins into a single slur.)

Editorial alterations like these are problematic. Even when they manage to avoid indicating erroneous groupings, "phrase marks" often say too much by precluding multiple implications and essential ambiguities, while the "summarizing" ligatures fail to convey the local rhythmic effects of Beethoven's shorter slurs when pitches or groups are *not* bound, especially when, as above, the sense of "adding on" is so palpable. Also, the appearance of "phrasing slurs" and "summarizing" ligatures where short slurs are meant to be detracts from the visual effect of slurs that really *are* long. Especially in the early sonatas Beethoven's long slurs are cues for special events, like the mysterious, winding ascent of the opening eight bars of the *Allegretto* of Op. 10, no. 2 (Example 27)—six bars in the strictest legato released only after the line has flowered into six voices at the cadence.

Tovey, who like Krebs believed that "the classical composers did not arrive at a coherent system of marks of articulation," was another editor who used what he called "long slurs" to indicate "phrase length." He correctly observed that "articulation on the pianoforte . . . has no natural limits," but erred in assuming that Beethoven's practice is best seen in light of those who came after him, insisting that "the instinct of composers from Beethoven to Wagner is to indicate as long an

Example 27. Beethoven Sonata in F, Op. 10, no. 2, second movement, measures 1–8 (first edition, Vienna: Eder, 1798)

unbroken legato as possible, whatever means an instrument can use for concealing breaks." Since he believes that Beethoven "never makes two slurs meet," Tovey concludes that he "therefore has no means of indicating the numerous cases in which he wishes to have no break between his phrases."[118] But what about instances where Beethoven applies the term "legato" in passages where he is also using ligatures? Might not this place the groupings in a legato context? The notion that Beethoven's rhetoric was more articulate evidently seems out of the question to Tovey: when he finally proposes that "short sub-phrase indications concern matters of touch," he reveals that he views these matters of local "touch" as having nothing to do with articulative silence.[119]

Tovey speaks as if Beethoven's developing breadth of expression were a direct approach to what came to be called the "endless melody style" of Wagner. The term "endless melody" seems to me best applied to what might be described as the "purely lyric," for example the outer sections of Chopin's Nocturne in F-sharp, Op. 48, no. 2, but among Beethoven's sonatas the perpetual motion movements of Op. 78 and Op. 90 might seem the first to lend themselves to this sort of description, though not so much because of their lyricism as because they (purposefully) lack the local level of rhetorical content we ordinarily find in his writing.[120]

---

[118]It is not entirely true that Beethoven never makes two slurs meet; for example bars 3 to 4 of Example 24 show two slurs meeting, and holographic evidence abounds with slurs that appear to be segmented in various ways.

[119]Beethoven, *Sonatas*, Tovey and Craxton ed., preface, 7.

[120]In his study of the fantasy-style in Beethoven, Malcolm Bilson identifies "endless melody" texture in the rondos of the Sonatas Opp. 78 and 90. See his *The Emergence of the Fantasy-Style in the Beethoven Piano Sonatas of the Early and Middle Periods* (Ann Arbor, Mich.: University Microfilms, 1968), 15, 134, 138, 153, 157–58, and 168.

Eva Badura-Skoda, in her article "Performance Conventions in
Beethoven's Early Works," also opts for reading Beethoven's notation less articulately:

> Notational conventions taken for granted by every Viennese musi-
> cian around 1800 included the knowledge of how to indicate legato
> and the meaning of slurs ending at bar lines. Before 1800, com-
> posers eschewed long slurs, preferring to end them at the bar line
> even when the lyrical sweep of a melody suggested its execution
> without a break in the middle. This notational habit stems from
> violin bowing, and it was retained for some time even in keyboard
> and wind parts. On the other hand, Viennese musicians distin-
> guished clearly between two types of slurs. The first was the short
> slur over two or three notes, which required the player to shorten
> and detach the last note under the slur. The second was the slur
> found in cantilenas over several notes, which—regardless of wheth-
> er it ended at the bar line or not—was simply indicated legato.
> Making these distinctions created no difficulties for eighteenth-
> century Viennese musicians, though a modern musician can be
> vexed by such broken slurs, which are meaningless if performed
> literally.[121]

To support her argument, Badura-Skoda refers generally to Türk's
explanation of slurring in his chapter on execution. However, Türk
does not say that slurs "found in cantilenas over several notes" indicate continuous legato, but rather that "if all tones of a composition *or
most of its parts* [italics mine] are to be slurred, then this manner of
treatment is indicated at the beginning by the word *legato*." Then he
adds: "Often curved lines are written *only over the first measures* [italics
mine] and serve to indicate to the player that he should continue to use
this form of execution, until the contrary is designated by strokes or
rests."[122] Though he equates slurs over several opening measures

[121]Robert Winter and Bruce Carr, eds., *Beethoven, Performers, and Critics* (Detroit:
Wayne State University Press, 1980), 71.
[122]"Sollen alle Töne oder die meisten Stellen eines Tonstückes geschliest werden, so
bestimmt man diese Behandlungsart durch das zu Anfange beygefügte Wort *legato*.
Oft schreibt man nur etwa über die erstern Takte solche Bogen, und will dadurch

with general legato, Türk immediately makes it clear that longer slurs may need to be articulated, as his advice on the performance of a slur over eight notes makes clear: "The note on which the curved line begins should be very gently (and almost imperceptibly) accented."[123] Türk revealed his sensitivity to these subtle groupings in clavichord playing in his discussion of continuity and separation earlier in the same chapter:

> For a very refined execution, with regard to the lifting up of the finger, one must take into consideration whether the periods are larger or smaller and more or less joined to each other. The finger is lifted sooner from the key at the end of a full cadence, or such a conclusive note is played with a shorter duration than when only a phrase member of the composition has been completed.[124]

Türk's description of the way articulation reflects the subtleties of cadential action calls to mind passages in the sonatas of Haydn, Mozart, and Beethoven in which a texture of measure-long slurs is interrupted by, for example, a slur that is two measures long. Consider the fifth variation of the first movement of Beethoven's Sonata in A-flat, Op. 26 (Example 28), in which the left- and right-hand slurs depart from their normal one-measure length in ways that highlight the part writing. This is the work whose finale Czerny cited for its resemblance to Cramer's legato passagework, so it may be significant that the slurring in this variation anticipates the double-layered slurs of later works like the Piano Sonata in A, Op. 101.

---

andeuten daß der Spieler bey dieser Art des Vortrages bleiben solle, bis das Gegentheil durch beygefügte Striche oder Pausen bezeichnet wird" (Türk, *Klavierschule,* 354–55; translation from Haggh, *School of Clavier Playing,* 344).

[123]"Die Note, über welcher der Bogen anfängt, sehr gelinde (kaum merklich) accentuirt wird" (Türk, *Klavierschule,* 355; translation from Haggh, *School of Clavier Playing,* 344).

[124]"Bey einem sehr feinen Vortrage muß man, in Ansehung des Abhebens der Finger, sogar auf die großern oder kleinern, mehr oder weniger mit einander in Verbindung stehenden Perioden Rücksicht nehmen. Man hebt nämlich bey dem Ende eines volligen Tonschlusses den Finger früher von der Taste, oder trägt eine solche Schlußnote kürzer vor, als wenn damit nur ein Einschnitt geendiget wird" (Türk, *Klavierschule,* 342; translation from Haggh, *School of Clavier Playing,* 331).

Example 28. Beethoven Sonata in A-flat, Op. 26, first movement, variation 5, measures 9–16 (holograph)

Eva Badura-Skoda also voices the popular notion that slurs in keyboard notation are a "notational habit . . . retained" from violin bowing or wind playing. Although there is little doubt that the marks for bowing and tonguing were later adopted in keyboard notation,[125] describing this as a "retained habit" is objectionable for two reasons. First, it disesteems bowing in much the same way that the modern wind player often disesteems breathing. To look at bowing or breathing in classical music as relatively unmusical but "necessary" aspects of performance, as obstacles that prevent "lyrical sweep," is to ignore their natural and vital role in musical rhetoric, whose analogue is a medium that breathes, the human voice sounding its inflections and its silences. Second, having been told that slurs are merely indicators of a sort of unmusical drudgery, we should be particularly suspicious of the idea that our greatest composers embraced them for use in their keyboard works when the keyboard, of all instruments, would find such "breaking up" of a musical texture the least necessary.

---

[125]Rosenblum, *Performance Practices*, 172–74. Here Rosenblum makes it clear that it is the expressiveness of bowing and tonguing that the sensitive keyboardist seeks to imitate.

A Definition of Articulation

The most important bias the approaches of Czerny, Krebs, Tovey, and Eva Badura-Skoda reveal is the idea that to articulate is to break apart something that really ought to be continuous: a "sentence" needs to be completed, the "lyrical sweep of a melody" must not be ruined by "a break." We need to be reminded of articulation's full meaning, that it is just as much a matter of binding, of uniting by forming a joint.[126] To insist that "such broken slurs" are "meaning-less if performed literally" is to misunderstand an essential aspect of classical articulation: that while certain articulations do indeed sepa-rate, many articulations, including those before destination notes on the far side of bar lines or major metric groupings, *join* the preceding legato group to the arrival note. These "fresh" arrivals sound dis-tinctly different from subsumed arrivals, a fact of which Beethoven seemed well aware when he made the comment to Karl Holz about copyist errors.[127]

Both Krebs and Tovey assume that—regardless of what Beethoven indicates—whenever slurs like these

appear in a quick tempo they are to be performed as

lest they suffer a "loss of energy." Actually the opposite is true: should the player make the mistake of subsuming the arrival pitches, a significant loss of energy would result and tempo would need to change to compensate for that loss. What Krebs and Tovey fail to realize is that the articulation can be made without making the arrival note at all late, without "breaking up" the figure.

For the musical orator this is the aspect of articulation that comes

---

[126] *American Heritage Dictionary,* s.v. "articulate—*intr.*"
[127] Beethoven, *Briefe,* Prelinger ed., vol. 3, 212.

closest to German speech. The short-slurred style is one in which the smallest breaks and the most minute "binding articulations" are like the consonantal closes and glottal stops of the language.[128] It is no accident that fresh arrivals and consonants of all kinds can be performed especially elegantly on the Viennese instrument; that is precisely what the swift action and highly efficient leather dampers were designed for. Perhaps even the soft oinking sound that occasionally accompanies leather damping was to some extent relished by the Viennese.

As for Beethoven, his orthography, his demands that it be heeded, and his continuing preference for responsive, clear-sounding fortepianos with light actions (especially Streicher's) all suggest that his cultivation of a legato common touch did not interfere with his sensitivity to articulation.[129] And despite the profound differences between his character and temperament and those of Haydn and Mozart, his articulation should in every sense be "observed" within the rhetorical tradition, remembering of course that breaks in ligatures bind or separate according to context. Whether in Mozart's music or in Beethoven's, touch within a legato group needs to be graded in a variety of ways in approaching or leaving a destination. On a Viennese fortepiano such gradations require subtlety but little physical effort, so that a wide range of articulation can sound "natural," from the almost legato to the highly disjunct (neither of these necessarily joining or separating musical *ideas*).

Even in instances where Beethoven is very concerned about binding, as in the passage marked *dolce e molto ligato* in the exposition of the first movement of the Piano Sonata Op. 53 (Example 29), he may continue to indicate slurs of varying length. This is the texture Czerny associates with Beethoven's "extraordinarily *characteristic* manner of playing . . . distinguished particularly by the strict *legato* of its *chords*." In this instance, I take Beethoven's "molto ligato" to mean "bind the chords so that all their voices seem legato; the slurs mark the groups to be shaped" rather than "bind everything as if I had written no slurs, but simply 'legato.'"

[128] *American Heritage Dictionary,* s.v. "articulation," definition 2b: "any speech sound, especially a consonant."

[129] William S. Newman, *Beethoven on Beethoven: Playing His Piano Music His Way* (New York: W. W. Norton, 1988), 55.

Example 29. Beethoven Sonata in C, Op. 53 (*Waldstein*), first movement, measures 35–50 (first edition, Vienna: Bureau des arts et d'industrie, 1805)

Beethoven's concern for local articulation never lessened. While the English frequently used the term "legato" to characterize the texture of whole movements, Beethoven retained it as a more local mark. Only twice in his sonatas does "legato" appear at the *beginning* of a movement: in the first movement of Op. 14, no. 2 (its first appearance in the sonatas), where within four measures of its appearance Beethoven notates staccato, half-measure slurs, portato, and sighing appoggiaturas; and in Op. 109, where the term appears over the opening texture, which lasts for only eight measures. It is reiterated seven times thereafter, always in association with the opening texture, but not simply as a replacement for ligatures, which appear as well. The *Adagio espressivo* with which this texture alternates is characterized by much shorter slurring, including expressive two-

Example 30. Beethoven Sonata in B-flat, Op. 106 (*Hammerklavier*), first movement, measures 1–16 (first edition, Vienna: Artaria, 1819)

note slurs, some of which are portato. Curiously, the term "legato" does not appear at all in the perpetual motion movements reminiscent of Cramer's passagework. In light of all this, it appears that Beethoven used the term as he used his more expansive ligatures in the later works: more as an enrichment of his notation than a means of replacing shorter slurs.[130]

Articulation is certainly very rich in the late piano sonatas. In the first sixteen measures of the first movement of the *Hammerklavier* Sonata Op. 106 (Example 30), Beethoven calls for everything from

[130]Newman disagrees, claiming that the later the date, the more Beethoven tends to replace articulated arrivals with subsumed arrivals (ibid., 135–36).

eighths in pairs or fours to sixteen eighths bound 'so as to include repeated pitches (in the right hand of bars 12–14). In the second movement (*Prestissimo*) of the Sonata Op. 109 (Example 31), ligatures are applied to the half-measure or measure in the intensity of the opening *ben marcato,* only to be replaced by indications of two-measure legato for the more lyrical gestures with hairpins in bars 11–12, 15–16, and 19–20 (and presumably 23–24). After the four lyrical gestures, the last two marked *legato* (probably to ensure that the syncopated alto line will also be bound), Beethoven returns to single-measure units until the *un poco espressivo* in bars 29–30 results in another pairing in bars 31–32. Legato connections between single-measure units in this passage would only weaken the distinctions between breathless intensity and yearning.

We find some of the subtlest local articulation in a late work, one of Beethoven's masterpieces of concision, the *Allegretto* of the Sonata in A, Op. 101.[131] To be sure, with its profusion of avoided cadences, pivot chords, ambiguous gestures, and hesitations, there is no significant point of rest on the tonic until the final measure. But despite the sense of continuous unfolding from the opening gesture onward, this *Allegretto ma non troppo (Etwas lebhaft, und mit der innigsten Empfindung)* retains an approach to singing that is anything but Wagnerian. It is simply not concerned with "endlessness," or even "breadth" for that matter. Beethoven is employing, with astonishing economy, a rhetoric of elisions, of unfinished gestures, of antecedents awaiting local closure, all very speechlike and all for the purpose of furthering a kind of continuous speculation.[132] It "sings" in an eighteenth-century sense: gentle vocal declamation is at the fore.[133]

The movement could scarcely be more unlike, say, the Rondo of Op. 90, with its regular 4 + 4 measure structure and its broadly

---

[131]Because the examples from Op. 101 are extensive, I refer the reader to any reliable score.

[132]The elliptical nature of the rhetoric here stands in striking contrast to the style adopted in the first movement of Op. 106, with its far more distant horizons; the movements taken together furnish another example of Beethoven's toying with extremes.

[133]See Arnold Schering's comments on "singing" as understood in the eighteenth century in "Carl Philipp Emanuel Bach und das 'redende Prinzip' in der Musik," *Jahrbuch der Musikbibliothek Peters, 1938* 45 (1939): 15.

Example 31. Beethoven Sonata in E, Op. 109, second movement, measures 1–32 (first edition, Berlin: Schlesinger, 1821)

singing melodies (marked *"sehr singbar vorgetragen"*). Unlike the Rondo, the *Allegretto* is filled with indications for articulation and grouping: fresh arrivals within the measure (bar 6), short slur groups with articulation at bar lines (bars 9, 10, 100, 101, etc.), portato (bars 15 and 67), and even longer slurs over shorter slurs to make the shorter articulation more subtle (as in bars 14, 17, and 19).[134] The working out of the material gives the strong impression of "the way things

---

[134]A good description of the performance of these double-layered slurs may be found in Türk: he suggests that shorter slurs under a longer ligature (and I would include here shorter slurs in a passage marked legato, as in Example 29, from Op. 53) should begin with a very gentle marking for attention: "Durch die Bezeichnung . . . will man andeuten, daß zwar alle Noten geschleist werden müssen, doch soll der erste, dritte, fünfte und siebente Ton sehr schwach markirt werden" (Türk, *Klavierschule,* 355).

happen" in speech. Viewed in terms of a monologue it could be evocatively described with the ancient terms: *dubitatio, parenthesis, ellipsis, confirmatio*, much of it effected by *irregularities* of periodicity (as in the retrospective additions to apparently closing measure groups through the use of rhythmic and tonal pivots in bars 13, 15, 21, and 92).

If neither "endless melody" nor "increased breadth of cantabile lines" adequately describes the goal of Beethoven's legato and the stretching of ligatures in his more mature works, then what will? Tovey hints at it when he notes that "the sonata forms accomplish their designs more quickly than they can satisfy their emotional issues."[135] From the beginning, many of the emotional issues Beethoven raised needed to be worked out on a grand scale. By the time he was composing his middle-period sonatas a mere movement seemed too small to contain them, and the sonata as a whole became his working ground. This is where we observe his ever-increasing use of continuously unfolding fantasy, as Malcolm Bilson points out.[136] It is a kind of speculation that comes directly out of his fragmentary melodic rhetoric, and it enables him to deal with "issues" raised by those fragments in the course of whole works, as in the Sonata Op. 27, no. 1, or the *Waldstein* (in which the "Gilbert and Sullivan" close of the first movement is called into question by the *Introduzione* and only satisfactorily answered by the working out of the Rondo). This sort of fantasy can "explode" form and greatly slow large-scale harmonic motion by removing all fragmenting articulation (as in parts of the variations in extreme diminution in the Sonata Op. 111), or it can delay closure by relying on fragments alone (as in the Sonata Op. 101).[137]

---

[135]That sonatas are divided into separate pieces is seen by Tovey as something "retained." It is "inherited from the earlier suite forms which are their decorative prototypes" (Donald Francis Tovey, *A Companion to Beethoven's Pianoforte Sonatas* [London: Associated Board of the Royal Schools of Music, 1931], 263).

[136]Bilson, *Fantasy-Style*, 161–62.

[137]See Newman's penetrating analysis of Beethoven's increasing use of variation technique and the concomitant slowing of harmonic motion in his music (Newman, *The Sonata in the Classic Era*, 2d ed. [New York: W. W. Norton, 1972], 130 and 149–50).

Beethoven's Syntactical Markers: The Seen and Unseen

Beethoven often made it clear how much he cared about proper emphasis, and in warning Czerny about the dangers of memorizing he revealed his belief that this was something the notation could at least in some important measure convey. We have seen how Czerny's ligatures and marks of expression can obscure Beethoven's syntax. But even if we try to perform from the information we find in holographs and in first and early editions, which offer much more varied and expressive slurring, beaming, and stemming than even the most authoritative modern editions, we still face a question about syntax. We learned from Czerny and Schindler that a great deal of tempo modification can inhere in the music itself without being specifically notated in the score: to read properly is to "see" this and respond to it. What about emphasis? What emphasis did Beethoven expect that we would "see" beyond what he indicates with slurs, dynamics, and markings for special attention like sforzati, dots, strokes, wedges, and fermati? No doubt he expected that we would see the emphasis that arises, in Heinrich Christoph Koch's words, "partly from a certain stress on length, in which it appears that the accented tone is held an instant longer than its prescribed length."[138]

Theorists like Türk who used rhetorical metaphors insisted, like Beethoven, that emphasis was essential to clear communication at the keyboard. Türk saw it as a way to bind or separate musical periods.[139] He describes agogic emphasis as "another means of accent, which is to be used much less often and with great care":

> The orator not only lays more emphasis on important syllables and the like, but he also lingers upon them a little. But this kind of

---

[138]"Genau genommen bestehet sie theils in einer mit getragener Stimme vermehrten Stärke des Tones, theils in einem gewissen nachdrücklichen Verweilen, wobey es scheinet, als halte man sich bey einem solchen accentuirten Tone einen Moment länger auf, als es seine bestimmte Zeitdauer erfordert" (Heinrich Christoph Koch, *Musikalisches Lexikon* [Frankfurt am Main, 1802], col. 50; Koch's expression is "besser empfinden, als beschreiben"; translation from Ratner, *Classic Music*, 191).

[139]Türk, *Klavierschule*, 334 (324 in Haggh).

lingering, when it occurs in music, cannot, of course, always be of the same duration, for it appears to me to depend upon (1) the greater or lesser importance of the note, (2) its length and relationship to other notes, and (3) the harmony which is basic to them.[140]

Türk reasons that, since the need to linger "somewhat longer on a very important note" is universally recognized, he need only answer the question "What are the more important notes and how long can they be held out?" "Depending on the circumstances," he concludes, they are "the many notes which can be accented." These he lists as:

1. "good" beats in the traditional hierarchy of "good" and "bad";
2. the first tone of every *Abschnitt* or *Einschnitt;*
3. appoggiaturas;
4. intervals dissonant with the bass;
5. syncopations;
6. notes that do not belong to the diatonic scale of the key;
7. tones that are markedly long, high, or low;
8. intervals that take on special harmonic importance; and
9. a variety of others "for which it would be difficult to establish rules."

In many ways Türk was a conservative theorist (not least in continuing to champion the beauties of the clavichord), and he approaches the whole subject of agogics with caution, perhaps in response to bad habits he encountered. The increase in note length is usually "scarcely perceptible" and never more than half the value of the note; and the economy is one in which time is simply paid back: "the following

---

[140]"Der Redner legt auf die wichtigern Silben &c. nicht nur mehr Nachdruck, sondern er verweilt auch etwas dabey. Dieses Verweilen kann aber in der Musik natürlicher Weise nicht immer von gleicher Dauer seyn; denn es kommt hierbey, wie mich dünkt, vorzüglich 1) auf die mehr oder weniger wichtige Note selbst, 2) auf die Länge und auf das Verhältniß derselben zu den andern Noten, und 3) auf die zum Grunde liegende Harmonie an" (Türk, *Klavierschule,* 338; translation from Haggh, *School of Clavier Playing,* 327–28).

note loses as much of its value as has been given to the accentuated note."[141] But despite his warning that agogic accents are "to be used much less often" than dynamic accents, his list is a long one, and in the normal course of music making the events Türk associates with note lengthening occur quite frequently.

It is important to note the distance between Czerny and Schindler on the question of emphasis. They agree that all the subdivisions of the bar must be somehow made palpable in order to clarify *meter*. But their descriptions of meter differ. Czerny describes subdivision by accent, with no explicit mention of time, syllable length, or articulation:

> Since it is one of the first responsibilities of the player never to leave the hearer in doubt as to the subdivision of the bar, it follows of course that where it is necessary, one should mark by a small accent the beginning of each bar, or indeed even of every good part of the bar.[142]

We have seen Czerny attempt to replace the effect of missing slurs with a hairpin, a kind of accent, and this certainly tells us something about his idea of the function of articulation. But how does he approach the function and nature of accent itself? His description (which Beethoven may have found overly optimistic) might at first lead us to believe that he is interested in a musical analogue to syllable length, except that "long" is immediately rendered "with weight, and on which the *accent* comes":

> It is known that every language consists of long and short syllables; that is, of those that must be pronounced long or with weight,

---

[141]Haggh, *School of Clavier Playing*, 328.

[142]"Da es eine der ersten Pflichten des Spielers ist, den Hörer nie über die Takteintheilung in Zweifel zu lassen, so führt dieses schon von selber mit sich, dass man, wo es nöthig ist, jeden Anfang eines Takts, oder gar wohl jeden guten Takttheil durch einen kleinen Nachdruck merkbar mache" (Czerny, *Pianoforte-Schule*, vol. 3, 6).

and on which the *accent* comes, and of those that sound short and unstressed. . . .

The case is much the same with musical ideas, in which expression must always occur on the proper note. Although in music this cannot be as exactly stipulated by means of rules as in language, we are guided in this so much by a proper feeling for euphony, clarity, rhythm, and above all for the character of each passage we play, that the musical declamation does not fail, and as much as possible is made understandable to the listener through the expression of his feelings.[143]

Czerny is not about to distinguish meter from rhythm, nor does he wish to establish distinctions between kinds of accent; rather he is preparing to discuss emphasis on long tones and on dissonance, both of which he describes exclusively in terms of dynamics.

In contrast to Czerny, Schindler insists that Beethoven united the old and the new in his mature style, using the metric and accentual hierarchies of prosody to clarify the "freedom" of the new Romanticism. As we noted earlier, Schindler claims that in adopting this oratorical approach to metrics and expression Beethoven was influenced by Clementi, who

as a self-taught singer, . . . attempted to carry over the prosody of the language and the rules of verbal and sung declamation into instrumental forms. Through this he arrived at the point where his playing itself became singing, and in certain works, where the rep-

[143]"Man weiss, dass jede Sprache aus langen und kurzen Silben besteht, das heisst, aus solchen, welche gedehnt, oder gewichtig ausgesprochen werden müssen, also auf welche der *Accent* kommt, und aus solchen, welche kurz und ohne Nachdruck lauten. . . . Ganz dasselbe ist mit den musikalischen Jdeen der Fall, wo der Ausdruck stets auf die geeignete Note kommen muss. Wenn sich dieses in der Musik auch nicht so genau durch Regeln festsetzen lässt, wie in der Sprache, so leitet doch das richtige Gefühl für Wohlklang, Deutlichkeit, Rhytmus, und vorzüglich für den *Charakter* jeder eben vorzutragenden Stelle darauf, dass man die musikalische Deklamation nicht verfehle, und sich dem Zuhörer im Ausdruck seiner Gefühle möglichst verständlich mache" (ibid., 5).

resentation of a particular state of the soul was called for, as for example his *Didone abbandonata,* was shaped into understandable speech. Clementi showed me the indispensable necessity, for an expressive performance, of knowing with each melody which of the various verse meters, of which music makes use, could be put to the melody, whether the iambic, trochaic, etc., because of the shifting of the main accent and the *caesura,* of which one must take note also in the performance of instrumental music, above all in *free* performance.[144]

According to Schindler, Clementi further directed that "in passages and runs the long and short accents must have audible nuances, even if they have not been written in."[145] Much the same advice appears in the controversial annotations to the Cramer Etudes, attributed by Schindler to Beethoven. The annotations come to us only in Schindler's hand, and for this reason their authenticity—at least with regard to particulars—is necessarily suspect but, as Newman points out, the suggestions contained in them receive indirect support both from Beethoven's own annotations and from his related works. Newman decides (as Czerny did), to clarify the reference to "longs and

---

[144]"Als selbst gebildeter Sänger versuchte er die Prosodie der Sprache und die Regeln der Wort- und Gesang-Declamation in die Instrumental-Musik hinüber zu tragen. Dadurch gelangte er dahin, dass sein Vortrag selbst Gesang ward, und in gewissen Werken, wo es galt besondere Seelen-Zustände darzustellen, z. B. in seiner *Didone abbandonata,* zur verständlichen Rede sich gestaltet hat. Mir zeigte Clementi die unerlässliche Nothwendigkeit zum ausdrucksvollen Vortrage, bei jeder Melodie zu wissen welches von den verschiedenen Versmaassen, deren sich die Musik bedient, der Melodie unterlegt werden könne, ob das jambische, das trochäische u.s.w., wegen Verlegung der Haupt-Accente und der *Cäsur,* von welcher auch im Vortrage der Instrumental-Musik, vornehmlich im *freien* Vortrage, Kenntniss genommen werden müsse" (Anton Schindler, "Für Studirende von Beethoven's Clavier-Musik," *Niederrheinische Musik-Zeitung für Kunstfreunde und Künstler* 20 [20 May 1854]: 156–57; translation from Drake, *Sonatas of Beethoven,* 106). (Drake's citation incorrectly cites the issue as no. 48.) Schindler's definition sounds more like Mattheson's or Emanuel Bach's. See also Schindler and MacArdle, *Beethoven,* 417.
[145]"In Passagen und Gängen die Längen und Kürzen hörbar nuancirt werden müssen, wären sie auch nicht geschrieben" (Schindler, "Für Studirende," 157; translation from Drake, *Sonatas of Beethoven,* 111).

shorts" by adding "[for which read, strongs and weaks],"[146] perhaps because he assumes that Latin *quantitas* can not be imported into a Germanic model of musical prosody, since long and short are not real aspects of the German language. But we need to look more closely at the first four bars of no. 4, the example to which the annotation is appended (Example 32):

> Here longs and shorts are to be performed throughout—that is, the first note long (—), the second short (˘), the third long again, the fourth short again. The same method as in scanning trochaic meter. At first lengthen the first and third notes deliberately so as to distinguish the longs clearly from the shorts, yet not to the extent of making the first and third notes dotted. Only later speed up the flow, thereby gently rounding off the sharp edges. The student's gradually heightened perception will contribute and legato will result.[147]

Example 32. Johann Baptist Cramer, *21 Etüden für Klavier,* no. 4, measures 1–4 (after the Haslinger edition, annotated by Anton Schindler)

---

[146]Newman, *Beethoven on Beethoven,* 178. For further information on the annotations see idem, "Beethoven Forgery," 397–422.

[147]"Hier sind durchgehends Längen u. Kürzen zu beobachten, d. h. die 1te Note lang (—), die 2te kurz (˘), die 3te wieder lang, die 4te wieder kurz. Gleiches Verfahren wie im Scandiren des trochäischen Versmaßes. Anfangs verlängert man absichtlich die 1te und 3te Note, damit sich Länge von Kürze recht merkbar unterscheide, ohne Verlängerung der 1ten und 3ten Note durch Punkte. Erst später beschleunige man die Bewegung, wobei dann die scharfen Ecken leichtwegfallen; der nach u. nach gebildetere Sinn des Schülers wird schon mitwirken u. Bindung erzielt werden" (Cramer, *21 Etüden,* Kann ed., 8).

Clearly the concern *here* is not with dynamic accent at all, but with duration. This interest in prosodic rhythm is, as mentioned in the preceding, in keeping with the inscription found beneath the two C-major melodies in the "Rolland" sketchbook of 1823.[148] What Schindler may not have realized is that the annotations also receive support from two of the eighteenth-century theorists Beethoven respected most highly. Both Mattheson and Emanuel Bach describe the two aspects of accent discussed by Koch and Türk: time, the *quantitative* aspect, and dynamics, the *qualitative* aspect.[149] Like Koch, Mattheson defined accent in terms of both quality and quantity, the former:

> An accent on a note is its own inner content and emphasis, so placed that a note stands out from another, without consideration of its apparent size and its ordinary value in a given time.[150]

To describe the *quantitative* aspect of accent Mattheson employs the term *rhythmus*. In his chapter entitled "On the Length and Shortness of Sound, or the Construction of Tone-Feet" he defines *rhythmus* in accord with his theory of time measurement by thesis and arsis:

> What a *rhythmus* is, is taught to us by prosody, or that instruction in the art of speaking by means of which it is ascertained how one should properly place the accent, and whether one should utter a long or a short. The meaning of the word *rhythmus* however is merely *quantitative*, namely, a certain measuring or counting out, there the syllables, here the sounds, not only with regard to their multiplicity; but also with regard to their *brevity and length*.[151]

---

[148]Johnson, Tyson, and Winter, *Beethoven Sketchbooks,* 401, 403.

[149]See Ratner's discussion of "scansion" in *Classic Music,* 319–20.

[150]"Ein Accent in den Noten ist der innerliche Gehalt und Nachdruck derselben welcher so placirt ist dass dadurch eine Note vor der andern ohne Ansehen ihrer äusserlichen Gestalt und gewöhnlichen Geltung zu gewissen Zeiten hervorraget" (Johann Mattheson, *Critica musica* [Hamburg, May 1722], 43; translation from George Houle, *Meter in Music, 1600–1800: Performance, Perception, and Notation* [Bloomington: Indiana University Press, 1987], 126).

[151]"Was ein *Rhythmus* sey, solches lehret uns die Prosodie, oder diejenige Anweisung in der Sprach-Kunst, mittelst welcher festgesetzt wird, wie man die Accente

Once again, Mattheson's notion of measuring quantity has nothing to do with "equality" of parts in the modern sense (where, for example, each beat may be one second long). Rather it has to do with marking regular recurrences, with the recognition of shapes: "a certain measuring or counting out" of syllables in speech and sounds in music that differentiates "long" from "short." Mattheson's next step is to define relationships between recurrent groups of two, three, or four notes—the poetic feet (which he lists later)—and thereafter to show how these feet accumulate to form larger units apprehensible to the ear. This is the defining of scansion, which he calls *rhythmopöia:*

> What meters are in poetry, rhythms are in music, for this reason we will call them tone-feet, since song as it were walks along on them. But the uniting and other manipulation of these tone-feet is technically called *rhythmopöia.*[152]

Often the relationships between the notes within these two- and three-note groupings are left unmarked. For example, a strongly trochaic gesture can easily be represented by notes of different length, such as ♩ ♪; but a more subtle trochaic gesture is often better represented by notes of equal outer worth, for example, ♩ ♩, that are nevertheless performed so as to be recognizable as a trochee. In the rhetorical tradition, metric schemes in themselves carry the power to

---

recht anbringen, und lang oder kurtz aussprechen soll. Die Bedeutung aber des Worts *Rhythmus* ist nichts anders als eine *Zahl,* nehmlich, eine gewisse Abmessung oder Abzehlung, dort der Sylben, hier der Klänge, nicht nur in Betracht ihrer Vielheit; sondern auch in Ansehung ihrer *Kürze und Länge"* (Johann Mattheson, *Der vollkommene Capellmeister* [Hamburg: Christian Herold; facsimile, Kassel: Bärenreiter-Verlag, 1954], 160 [Von der Länge und Kürtze des Klanges, oder von Verfertigung der Klang-Füsse]; translation from Harriss, *Johann Mattheson's "Der vollkommene Capellmeister,"* 344).

[152]"Was die Füsse in der Dicht-Kunst bedeuten, solches stellen die Rhythmi in der Ton-Kunst vor, deswegen wir sie auch Klang-Füsse nennen wollen, weil der Gesang gleichsam auf ihnen einhergehet. Die Zusammenfügung aber und übrige Einrichtung dieser Klang-Füsse heisset mit ihrem Kunst-Worte *Rhythmopöie* . . . " (Mattheson, *Capellmeister,* 160; translation from Harriss, *Johann Mattheson's "Der vollkommene Capellmeister,"* 344).

inflect values in this way, and these are often strengthened by the visual aids of beams and slurs. Emanuel Bach refers to the differing "inner values" of notes of outwardly equal value in the opening chapter of the second volume of his *Versuch,* and distinguishes them in terms of length and shortness:

> If the accompaniment falls directly on the notes that are *long in terms of their inner value,* then the *passing tone* is *regular (transitus regularis).* With notes of equal value, the first, third, etc., are (virtually) long in terms of their inner value, and the second, fourth, etc., short.

> If the accompaniment that belongs to the virtually short note is taken before it, and is played on the long note, then the *passing tone* is *irregular (transitus irregularis)* and the notes are called *changing notes:*[153]

[153]"Wenn alsdenn das gehörige Accompagnement blos auf die *dem innerlichen Werthe nach lange Noten* fällt: so ist der *Durchgang regulär (transitus regularis).* Unter Noten von gleicher Geltung ist die erste, dritte u.s.w. dem innerlichen Werthe nach *(virtualiter)* lang; und die zweyte, vierte u.s.w. kurz: . . . Wenn die Begleitung, welche der *virtualiter* kurzen Note zukommt, vorausgenommen, und zur langen Note angeschlagen wird, so ist der *Durchgang irregulär (transitus irregularis)* und die Noten heißt man alsdenn *Wechselnoten:* . . . " (Carl Philipp Emanuel Bach, *Versuch über die wahre Art, das Clavier zu spielen,* 1st ed. [Berlin, 1753 and 1762]; facsimile, ed. Lothar Hoffmann-Erbrecht [Leipzig: Breitkopf and Härtel, 1957], part 2 [1762], 30). See also Bach's description of the "scarcely noticeable increase of pressure" on appropriate notes in "patterns" of two, three, and four slurred notes (Carl Philipp Emanuel Bach, *Essay on the True Art of Playing Keyboard Instruments,* trans. William Mitchell [New York: W. W. Norton, 1949], 154). The notion of "inner" or "virtual" worth is addressed by other theorists as well, including Ernst Wilhelm Wolf, in his *Musikalischer Unterricht* of 1788: "One says of two notes that have the same length, such as ♪ ♪ that the heavier note, designated with a ▼, is *intrinsically and extrinsically* long . . . the lighter note, however, designated here with a ⌣, is only *extrinsically* long, and intrinsically short" (Ernst W. Wolf, *Musikalischer Unterricht* [Dresden, 1788], 25; translation from Ratner, *Classic Music,* 71). See also Johann G. Walther, *Musikalisches Lexikon* (Leipzig, 1732), 507.

Bach also describes quantitative accent as a means of serving explicitly affective ends. This was sometimes referred to as "oratorical" accent, and in its extreme form was further differentiated as "pathetic" accent.[154] In Example 33 Bach illustrates both:

> [Example 33] shows us various instances where for the sake of affect one allows the notes and rests to have a longer value than that required by the notation. Some of these broadenings I have clearly written out, others are indicated by small crosses.[155]

Example 33. Emanuel Bach's notation for agogic accentuation (*Versuch,* part 1, tab. 6, fig. 13)

That these traditional means of agogic accentuation were used by Beethoven to mark both meter and gesture is supported by Schindler's description of Beethoven's accentuation. But his use of the terms "rhythmic accent" and "melodic accent" needs to be clarified:

[154]Although Bach did not discuss these distinctions explicitly, several theorists did, among them Jean-Jacques Rousseau, Johann A. Hiller, Heinrich Christoph Koch, and Johann F. Christmann (Ratner, *Classic Music,* 191, cites Rousseau, *Dictionnaire de musique* [Paris, 1768], 2–4; Hiller, *Anweisung zum musikalisch-zierlichen Gesange* [Leipzig, 1780], 27f.; Koch, *Lexikon,* 50–53; and Christmann, *Elementarbuch der Tonkunst* [Speyer, 1782–89], 207).

[155]"[Example 33] zeigt uns unterschiedene Exempel, wo man aus Affeckt bißweilen so wohl die Noten als Pausen länger gelten läßt, als die Schreib-Art erfordert. Dieses Anhalten habe ich theils deutlich ausgeschrieben, theils durch kleine Kreuze angedeutet" (Emanuel Bach, *Versuch,* part 1 [1753], 129). The upper ligatures in the examples reproduced here are visual aids that extend over Bach's written-out versions (those without the small crosses). They are not indications for legato binding.

As for Beethoven's particular style of accentuation, the author can speak partly from Beethoven's critical remarks on Czerny's playing and partly from the piano instruction that Beethoven gave to him directly. It was above all the *rhythmic* accent that he stressed most heavily and that he wanted others to stress. He treated the *melodic* (or grammatic, as it was generally called) accent, on the other hand, mostly according to the internal requirements. He would emphasize all retardations, especially that of the diminished second in *cantabile* sections, more than other pianists. His playing thus acquired a highly personal character, very different from the even, flat performances that never rise to *tonal eloquence*. In *cantilena* sections he adopted the methods of *cultivated* singers, doing neither too much nor too little. Sometimes he recommended putting appropriate words to a perplexing passage and singing it, or listening to a good violinist or wind player play it.[156]

"Rhythmic accent" suggests a relationship to *rhythmus,* meter, scansion, and therefore to "grammatical" accent. But Schindler mistakenly associates the term "grammatical accent" with "melodic accent." Since Beethoven's "melodic accents" were dependent upon "inner requirements," apparently including the stressing of diminished seconds and other highly affective intervals, it seems likely that "melodic accent" would be better associated with the oratorical and pathetic.

---

[156]"Was Beethoven's Eigenheit in der Accentuation betrifft, so kann der Verfasser anführen, was sich theils aus den kritischen Anmerkungen über Czerny's Vorträge, theils aus den unmittelbaren Belehrungen am Piano ergeben. Vorzugsweise was es der *rhythmische* Accent, den er meist kräftig hervorhob und hervorgehoben wissen wollte, dagegen behandelte er den *melodischen* (gewöhnlich der *grammatische* genannt) meist nach Erfordernitz, pflegte nur alle Vorhalte, den der kleinen Secunde im Cantabile ganz besonders, immer mehr zu betonen, als man es von Andern gehört. Dadurch erhielt sein Spiel ein Prägnant-Charakteristisches, fern von dem Glatten, Flachen, das sich niemals zur *Tonsprache* erhebt. Bei der Cantilene verwies er auf die Methode *gebildeter* Sänger, die nicht zu viel und nicht zu wenig thun, rieth ferner bisweilen passende Worte einer streitigen Stelle unterzulegen und sie zu singen, oder auch solche Stellen von einem gebildeten Violinisten oder Bläser zu hören" (Schindler, *Biographie,* 4th ed., 236–37; translation from Schindler and MacArdle, *Beethoven,* 416; original emphasis restored).

To sum up we must weigh the nineteenth-century views of Czerny against the somewhat muddled report from Schindler. It seems clear from both sources that Beethoven used agogics for oratorical accent, and from Schindler that he used them for the establishment of "rhythmic accent" as well. Because Beethoven spent most of his life steeped in the rhetorical tradition in a world without metronomes, it seems likely that Schindler was right in suggesting that he practiced that tradition, marking a metric stress as he would have marked the quality and quantity of a long syllable. But Beethoven probably needed agogics for another reason. Though his syntax was preeminently classical, his playing was based on legato: in some measure agogic stress could replace the consonant in articulating structure. As for his handling of oratorical or pathetic accent, it evidently depended on combinations of greater length, a higher dynamic, and, where appropriate, evocative silence. Normally metrical accent bows to the accent of phrase rhythm, and phrase rhythm in turn bows to expressive accent.[157] But whatever the hierarchy, we aim to capture a style that was, in Czerny's words, "gigantic."[158]

After Beethoven, when dynamic accent finally came to be seen as the only way to mark meter, and the importance of *rhythmopöia* diminished, metrics were, indeed, based on "equal" beats, but in this respect Beethoven's inclinations were not modern. I regard Czerny rather than Beethoven as the foremost exponent of the new practice.[159]

---

[157]Rosenblum, *Performance Practices*, 93. I recommend Rosenblum's lucid, thorough, and well-balanced discussion of classical accentuation.

[158]Forbes, *Thayer's Life of Beethoven*, 369.

[159]I have always felt that Beethoven's annoyance with Czerny's interest in pearly effects has some bearing on this. I refer here to Beethoven's well-known letter of advice on the instruction of his nephew Karl, to the effect that Czerny should encourage the lad to use all the fingers in runs of broken thirds ascending or descending to create a more gliding effect, that is, more legato. "Of course such passages sound 'pearly' or 'played like pearls' when fewer fingers are used, but one wishes for other jewellery occasionally" [Freilich klingen d. g., wie man sagt, 'geperlt gespielt (mit weniger Fingern) oder wie eine Perle,' allein man wünscht auch einmal anderes Geschmeide] (quoted in Badura-Skoda's introduction to Czerny, *Proper Performance*, 3; and *Über das richtigen Vortrag*, 9).

4 Applications, Both "Modern" and "Translated"

A "Strict" Performance of the Introduction to Op. 5, No. 1

If Czerny did not intend his repeated recommendations for "strict tempo" to be taken too literally, he has in that case been misunderstood by generations of musicians. To this day the influence of his metronomic ideal can be heard in performances of many of the best-known recitalists. Consider, for example, the recording of the Sonata for Piano and Violoncello, Op. 5, no. 1 by Sviatoslav Richter and Mstislav Rostropovich, which thoroughly satisfies Czerny's demand for "strict tempo" in the opening *Adagio sostenuto*.[1] Rostropovich and Richter offer us here a realization of what I call "modern meter," that is, meter as Czerny described it: dynamic tendencies alone clarify meter, and because time comprises "equal" parts and note values are read as literally as possible, rhythm distinct from meter has ceased to exist. This is "early Urtext" playing of the kind that began to show up in the 1950s: scrupulous, and earnest to a fault, the fault being that playfulness, humor, double entendre, and topical content are too of-

[1] I refer to the performance of the Sonata in F major for Piano and Violoncello, Op. 5, no. 1 on Philips compact disc set 412 256–2, *Beethoven: The Sonatas for Piano and Cello*, Sviatoslav Richter, piano; Mstislav Rostropovich, cello; recorded July 1961. (The timing of the *Adagio sostenuto* is two minutes thirty-four seconds.)

ten overlooked. In this recording the duo's earnestness actually serves to magnify the consequences of their superficially "strict tempo."

But if we draw instead from Czerny's more sensitive theorizing (for example, his explication of the *Andantino espressivo* in Example 1), and from Beethoven's hints (supported by Schindler, Beethoven's colleagues, and many of the theorists Beethoven most admired), our picture of the aesthetics of the day suggests that this approach to the *Adagio* is both naive and anachronistic. To read the surface of a score in this way—without a metric structure independent of rhythm, without grammatical accent distinguished from oratorical accent—is to misread. Like the poet who recites with varied stress but in equal time, Richter and Rostropovich spare some of the sense but none of the evocative freedom of the "speaking style."

A Rhetorical Analysis of the Introduction to Op. 5, No. 1

To my way of thinking the *Adagio* of Op. 5, no. 1 has a great deal more to say than Czerny's description would lead us to believe. We may forgive him his brevity, but we do need more substantial advice on how to deliver the goods. In my analysis here, which is necessarily and decidedly ad hoc and individual, I suggest a way of unfolding the *Adagio* with the strength and flexibility of declamation. I identify two principal figures in the *Adagio*: the first a "question" and the second an "answer," represented by Q and A respectively in the diagram here (Figure 1) and in the annotated score (Example 34).[2] (The questions are given superscripts that represent the scale degrees of their initial notes; the answers are simply numbered.) I use "question and answer" rather than more generic terms like "incomplete and complete

[2]In Figures 1 and 2, pitches in specific octaves are designated as follows: C_2 C_1 C c c^1 c^2 c^3, where "c" is middle C; moving upward, the form of the name alters with each C. In the annotated examples that follow, all tempo indications, pitches, note values, slurs, accidentals, rests, fermatas, dynamics, and signs of articulation appear in the cited editions. Stemming is altered only where additional stems are beamed to connect the pitches of a motive. In the Op. 5 analysis the designations *"dubitatio," "cantabile," "variation on cantabile,"* etc. are my own.

Bars 1–21 (tonic):   *Abschnitten* ↓

1–3	Q^1		A1	(cello hesitates to descend the
	(1 bar	**+**	**2 bars)**	arpeggio: *dubitatio* and link to . . .)
4–6	Q^2 (more intense)		A2	(cello traces beginning of A2, then
	(1 bar	**+**	**2 bars)**	turns away and rises to . . .)

7–10 cello *cantabile* with ornate Q^3 in final bar
      (4 bars)

11–(14) keyboard variation: *cantabile* turning toward minor in *crescendo*; Q^4 **p** in bar 14
         (should be 4 bars, but bar 14 is "wrong"; reinterpreted as first bar of . . .)

14–16 two-bar pair: Q^4 + Q^7 in keyboard Q^3 reiterated by keyboard in F
       (pair of figures linked by run suggests   minor
       shape of *cantabile* in diminution)
       (2 bars   +   1 bar)

17–21 bars 17–19: cello's **sf** tenor line = Q^2;   bars 20–21: second variation on
       reinforced by keyboard, bar 18 = Q^5 *cantabile* in minor (by cello as it
       = a recomposition of bar 6, the   attains *f*), this time as a hesitant
       swing into the *cantabile;*   placement of the dominant; bass
       bar 17: three **sf**s in keyboard bass =   double-dotted figure = Q^4 with
       Q^4;   crescendo to high note
       bars 19–20: Q diminutions in soprano
       (3 bars   +   2 bars)

Bars 22–34 (on the dominant):

22–25 (cf. 1–6, but here in pairs of bars and more static) keyboard strums dominant
       chord; cello (no questions asked) descends it staccato;
       keyboard figures = variations on A1 and A2, but less declamatory
       (4 bars)

26–28 whimsical cello variation on A2   variation on A2 repeated by
       closing with a soft reiteration of Q7   keyboard; startling **ff** set off by cello
                                                for Q^2 in keyboard;
                                                chromatic extension in bass
       (1 bar   +   2 bars)

29–31 peroration on dominant 9th   repeated;
                                                chromatic extension in bass
       (1 bar   +   2 bars)

32–34 final reference to *cantabile;* hints of A   Q diminutions similar to those in
                                                bar 19 now outline a turn around *f*
                                                descending from *g* [but *f* destination
                                                is avoided in first bar of *Allegro*]
       (2 bars   +   1 bar)

Figure 1. An interpretation of rhetorical content and periodic structure in the introduc‐
tion to Beethoven's Sonata in F for Piano and Violoncello, Op. 5, no. 1

Example 34. Beethoven Sonata in F for Piano and Violoncello, Op. 5, no. 1, first movement, measures 1–34 (after the first edition, Vienna: Artaria, 1797), with my annotations

Example 34. (Continued)

Example 34. (Continued)

statement" or "antecedent and consequent" because the conversation-
al terms suggest inflections appropriate to the play of figures throughout the introduction. The hierarchy of elongated numbers above the
bar lines is my way of illustrating what Mattheson and Kirnberger
called the *Einschnitten,* and their groupings into *Abschnitten* and
Perioden, as shown in boldface on the diagram, the whole of the
Adagio being equivalent to a *Paragraphus,* despite the fact that it
reaches no final perfect cadence.

The first *Einschnitt,* the question asked in unison by piano and cello,
takes a measure to itself. The first answer proves to be an occasion for
some disagreement: the piano replies in two bars, but the cello seems
suspicious and descends its arpeggio much more hesitantly than the
piano, finally sharping the tonic as a way to raise the question once
again (while literally raising it to the next scale degree).

The piano, apparently well aware that its pat answer would never
be accepted, proves ready and willing to join with the cello in asking
the question again, this time more urgently. But the cello is even less
inclined to go along with the piano's second answer, and refuses to
budge from its B-flat. With a luxurious upswing outlining a first-
inversion triad the cello moves to the fore, ushering in the opening of
the second *Abschnitt* as it sings a whole new cantilena with a beautifully ornamented question at its close, this one raised by yet another
scale degree. When the piano takes up the *cantabile,* varying it in the
minor, the question disrupts everything by appearing on a "wrong
note" atop a "wrong chord"—but again one scale degree higher.
Now we are "lost": the piano mutters a couple of questions softly out
of sequence (Q^7 and Q^3). But just as abruptly resolution returns with
the bass sforzati in the piano, and by the downbeat of bar 19 a syncopated sforzato question on the fifth scale degree has enabled us to
attain E-flat, which needs only to be naturalized to become the major
third of the dominant.

I am of the opinion that this sort of storytelling is something one
does oneself, alone, and in one's own way. I am going to these lengths
here to show how *"streng im* Tempo*"* fails as a substitute for comprehension, and, much more important, to show how Beethoven's
far more detailed slurring suggests precisely the nuances that the
declamation needs. Whereas Czerny submerges both the tonic and

the third of the opening question beneath a slur, Beethoven leaves both pitches articulate, thereby encouraging the players to project the question with delicacy and at the same time enabling them to make clear the relationship between it and its inversion in bar 3: the staccato falling third played by the piano at the end of its "lame answer." The discrepancies in first-edition slurring between piano and cello in bars 4 and 5 can also work to good effect. The cello approaches the B-flat first softly and without articulation in bar 4 (so that the final eighth evaporates in the diminuendo as the end of a question of this sort should), but then with subtly increased intensity and clearer articulation in bar 5 (so that the B-flat is reached for and gently prolonged) as a preparation for the singing B-flat that will bring its *cantabile* to the fore by bar 7. The piano all the while remains stuck in the pattern it first established, which, just as it should, sounds progressively less convincing.

The hypermetric structure of the *Adagio* is symmetrical: three bars for each of the first two question-and-answer pairs, making *six* bars; the *cantabile* with the question at its close, interrupted in its varied reiteration, making *seven* bars; followed by the *eight* bars leading up to the dominant, with their disturbing intensifications of the question in the bass and tenor registers. The arrival at the dominant clears the air, and it seems at first that there are no more questions, only variations on the answer. Six downbeats pass with delicate play between the instruments before the explosion of the question and its chromatic prolongation stretch this *Abschnitt* to *seven* bars, the peroration and final return to *cantabile* bringing us to the fermata in *six* bars.

The large-scale symmetry is significant because it represents the shape of the drama as a whole, but even more pronounced are the effects of the asymmetries within the local measure groups, wherein odd groupings disturb while even groupings stabilize. One-bar questions are first met with two-bar answers. After the dominant is achieved, tension is dissipated with the languid pairings in bars 22–25. For reasons like these the two seven-measure *Abschnitten* are clearly dissimilar: the first is cut short when the "wrong chord" in bar 14 causes us to reinterpret this measure as the first of a new *Abschnitt* filled with questions, while the second occurs for the opposite reason, when after the explosive fortissimo question in bar 27, the dominant ninth of the peroration can be reached only through the mighty broadening of the chromatic extension.

As usual Beethoven's musical idea "everywhere predominates"; the question is at work on many levels, some completely explicit (like the first two questions), some on the order of details (like the tiny diminutions of the rising figure in bar 19), and some more subterranean (like the bass tones marked by sforzati in bar 17, or the jagged rhythms in the bass in bars 20–21).

But in line with the best aims of the rhetorical tradition, Beethoven's plan extends well beyond the *Adagio:* this drama of question and answer proves essential to the large-scale architecture of the entire first movement. As in many rhetorical introductions, questions in the *Adagio* far outnumber answers (just as they do in the introductory part of Op. 31, no. 3). As a result the *Allegro* that follows has work to do, questions to answer.

From the outset Beethoven uses figures from the *Adagio,* cleverly redesigning some of them (Example 35) to make them more assertive while allowing others (Examples 36 and 37) to retain more of their questioning aspect (again as in Op. 31, no. 3).[3] Yet it clearly remains for the *Allegro* to answer the opening questions in some final way, since none of the answers in the *Adagio* is able to balance the astonishing outburst in its twenty-seventh bar.

To set the stage for the *Allegro* to satisfy this need, the *Adagio* must be supremely effective, its "one grand idea" made especially vivid. If the opening "question" (Q^1) can be made to *sound* like a question (with appropriately curtailed final note followed by a silence that is brief but fraught with significance), and if the first answer ($A1$) can be made to sound sufficiently pat (with rubato shaped around its sforzato high note, and absurdly deadpan and rather pointed staccato eighths to end it), and if the cello's hesitant mulling-over of the first answer (*dubitatio*) and its sly reiteration of the question (Q^2) and its subsequent refusal to accept the varied answer (the retained B-flat in bar 6

---

[3]I have indicated the musical question with an inverted question mark in Examples 36 and 37.

Example 35. Beethoven Sonata in F for Piano and Violoncello, Op. 5, no. 1, first movement, measures 37–38 (after the first edition, Vienna: Artaria, 1797)

Example 36. Beethoven Sonata in F for Piano and Violoncello, Op. 5, no. 1, first movement, measure 44 (after the first edition, Vienna: Artaria, 1797), with my annotation

Example 37. Beethoven Sonata in F for Piano and Violoncello, Op. 5, no. 1, first movement, measures 161–64 (after the first edition, Vienna: Artaria, 1797), with my annotation

and the swing into the *cantabile*) can sustain the rhetorical line, we have achieved the essential first steps in a trajectory that points all the way to the climax at the coda of the *Allegro*.

Following the Rhetorical Trajectory into the *Allegro* of Op. 5, No. 1

In both the exposition and the recapitulation of the *Allegro,* Beethoven focuses on the motif of the rising third in remarkable ways. In this bracing tempo, the questions, while they still sound "unfinished," are often far more assertive (Figure 2[4] and Example 38[5]). At times they lead us on (Example 39), and sometimes they become downright obsessive (Examples 40 and 41). At length there is a pronouncement equivalent in vehemence to the outburst in bar 27 of the *Adagio* (Example 42). In the coda that follows, Q^2 is at first quietly linked with Q^6 (Example 43). But this is almost immediately questioned (especially in the ensuing *Adagio* in which the cello reminisces about the first half of its original answers in the opening *Adagio*. With the timid arrival on I_4^6 a *Presto* begins in which the piano reminds us obsessively of the second half of those original answers, then cadences grandly with the cello to return to *Tempo primo*. Now the stage is set: the final answer in bars 391–95 at last puts all doubt to rest by absorbing Q^3 (with a naturalized B) into its structure (Example 44).[6] In celebration, the final two bars of the peroration show the link with Q^6 that had been suggested at the very opening of the coda (Example 45).

[4]Figure 2 is most easily understood with a reliable score of the Op. 5 sonata at hand.
[5]In measure 247 the doubled slurs for the piano right hand are original.
[6]Lewis Lockwood says that "this touch of sophistication utterly separates Beethoven, no matter how early in his career, from virtually all his contemporaries but Haydn and Mozart, and reminds us once again of his power to assimilate not only the central resources of their compositional styles but their subtleties as well" (Lewis Lockwood, "Beethoven's Early Works for Violoncello and Pianoforte: Innovation in Context," *The Beethoven Newsletter* 1 [1986]: 20).

Bars 35–160, exposition: *Allegro* **(tonic to dominant):**

35–38	**4 bars:** begins by avoiding *f*; arpeggio now descends from c^1, partially filled in by appoggiaturas; achieves harmonically in 4 bars what *Adagio sostenuto* needed 6 bars to complete, but here pitches descend ($c^1 \to b^b$)
39–40	**2 additional bars** → *a* in what will be vi$^6_5$
41–48	**8 bars:** closing with keyboard *a* → *b*♭ to . . .
49–56	**8 bars:** cello's *c*; still toying with *c* → *B*♭ to . . .
57–64	**8 bars:** keyboard's a^1 (new register) → b^{b1} (with mordent reminiscent of original Q^3) → c^2 (additional mordent allows extension to sforzato d^2 in bar 65)
65–72	**4 + 4 bars:** with arrival *on* V, Q^2 ($g^1 \to a^1 \to b^{b1}$) asked in keyboard (bars 65–66), then varied in 67–68, both marked by sforzati; 4 bars celebrating C
73–80	**4 + 4 bars:** questions now arise from C: Q^5 in major ($c \to d \to e$) in cello in bars 75–76; Q^6 ($d \to e \to f$) in cello in bars 79–80. . .
85–92	**4 + 4 bars:** keyboard variation on bars 73–80: same questions an octave higher
93–97	**5 bars (interrupted 6):** reiteration and intensification of Q^6 in bars 95 and 97 . . .
102–3	obsessive reiteration of Q^6 . . .
108–16	**9 bars:** $g^1 \to a^1 \to b^{b1} \to c^2 \to d^2$ then triple reiteration of Q^6: $d^2 \to f^2$ . . .
117ff.	dominant preparation
126ff.	deceptive cadence: ♭VI/V
137–42	dominant preparation completed with V$^6_4$, V^7/V, V ($e^2 \searrow d^1 \to [c^1$ in bar 143]) . . .

Bars 161–220, development: (begins in remote key of III; much figural play on motives from bars 35–36) . . .

Bars 221–341, recapitulation:

. . .	
246–53	**4 + 4 bars:** equivalent to 65–72: Q^2 with varied reiteration; celebration of C
254–61	**4 + 4 bars:** transposition of 73–80 so that cello's questions are now Q^1 and Q^2 . . .
266–73	**4 + 4 bars:** keyboard variation on bars 254–61: same questions an octave higher
274–78	**5 bars (interrupted 6):** reiteration and intensification of Q^2 in bar 276, 278 . . .
283–84	obsessive reiteration of Q^2 . . .
289–97	**9 bars:** Q^2 still being asked in bars 293, 294 . . .
308ff.	deceptive cadence with return to I$^6_4$ at bar 318;
339–47	**4 bars:** $g^{\#1} \to a^1 \to (!)b^{b1}$ in fortissimo as a dramatic equivalent to Q^2 in bars 27–28 of the *Adagio sostenuto;* chromatic extension attains f^2 at fermata on I$^6_4$

Bars 348–85, coda:

. . .	
354–56	three reiterations of Q^2 with original F♯ upbeat
357	one quiet statement of Q^6 ($d^2 \to e^2 \to f^2$ in I$^6_4$)
362	*Adagio* = point of furthest remove: f^2 reinterpreted within V^7/E♭, then again within . . .
368ff.	I$^6_4$ in *Presto:* triplet runs outline descending and ascending arpeggio of F major, followed by conventional cadence with fermata into . . .

Bars 386–400, codetta: *Tempo primo:*

386–89	**4 bars:** cello moves from $A \to B♭$
390–91	**2 additional bars:** cello moves from $B♭ \to c$ (pitches of Q^3 have now been traversed)
392–94	**3 bars:** Q^3 with naturalized B absorbed into final answer with cadence closing into . . .
395–400	**6 bars (2 + 2 + 1 + 1):** peroration celebrating F and final reiterations of Q^6 in bars 399 and 400 ($Q^3 + Q^6 = \hat{3}\,\hat{4}\,\hat{5}\,\hat{6}\,\hat{7}\,\hat{8}$)

Figure 2. An interpretation of rhetorical content and periodic structure in the first movement *Allegro* of Beethoven's Sonata in F for Piano and Violoncello, Op. 5, no. 1

Example 38. Beethoven Sonata in F for Piano and Violoncello, Op. 5, no. 1, first movement, measures 246–47 (comparable to measures 65–66 in the exposition) (after the first edition, Vienna: Artaria, 1797), with my annotations

Example 39. Beethoven Sonata in F for Piano and Violoncello, Op. 5, no. 1, first movement, measures 253–61 (comparable to measures 72–80 in exposition) (after the first edition, Vienna: Artaria, 1797), with my annotations

Example 40. Beethoven Sonata in F for Piano and Violoncello, Op. 5, no. 1, first movement, measures 276–78 (comparable to measures 95–97 in exposition) (after the first edition, Vienna: Artaria, 1797), with my annotations

Example 41. Beethoven Sonata in F for Piano and Violoncello, Op. 5, no. 1, first movement, measures 283–84 (comparable to measures 102–3 in exposition) (after the first edition, Vienna: Artaria, 1797), with my annotations

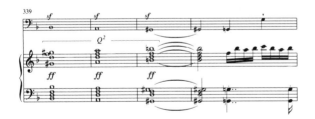

Example 42. Beethoven Sonata in F for Piano and Violoncello, Op. 5, no. 1, first movement, measures 339–42 (after the first edition, Vienna: Artaria, 1797), with my annotations

Example 43. Beethoven Sonata in F for Piano and Violoncello, Op. 5, no. 1, first movement, measures 353–57 (after the first edition, Vienna: Artaria, 1797), with my annotations

Example 44. Beethoven Sonata in F for Piano and Violoncello, Op. 5, no. 1, first movement, measures 390–97 (after the first edition, Vienna: Artaria, 1797), with my annotations

Example 45. Beethoven Sonata in F for Piano and Violoncello, Op. 5, no. 1, first movement, measures 399–400 (after the first edition, Vienna: Artaria, 1797), with my annotations

"Temporal Dissonance": Bartók's Performance of Op. 34

Having seen that Czerny's insistence on strictness is sometimes inappropriate, let us now examine one final example of his instruction in which he makes no mention of "strict tempo," but perhaps should. Here is his advice for the performance of the Variations on an Original Theme, Op. 34:

> In this excellent work, each *variation* is in another key, meter, and of a completely different *character*.
>
> The metronomic indications are given in the above-mentioned edition.[7] These *variations* require a style of performance as dexterous and thoroughly refined as it is fully expressive, and the *character* of each is so decidedly marked that the player can hardly miss it if he takes the right tempo.[8]

In Czerny's estimation the character of each variation will be obvious to any player. But he speaks in only the most general terms about a work that is, naturally, full of subtlety, as Ries discovered in a session with Beethoven:

> In the Variations in F major, dedicated to Princess Odescalchi (Op. 34), I had to repeat the last Adagio variations entirely seventeen times. Still he was not satisfied with the expression in the little cadenza, even though I thought I had played it just as well as he did.

---

[7]Czerny refers to an edition by Haslinger.

[8]"Jn diesem ausgezeichneten Werke ist jede *Variation* in einer andern Tonart, Taktart, und vom einem ganz verschiedenen *Character*.

"Die Metronombezeichnung findet man in der oben angezeigten Auflage. Diese *Variationen* bedürfen eines eben so gewandten und ausgebildeten, wie gefühlvollen Vortrags, und der *Character* einer jeden ist so bestimmt gezeichnet, dass der Spieler ihn nicht wohl verfehlen kann, wenn er das Tempo richtig nimmt" (Czerny, *Über den richtigen Vortrag der säntlichen Beethoven'schen Klavierwerke* [Vienna: Diabelli, 1846; facsimile, ed. Paul Badura-Skoda, Vienna: Universal, 1963], 64). Czerny's incipit mistakenly binds the upbeat into the first bar, lacks a bar-long slur over the stem-up thirds in the bass clef of bar 1, lacks a staccato point above the second rolled chord in bar 2, and substitutes broken rolls for continuous rolls for both chords in bar 2, all of which make us wonder about his perception of its "so decidedly marked" character.

I received nearly two full hours of instruction that day. If I made a mistake somewhere in a passage, or struck wrong notes, or missed intervals—which he often wanted *strongly emphasized*—he rarely said anything. However, if I lacked expression in crescendos, etc. or in the character of a piece, he became angry because, he maintained, the first was accident, while the latter resulted from inadequate knowledge, feeling, or attention.[9]

By the end of the lesson Ries should have been the last to underestimate the difficulties here; Beethoven surely did not. Seventeen times and still the little cadenza was not realized to his satisfaction! Yet given the nature of that cadenza it is hardly surprising, for although it may at first appear that the pitches to be stressed fall on the high points, the cadenza is really much more peculiar than that: harmonic syntax suggests échappées that outline the second inversion of the suspended F-major chord (Example 46).[10]

The last note emphasized is of course the first beyond the run, B-flat. A delicate performance of these irregular groupings requires a great deal of finesse, and one can imagine why even an advanced

[9]"In den Variationen in F dur, der Fürstinn Odescalchi gewidmet (Opus 34), habe ich die letzten Adagio-Variationen siebenzehnmal fast ganz wiederholen müssen; er war mit dem Ausdrucke in der kleinen Cadenze immer noch nicht zufrieden, obschon ich glaubte, sie eben so gut zu spielen, wie er. Ich erhielt an diesem Tage beinahe zwei volle Stunden Unterricht. Wenn ich in einer Passage etwas verfehlte, oder Noten und Sprünge, die er öster *recht herausgehoben* haben wollte, falsch anschlug, sagte er selten etwas; allein, wenn ich am Ausdrucke, an Crescendo's u.s.w. oder am Charakter des Stückes etwas mangeln ließ, wurde er aufgebracht, weil, wie er sagte, das Erstere Zufall, das Andere Mangel an Kenntniß, an Gefühl, oder an Achtsamkeit sei" (Ferdinand Ries, *Biographische Notizen über Ludwig van Beethoven von Wegeler und Ries,* ed. Alfred C. Kalischer, 2d ed. [Berlin: Schuster and Loeffler, 1906], 113–14; translation from *Beethoven Remembered: The Biographical Notes of Franz Wegeler and Ferdinand Ries,* trans. Frederick Noonan [Arlington, Va.: Great Ocean Publishers, 1987], 82–83 [emphasis restored]). Ries uses the plural "variations" when speaking of the final *Adagio molto.* Whatever he means, it should be noted that this section contains only one statement of the theme interrupted in its penultimate bar by the aforementioned cadenza, and then completed with a double-time reiteration of the approach to the penultimate bar and two variations on the final bar. Note Ries's corroboration of Schindler's claim that Beethoven wanted certain intervals to be emphatically expressed.

[10]This reading was first suggested to me by Samuel Rechtoris.

Example 46. Beethoven Variations on an Original Theme, Op. 34, Variation 6, measures 59–60, with my annotations

player like Ries might have found it difficult to satisfy Beethoven. Yet the cadenza is but one of many elements in the work that seem at first awkward or ill-conceived: almost every variation discloses some new problem for the performer, which if solved proves to strengthen further Beethoven's large-scale plan.

When we recall Beethoven's anger with those who were "inattentive," we might wonder what he would have made of the superficiality of Czerny's advice for performing this, the first variation set in his *ganz neue Manier*.[11] Although Czerny emphasizes the variety in the set and the necessity for a style that he characterizes as dexterous, thoroughly refined and *"gefühlvoll,"* he nevertheless stresses that success depends upon the player's choosing the right tempo. But while expressive flexibility of gesture is essential to the work's coherence, it is in fact a flexibility that occurs within the context of a *tempo giusto*.

---

[11]The term had a history of use in sales pitches, but Beethoven had more than this in mind when he wrote to his publishers about the Variations Opp. 34 and 35; see his two letters to Breitkopf and Härtel in Emily Anderson, trans. and ed., *The Letters of Beethoven,* 3 vols. (New York: St. Martin's Press, 1961), vol. 1, 76–77 (letter 62) and 83–84 (letter 67), and the discussion in Alan Tyson's "Steps to Publication—and Beyond," *The Beethoven Companion,* ed. Denis Arnold and Nigel Fortune (London: Faber and Faber, 1971), 483.

Béla Bartók illustrated this "expressive *tempo giusto*" in his recording of a fragment of the variations, a work he knew very well, having edited it in the Beethoven editions for Rozsnyai in 1910.[12] Bartók was, of course, accustomed to distinctions in the Central European folk musics between *parlando rubato* and *tempo giusto*. But as László Somfai notes, he never approached *tempo giusto* mechanically, since he saw it as displaying a subtle flexibility, a flexibility of a certain cast: springy, resilient, in quicker tempos sometimes suggesting "rhythmic movement that is elastic and tight like dance-steps, full of tiny follow-throughs."[13] Just as *tempo rubato* gains much of its evocative power by operating within certain strictures, whether they are defined by the imitation of speech or simply by local or more distant periodicities, *tempo giusto* gains expressive power from its own kind of flexibility.

The theme of Op. 34 suggests an underlying *tempo giusto* strong enough to allow for a flexible foreground: no one voice needs to express the *tempo giusto,* but underneath the surface it regulates all the expression. Examples 47 and 48 are fragments from the theme and Example 49 the opening of the first variation; Bartók's lengthened "good" syllables are indicated with a + and his lightened "bad" syllables with a ‿.

In Bartók's hands both the theme and first variation remain flexible while maintaining a deep structural pulse, the largest "beat" of the variation based on the theme itself. His minute displacements in time distinguish "good" notes from "bad" and point up dissonance. Indeed it all calls to mind Schindler's description of Beethoven's marking of scansion and his agogic enhancement of dissonance. In the end it is

[12]I refer to the *Thema* and fragment of Variation 1 from the Variations on an Original Theme in F major, Op. 34, from *The Centenary Edition of Bartók's Records* (complete), vol. 2, *Bartók Record Archives, Bartók Plays and Talks, 1912–1944: Private and Family Recordings/Fragments,* Hungaroton LPX 12335-A, band 2. The original is an "X-ray foil" recording (see the notes by László Somfai, 21–23). The quality of the recording is very poor, but despite the fact that many of the highs are obscured by surface noise (especially in the fragment of Variation 1) one can still distinguish timings and inflections.

[13]László Somfai, *The Centenary Edition of Bartók's Records* (complete), vol. 1, *Bartók at the Piano,* notes, 29. Bartók's use of rubato styles from folk music is cogently discussed on 29–31.

Example 47. Beethoven Variations on an Original Theme, Op. 34, Theme, measures 1–4, with my annotations

Example 48. Beethoven Variations on an Original Theme, Op. 34, Theme, measures 9–13, with my annotations

Example 49. Beethoven Variations on an Original Theme, Op. 34, Variation I, measures 1–2, with my annotations

not the ticking of a metronome but rather Bartók's ability to convey the subtle curves on multiple levels with a sense of simplicity and directness that enables him to achieve such a successful sense of *tempo giusto*. His large-scale framework is, by the clock, very strict: a projection of the incomplete first variation based on its tempo and prevailing inflections would suggest an overall duration of approximately one minute thirty-nine seconds, remarkably close to the one minute thirty-seven seconds of the theme. And given Bartók's renowned sensitivity to clock time, variations of two seconds begin to seem like meaningful large-scale planning, some scarcely believable sensitivity to "temporal dissonance" between mechanical time and rhetorical time that he can use for expressive purposes.[14]

In this kind of playing the audible curving of time within subbeats (which makes them sound iambic, trochaic, etc.) focuses attention on dissonance in the next higher time dimension, the units of which are colored in turn by the nature of the curvature within them. In Viennese music, as in the music of Bartók's culture, the curves occur on more than one level at a time; what rises to the surface as sound speaks of these many influences. But even in this context of multiple curves, when the structural posts are placed with a certain firmness, a *tempo giusto* results. Although it might at first seem that Bartók's relationship to Beethoven was, culturally and historically speaking, somewhat oblique, his musicological writing, his extensive experience as an editor of classic music, and his playing all attest to a deep sensitivity to Viennese practice and its history. In my opinion his recordings offer some of the most inspired declamatory playing anywhere available.

[14]Bartók knowingly or unknowingly followed Czerny's advice by marking timings in minutes and seconds at the end of many of his works and at times even within movements (Czerny advocates noting the exact duration of each composition in minutes and seconds [die *Dauer* eines jeden Tonsatzes *an der Uhr* zu bemerken, und dann genau nach Minuten und Sekunden zu notieren] in *Über den richtigen Vortrag*, 113).

5 Imagining More Vivid "Modern" Performance

Obviously it has been my intention in this book to suggest that those who would flock to Czerny and abandon Schindler because of the revelations about the latter's forgeries are going to lose a lot. Not only are there dangers in relying too much on Czerny, for whom the ability to generalize was both a strength and a weakness; there are dangers, too, in belittling Schindler. It looks as if Schindler's response to his own limitations led him down the path of the paranoid, the one who suffers to preserve the secrets of the past against all odds in an insensitive and unbelieving world. We can sense this in his introductory remarks to the annotated Cramer Etudes:

If the question should arise why I haven't published the general practical applications of these Etudes in the interest of Beethoven's music, let this serve as an answer: that for the past 30 years the reigning tendency in pianoforte playing that recognizes technique alone as the sole necessity would have taken no notice of this entirely opposing method. Another age must come that is again eager to apprehend instrumental music of every kind from the spiritual side; only then will the way be paved for the comprehension of Beethoven's intentions. Discerning musicians will understand this.

For my part I can assert that this path, nevertheless, is a very trying one.[1]

But as intellectuals of such a stripe often do, Schindler in fact managed to preserve some important teachings that *were* being forgotten. He reminds us that

> without the previous study of (German) prosody, without a detailed understanding of iambic, trochaic, dactylic and spondaic verse meters, as well as those poetic forms that lay the foundation for all instrumental music, the student will gain nothing, because the art of proper accentuation and the discrimination of longs and shorts in groups of tones is based on this understanding.[2]

And in this Schindler was a throwback. Even the late-eighteenth-century theorists who had made a point of emphasizing rhetorical principles in their treatises had done so in reaction to rhetoric's waning influence. That was Johann Friedrich Daube's aim when he wrote from Vienna in 1770 exhorting composers to "consider carefully the rules of oratory."[3] And the comprehensive outline of musical rhetoric

---

[1] "Sollte die Frage entstehen warum ich die gesammte Nutzanwendung dieser Etüden im Interesse von Beethoven's Musik nicht veröffentlicht habe, so diene zur Antwort, dass die seit 30 Jahren herrschende Richtung im Clavierspiel, die als einzige Erforderniss nur die Technik kennt, von dieser ganz entgegenstehenden Methode keine Notiz genommen haben würde. Es muss eine andere Zeit kommen, welche die Instrumental Musik jeder Gattung wieder von der geistigen Seite aufzufassen bestrebt ist, dann erst wird dem Verständniss der Beethoven'schen Intentionen der Weg gebahnt werden können. Einsichtsvolle Musiker werden das begreifen. Meinerseits kann ich bekräftigen, dass dieser Weg dem ungeachtet ein sehr beschwerlicher ist" (Anton Schindler quoted in Cramer, *Selection of Studies by J. B. Cramer, with Comments by L. van Beethoven, and Preface, Translation, Explanatory Notes, and Fingering . . . ,* trans. and ed. John South Shedlock [London: Augener (1893)], ii; translation mine).

[2] "Ohne vorheriges Studium der (deutschen) Prosodie, ohne genaue Kenntniss des iambischen, trochäischen, daktylischen und spondäischen Versmasses, als derjenigen Dichtungsformen, die aller Instrumentalmusik zum Grunde liegen, ist beim Schüler nichts zu erreichen, denn auf dieser Kenntniss beruht die Kunst der richtigen Accentuation und Unterscheidung von Längen und Kürzen in den Tongruppen" (Anton Schindler quoted in ibid.; translation mine).

[3] The quotation is from Daube's *Der musikalische Dilettant: eine Abhandlung des Generalbasses* (Vienna: Kurzböck, 1770–71), 10; translation from George J. Buelow, "Music

that Johann Nikolaus Forkel included in his *Allgemeine Geschichte der Musik* from Göttingen in 1788, was a decided anachronism on the day it was published, especially in its description of musical figures.[4] It is true that critics kept the rhetorical analogies alive: Dussek was praised for "his truly declamatory style" in 1802, and as late as July of 1823 in an anonymous review that appeared in the *Harmonicon,* Cramer was singled out as a master of keyboard oratory, though fittingly, the words used in the 1823 review were quoted from an article that had appeared "three or four years ago, in a daily paper": "His brilliancy of execution is astonishing; but this quality . . . amounts to little or nothing in the general estimate of such merits as are his in taste, expression, feeling, the power that he possesses of almost making the instrument speak a language. . . . those who love to have their sympathies awakened by the 'eloquent music' which this instrument may be made to 'discourse,' . . . should seize every opportunity that is afforded them of hearing Cramer.[5]

In the same year August Leopold Crelle, a mathematician and musician from Berlin, published in his piano method a discourse on what he believed to be essential distinctions between speech and music, and his was an unequivocally nineteenth-century view:

Speech does not adhere strictly to tempo and tone, but rather gives its durational elements only *arbitrary* relationships, no *fixed* measure; likewise its tones. Both time measure and tone measure are inferior to the certainty with which speech expresses feelings. On the other hand, in music, which arouses and communicates only general feelings, the measurement of time and tone is, conversely, predomi-

---

and Rhetoric," *New Grove Dictionary of Music and Musicians* 15.802; quoted in Sandra P. Rosenblum, *Performance Practices in Classic Piano Music: Their Principles and Applications* (Bloomington: Indiana University Press, 1988), 13. According to Rosenblum, Daube was trained largely in South Germany.

[4]Vincent Duckles, "Johann Nicolaus Forkel: The Beginning of Music Historiography," *Eighteenth-Century Studies* 1 (1968): 286.

[5]Rosenblum, *Performance Practices,* 15, 16. Another rather arresting description of Cramer's "vocal" keyboard style appears in an account by Ignaz Moscheles, in which he claims that Cramer's legato "almost transforms a Mozart *Andante* into a vocal piece" (Jerald C. Graue, "Johann [John] Baptist Cramer," *New Grove Dictionary of Music and Musicians* 5.19).

nant. In [music] time maintains a *fixed, equal* duration, tone a *definite, appropriate* pitch and a fixed position. Starting with recitative, the more music distances itself from speech, that is, the more music ascends toward harmony, or toward any of its characteristic works of art derived from fantasy and the intellect, the more palpable are the differences between speech and music, namely, that the former possesses an indefinite measure of time and tone and definite meaning, whereas music has indefinite meanings and a precise measurement of time and tone.[6]

Crelle's treatise evidences no progress at all in describing the content of music (it is still "general feelings") and shows little inclination to equate speech with fantasy, as Emanuel Bach had done. For Crelle "fantasy" engendered works that drew music *away* from speech-mimetic effects and *toward* the "exact measure of time and tone" wherein time comprises "equal durations."

How old-fashioned Beethoven is beginning to seem by this time, with his concern for the "most distinct and intelligible declamation."[7]

---

[6]"Die Rede hält sich an dem Zeitmaasse und dem Tone nicht strenge, sondern giebt ihren Zeittheilen nur *willkührliche* Verhältnisse, kein *bestimmtes* Maass; eben so ihren Tönen. Beides, das Zeit- und Tonmaass stehen gegen die Bestimmtheit zurück, mit welcher die Rede Empfindungen ausdrückt. In der Musik dagegen, die nur allgemeine Empfin[dun]gen erregt und mittheilt, ist umgekehrt das Zeit- und Tonmaass vorherrschend. Die Zeit erhält in ihr eine *feste, gleiche* Dauer, der Ton eine *bestimmte, gemaasene* Höhe und eine feste Stelle. Je weiter sich, vom Recitative ab, die Musik von der Rede entfernt, das heisst, je weiter die Musik zur Harmonie, oder zu einem ihr eigenthümlichen, aus der Fantasie und dem Verstande herkommenden Kunstwerke aufsteigt, je fühlbarer sind die Unterschiede der Rede und der Musik, nemlich, dass jene ein unbestimmtes Zeit- und Ton-Maass und bestimmte Bedeutungen, dagegen die Musik unbestimmte Bedeutungen und ein bestimmtes Zeit- und Ton-Maass hat" (August L. Crelle, *Einiges über musikalischen Ausdruck und Vortrag für Fortepiano-spieler* [Berlin: Maurerschen Buchhandlung, 1823], 15–16). William Newman, who describes this treatise as "penetrating and illuminating," has twice erred in his paraphrase of this section by attributing to Crelle the ideas that "speech proves less exact in its expression of emotions than music" and that "the more [music] changes from fantasy and the verbalized toward harmony or any other of its idiomatic means, the more apparent becomes the distinction between speech and music" (William S. Newman, *Beethoven on Beethoven: Playing His Piano Music His Way* [New York: W. W. Norton, 1988], 254). Crelle in fact says very nearly the opposite, as I point out.

[7]The quotation is from Anton Schindler, *The Life of Beethoven* (based on his *Biographie von Ludwig van Beethoven,* 1st ed.), trans. and ed. Ignaz Moscheles (London, 1841; reprint, Boston: Oliver Ditson [1842?]), 157.

And how fortunate that Schindler, for all his weaknesses, appreciated this. He had the intelligence to realize that the key to expressing eloquently the wholeness of a work by Beethoven lay not in metronomic truing-up but in penetrating more deeply his art of gesture, and that to accomplish this "the proper declamation of verbal poetry [was] useful in this regard as analogy."[8] In contrast to Czerny, Schindler often went to great lengths to give a moment-by-moment account of the unfolding of a work by Beethoven, and in this way he reminds us that character is ever inflecting local tempo. It is in his fascination with gesture and declamation that we find something well worth preserving, albeit in a more credible way than Schindler himself was able to do. More credible in that, unlike both Schindler and Czerny, we ought to take Beethoven's articulation as it stands: because of Beethoven's lifelong concern for the minutiae of notation, a single gesture with original articulation often provides more of a clue to understanding the whole than a metronome setting ever could.

Beethoven never abandoned small-scale articulation. When in addition to the short slurs and fresh arrivals of his first mature works appeared the longer slurs and subsumed arrivals of his middle period, his palette of articulation was finally growing rich enough to serve the transcendent rhetoric of his last works, in which silence remained an essential tool. The transformation of the highly articulated speaking music of Mozart and Haydn at Beethoven's hands was due not so much to the growing sonority of instruments, or to the heavier actions of the English pianos (which Beethoven, despite his interest in increased power of tone, finally rejected in favor of the lighter Viennese action), or to the increasing emphasis on lyricism found among those of the English school. Rather it arose from his development of the fantasy-style into a kind of continuous speculation that gave rise to diminution over ever-larger spans of "rhythmic harmony." Though tone life was an ideal for him, since a certain amount of it was essential to sustaining the broader outlines of his fantasy rhetoric, Beethoven continued to use speech-mimetic effects in his keyboard works up to the end. And because of his allegiance to the Viennese

---

[8]"Die richtige Declamation der Wort-Poesie dient hierbei als Analogie" (Anton Schindler quoted in Cramer, *Studies*, Shedlock ed., ii).

instruments, with their lightness of touch, quickness of damping, and vividness of response to gesture, the passages that required a close approximation to speech articulation never had to suffer from the lack of subtlety in touch or the lack of efficient damping of the English pianos.

While it would be unfair to think less of Czerny for his "modernizations"—these, too, were, after all, part of the tradition he felt himself entrusted with—we must not underestimate their effect on his "translations" of Beethoven's notation and his reminiscences of Beethoven's playing. Czerny helped to popularize the practice of substituting changes in dynamics for articulation, at least partly, I believe, because he was responding to changes in the instrument itself. With the continued growth of tone life, hammer size, compass, and dynamic range, lightness of touch and quickness of damping increasingly diminished. Small-scale articulation began to seem less and less natural. Beethoven, who taught Czerny to play Emanuel Bach's works with a legato touch, nevertheless lived during a time when he could innovate without letting go of everything that he had inherited. Czerny let go of a lot more, and in teaching the generations that followed to play Beethoven with an *ultralegato* touch, removing many of the microarticulations that remain, he began to leave the world of rhetoric behind. The power of Czerny's influence might be measured by the extent to which the expressiveness of articulation remains unrealized in most performance of classical piano music today, even among those who specialize in performance on period instruments.

Also because of Czerny's influence, from his time onward, the tone and imagery surrounding descriptions of tempo and tempo flexibility became associated more and more with the "objective accuracy" of the metronome. After musicians had learned to defer to it, begging its pardon when they could not "squeeze in" what they needed to say (to use Czerny's expression), the old ways of describing time seemed in retrospect like crude approximations. It was with the notion that time comprised "equal units" that the demise of the declamatory style was sealed.

Of course since those days automata have continued to fascinate and instruct us, and now we shall turn to them again for one more lesson. In our day a shy West Coast artist with a Bösendorfer Model

SE and a modem can record a recital directly onto a keyboard in the morning, edit it in real time during the afternoon, and send it note-and-nuance-perfect around dinnertime to the stage of Carnegie Hall for an eight o'clock recital featuring another Bösendorfer that is played by solenoids. Opportunities like these have enabled us to derive some data about human musical performance. We have learned, for example, that we human beings almost never *perform* the equalities suggested by our musical notation, even when we play "classical" works. Irregularities continually arise in our performance, some purposeful, others perhaps better described as unavoidable—and even the latter are generally welcomed by discerning musicians, and at once put to good use. In part it was the absence of metric shape and rhythmic nuance in some early electronically generated arrangements of well-known classical and Baroque works that made this especially obvious to us: as with the crudest mechanically cut player piano rolls of yesteryear, familiar pieces were sounding very peculiar. We became increasingly aware of the importance of systematic and unsystematic variation to our expression of time in classic music.[9]

Although it is no surprise that this kind of variation differs from performer to performer, the extent to which we avoid regularity is remarkable: a mechanical ear designed to perceive a quarter-note followed by an eighth-note on the basis of a two-to-one ratio would find almost none in our playing. We "sound" our two-to-one ratios at roughly one and three-quarters to one, but "hear" them as two to one.[10] In short, performances that seem to us to be exemplary, natural, or just plain ordinary are frequently exceedingly complex with respect to physical parameters like duration, intensity, envelope, and the like; whereas performances comprising the "simple" sound

[9]On the other hand, the prevalence of naively computerized renditions seems also to have fostered the proliferation of performance that sounds mechanical, perhaps because we always face the danger of "becoming what we behold."

[10]In the extensive observations of professional and semiprofessional performers by the psychologists Ingmar Bengtsson and Alf Gabrielsson, almost every performance of the notated two to one deviated markedly from this ratio (in most cases the longer note was shortened and the shorter note lengthened so that the ratio was much closer to one and three-quarters to one), yet all of them "sounded" like two to one (Ingmar Bengtsson and Alf Gabrielsson, "Analysis and Synthesis of Musical Rhythm," in *Studies of Musical Performance,* ed. Johan Sundberg [Stockholm: Royal Swedish Academy of Music, 1983], 58).

qualities associated with mechanical durations, constant intensities, and equivalent envelopes typically seem awkward to us. These human responses are strong enough to suggest an inverse relation between psychological and physical "simplicity": that which seems psychologically "simple" to us is physically complex, and the physically "simple" is, to *our* psyches, notably alien.[11]

Is it surprising that our notation should employ a system of symbols that seems on the surface to equate tones that are in effect never sounded alike? This is part of its strength: identity is not superficial, correspondences are beguiling and rich. Just as "one can never equal one" in the physical world, so it is with classic music.

Modern instruments require of us that we "transcribe" Beethoven's rhetoric: even readings that attempt to be faithful to the details of his notation require adjustment for the vast differences between modern pianos and Beethoven's pianos. If we are transcribing we need alternatives for those aspects of modern common practice that lie perilously close to Czerny's less imaginative prescriptions. Foremost among the alternatives is diastolic theory. It remains a most helpful tool for suggesting a living balance between quality and quantity in metric accent, and proper proportionality on successively deeper structural levels. From the standpoint of the poetic meters, it is important for us to remember that musical meter was generally described as an already-inflected field. The tones entered it with wills of their own, which reflected the "morality" of their mode and the affective content of the gestures or figures they formed, including the content that accrued by reiteration, reference, and association.

When we think on the largest scale, our observations on *parlando rubato* and *tempo giusto* remind us of the paradox of diversity within unity and unity within diversity: the *tempo rubato* gains much of its evocative power by operating within certain appropriate boundaries, while the *tempo giusto* normally displays a subtle flexibility.[12] Beethoven's 1825 annotation to the last movement of the Ninth Sym-

[11]Ingmar Bengtsson and Alf Gabrielsson quoted in Jonathan D. Kramer, *The Time of Music: New Meanings, New Temporalities, New Listening Strategies* (New York: Schirmer Books, 1988), 75.

[12]See John Kirkpatrick's exploration of the relationship between meter, rhythm, and structural proportion in his "Performance as an Avenue to Educational Realities in Music," *College Music Symposium* 4 (1964): 40–41.

phony, "in the manner of a recitative, but in tempo," is, then, no contradiction. It is not a call for metronomic regularity but rather one example among many illustrating the need for structural rigor within a declamatory context—here, at bar 8, a rigor that would enable the cellists and bassists to achieve enough unity to declaim as a single vocal soloist.

Finally, in my opinion it would be no loss to the world of classical performance if use of the metronome were restricted to that envisioned by the early inventors of chronometers, as a tool for communicating some information about beginning tempi. If it can be said to offer something more—for example, a means for organizing physical acts in sequence—it must be remembered that sequence is precisely what it offers, not insight into musical proportion. Even when proportions in a musical work suggest inflections so subtle that in the presence of a ticking machine we observe a simple correspondence, unless the effect is meant to be mechanical that fact may be of only incidental artistic interest: bringing rhythm closer to the metronomic may carry the piece further from its most eloquent shape in that world where "time knows no equality of parts."

Appendix   Descriptions of the Diastolica
from Selected Eighteenth-Century Treatises

Michel de Saint-Lambert, *Les principes du clavecin*
(Paris: Christophe Ballard, 1702)

A piece of music somewhat resembles a piece of rhetoric [une Pièce d'Éloquence], or rather it is the piece of rhetoric which resembles the piece of music, since harmony, number, measure, and the other similar things which a skillful orator observes in the composition of his works belong more naturally to music than to rhetoric [la Rhétorique]. In any case, just as a piece of rhetoric is a whole unit which is most often made up of several parts [parties], each of which is composed of sentences [périodes], each having a complete meaning, these sentences being composed of phrases [membres], the phrases of words [mots], and the words of letters, so the melody of a piece of music is a whole unit which is always composed of several sections [reprises]. Each section is composed of cadences [cadences] which have a complete meaning and are the sentences of the melody. The cadences are often composed of phrases [membres], the phrases of measures [mesures], and the measures of notes. Thus the notes correspond to the letters, the measures to words, the cadences to sentences, the sections to parts, and the whole to the whole. But these divisions in the melody are not perceived by all those who hear music sung or played on some instrument. One must be trained in music in order to be aware of them, except for some which are so glaring that everyone understands them. However, these divisions are marked in the notation by the bars which separate the measures and by some other characteristics which I will discuss in their place.[1]

Johann Mattheson, *Der vollkommene Capellmeister* (Hamburg, 1739)

This theory on incisions, which one also calls *distinctiones, interpunctationes, posituras*, etc., is the most essential in the whole art of composing melody, and is called *diastolica* in Greek; however, it is so neglected that hitherto only the smallest rule has been given thereupon or the slightest instruction: indeed, one does not even find it in the most recent musical dictionaries.[2]

Lipsius describes their force thus: *Comma sustinet*, the *Comma* makes a little pause; *Colon suspendit*, the *Colon* delays longer; *Periodus deponit*, brings the sentence to rest. In short, the *Comma* is a little part of the sentence through which the discourse obtains a little caesura [Einschnitt]; though there is not a rhetorical but only a grammatical and imperfect meaning; for very often a single word requires its own comma.[3]

The concept of a period obliges me not to make a *formal* close in the melody before the sentence is finished. But the concept of a paragraph prohibits me from using a *full* cadence anywhere except at the end. Both cadences are *formal*: but the first is not *full*.[4]

A period . . . , which we describe as a word-phrase in classifying it, is a *brief statement which includes a complete idea or an entire verbal*

[1]*Principles of the Harpsichord*, trans. Rebecca Harris-Warrick (New York: Cambridge University Press, 1984), 32–33 (14–15 in Saint-Lambert's *Les principes du clavecin*).

[2]Ernest C. Harriss, *Johann Mattheson's "Der vollkommene Capellmeister": A Revised Translation with Critical Commentary* (Ann Arbor, Mich.: UMI Research Press, 1981), 380 (180–81 in original).

[3]Ibid., 384 (184 in original).

[4]Ibid., 383 (182 in original).

concept. Whatever does not do this but contains less is not a period, no *sentence*; and that which does more is a paragraph, *section*, or *structure*, which can consist of several periods, and by all rights should.[5]

Leopold Mozart, *Versuch einer gründlichen Violinschule* (Augsburg, 1756)

The human voice glides quite easily from one note to another; and a sensible singer will never make a break [Absatz] unless some special kind of expression, or the [sections] [Abschnitte] or [caesuras] [Einschnitte] of the phrase demand one.*

*The stops [Abschnitte] and pauses [Einschnitte] are the Incisiones, Distinctiones, Interpunctiones, and so on. But what sort of animals these are must be known to great grammarians, or better still, rhetoricians or poets. But here we see also that a good violinist must have this knowledge. For a sound composer this [knowledge] is indispensable, for otherwise he is the "Fifth wheel on the wagon": [for] the Diastolica (from διαστολη) is one of the most necessary things in melodic composition.[6]

Friedrich Wilhelm Marpurg, *Principes du clavecin* (Berlin, 1756)

Caesura is a general term used to designate any repose which the music takes, no matter in what part of the piece or on what notes.[7]

[5]Ibid., 382 (182 in original).

[6]Adapted from *A Treatise on the Fundamental Principles of Violin Playing* (based on the first and third editions of *Versuch einer gründlichen Violinschule* [Augsburg, 1756 and 1787]), trans. Editha Knocker, 2d ed. (London: Oxford University Press, 1951), 101 (108 in original).

[7]*F. W. Marpurg's "Anleitung zum Clavierspielen" (Berlin, 1755) and "Principes du clavecin" (Berlin, 1756): Translation and Commentary,* trans. Elizabeth L. Hays (Ann Arbor, Mich.: University Microfilms, 1977), chap. 8a, 1. (These excerpts are all from a chapter entitled "Concerning the Caesura, the Cadence, and Rhythm" that appears in the *Principes* [as chapter 9, 44–50] but not in the *Anleitung* of 1755; Hays designates it "8a" and numbers the pages in this section beginning with 1.)

In particular, however, the term Caesura is used only to designate the lesser degrees of repose in the music, and the term Cadence is used to indicate greater repose. A cadence is either *Perfect* [or] *Imperfect*. . . .[8]

The distance from one caesura to another is called a Member. A succession of two or three members is called a Section, and a succession of several sections, the last of which ought to terminate with a perfect cadence is called a Period. . . .[9]

Two or three small periods form a Paragraph.[10]

Johann Philipp Kirnberger, *Die Kunst des reinen Satzes in der Musik* (Berlin, 1771–79)

Chords are in music what words are in language. Just as a sentence in speech consists of several words that belong together and express a complete idea, a harmonic sentence or period consists of several chords that are connected and end with a close. And just as a succession of many sentences constitutes an entire speech, a composition consists of a succession of many periods.[11]

Whoever has even a moderate sense of hearing will have noticed the greatest strength of music comes from its rhythm. Through rhythm the melody as well as the harmony of several measures are bound together into a single phrase so that the hearing grasps them all at once. And then several short phrases are again gathered together into a larger whole, forming one main sentence at the end of which comes a point of rest which enables us likewise to understand these several phrases all at once. . . . Just as in spoken discourse only at the end of a sentence has one grasped its meaning, and through this meaning one

[8]Ibid., 2.
[9]Ibid., 10–12.
[10]Ibid., 15.
[11]*The Art of Strict Musical Composition,* trans. David Beach and Jurgen Thym (New Haven: Yale University Press, 1982), 109 (vol. 1, 91 in original).

is more or less satisfied according as it is a more or less complete sentence, so it is with music.[12]

A principal section of a composition always ends with . . . a perfect cadence. Therefore it may be likened to [the end of] a paragraph in speech which concludes a succession of sentences that are individual yet related by a central topic, after which the speech pauses for a moment.

Just as a paragraph in speech consists of segments [Einschnitten], phrases [Abschnitten], and sentences [Perioden] that are marked by various punctuation symbols such as the comma (,), semicolon (;), colon (:), and period (.), the harmonic [equivalent of the] paragraph can also consist of several segments [Einschnitten], phrases [Abschnitten], and periods [Perioden].[13]

Each period [Abschnitt] generally consists of a greater or smaller number of phrases [Einschnitte], which are not cut off or separated from each other as they would be by cadences, but are nevertheless divided from each other by smaller points of repose. These small points of repose are marked in the melody by caesuras or rests, but in the harmony they are produced by restful chords, especially by dominant chords. Whenever the little point of repose occurs, at least a new consonant chord must be heard. One can also use cadence chords, but they must be weakened by inversions or dissonances so that the pause will not be too noticeable and the ear will maintain its anticipation of the harmony that is to follow.[14]

Heinrich Christoph Koch, *Versuch einer Anleitung zur Composition* (Leipzig, 1787)

Certain more or less noticeable resting points [of the spirit] are generally necessary in speech and thus also in the products of those

[12]Putnam Aldrich, "'Rhythmic Harmony' as Taught by Johann Philipp Kirnberger," *Studies in Eighteenth-Century Music: A Tribute to Karl Geiringer on His Seventieth Birthday*, ed. H. C. Robbins Landon and Roger E. Chapman (New York: Oxford University Press, 1970), 38–39 (vol. 2, 137 in Kirnberger's *Die Kunst des reinen Satzes in der Musik*).
[13]Beach and Thym, *Strict Musical Composition*, 114 (vol. 1, 96 in original).
[14]Aldrich, "Rhythmic Harmony," 39 (vol. 2, 142 in original).

fine arts which attain their goal through speech, namely poetry and rhetoric, if the subject they present is to be comprehensible. Such resting points [of the spirit] are just as necessary in melody if it is to affect our feelings. This is a fact which has never yet been called into question and therefore requires no further proof.

By means of these more or less noticeable resting points, the products of these fine arts can be broken down into larger and smaller sections. Speech, for example, breaks down into various sentences [Perioden] through the most noticeable of these resting points; through the less noticeable the sentence, in turn, breaks down into separate clauses [Sätze] and parts of speech [Redetheile]. Just as in speech, the melody of a composition can be broken up into periods [Perioden] by means of analogous resting points, and these, again, into single phrases [einzelne Sätze] and melodic segments [melodische Theile].[15]

Daniel Gottlob Türk, *Klavierschule, oder Anweisung zum Klavierspielen für Lehrer und Lernende, mit kritischen Anmerkungen* (Leipzig and Halle, 1789)[16]

I have often said that a complete composition could be suitably compared to a speech, for as the latter itself may be divided into smaller and larger parts or members, so is this also true of music. A main section of a larger composition is approximately the same as that which is understood as a complete part in a speech. A musical period (section) [Abschnitt], of which there can be several in a main section, would be like that which is called a period in speech and which is separated from that which follows by a dot (.). A *Rhythmus*

---

[15]Adapted from Heinrich Christoph Koch, *Introductory Essay on Composition: The Mechanical Rules of Melody, Sections 3 and 4* (from his *Versuch einer Anleitung zur Composition* [Leipzig, 1787]), trans. Nancy K. Baker (New Haven: Yale University Press, 1983), 1 (vol. 2, 342 in original).

[16]Daniel Gottlob Türk, *School of Clavier Playing or Instructions in Playing the Clavier for Teachers and Students,* trans. Raymond H. Haggh (Lincoln: University of Nebraska Press, 1982), 332 (343 in original).

can be compared with the smaller parts of speech which are indicated by a colon (:) or a semicolon (;). The phrase member [Einschnitt], as the smallest member, is like that which would be separated by a comma (,). If it is especially wished to include the caesura with these, then one would have to compare it with the caesura of a verse (see Sulzer's *Allgemeine Theorie,* article on *Einschnitt*).

References

Aldrich, Putnam. "'Rhythmic Harmony' as Taught by Johann Philipp Kirnberger." In *Studies in Eighteenth-Century Music: A Tribute to Karl Geiringer on His Seventieth Birthday*. Edited by H. C. Robbins Landon and Roger E. Chapman, 37–52. New York: Oxford University Press, 1970.

Allgemeine musikalische Zeitung 6, no. 15 (11 January 1804): cols. 243–44. Anonymous review of the Variations H. 14 (Wq. 118, no. 7) by Carl Philipp Emanuel Bach. Edited by J. F. Rochlitz.

American Heritage Dictionary of the English Language. Edited by William Morris. Boston: Houghton Mifflin, 1975.

Anderson, Emily, trans. and ed. *The Letters of Beethoven*. 3 vols. New York: St. Martin's, 1961.

——. *The Letters of Mozart and His Family*. London: Macmillan, 1985.

Bach, Carl Philipp Emanuel. *Essay on the True Art of Playing Keyboard Instruments*. Translated by William Mitchell. New York: W. W. Norton, 1949.

——. *Sonata c-moll: "Sanguineus und Melancholicus"* (Wq. 161, no. 1) for two violins and continuo. Edited by Klaus Hofmann. Stuttgarter Bach-Ausgaben, series E: Carl Philipp Emanuel Bach, Ausgewählte Werke, 4. Gruppe: Kammermusik. Neuhausen-Stuttgart: Hänssler-Verlag [1980].

——. *Versuch über die wahre Art, das Clavier zu spielen*. Facsimile of the 1st ed. of Berlin, 1753 (part 1) and 1762 (part 2). Edited by Lothar Hoffmann-Erbrecht. Leipzig: Breitkopf and Härtel, 1957.

Beethoven, Ludwig van. *Beethovens sämtliche Briefe*. 5 vols. Edited by Alfred C. Kalischer. Berlin: Schuster and Loeffler, 1906–08.

——. *Deux grandes sonates pour le clavecin ou piano-forte avec un violoncelle obligé . . . Oeuvre 5ᵐᵉ* (plate no. 689). Vienna: Artaria [1797].

——. *The Letters of Beethoven*. 3 vols. Translated and edited by Emily Anderson. New York: St. Martin's, 1961.

——. *Ludwig van Beethovens sämtliche Briefe*. Edited by Emerich Kastner. Tutzing: Schneider, 1975.

——. *Ludwig van Beethovens sämtliche Briefe und Auszeichnungen*. Edited by Fritz Prelinger. Vienna: C. W. Stern, 1907.

——. *Sonaten, neue Ausgabe* (published and sold separately). Vienna: Haslinger [1828–32?].

——. *The 32 Piano Sonatas in Reprints of the First and Early Editions*. 5 vols. London: Tecla Editions, 1989.

——. *Werke VII, 2: Klaviersonaten I*. Edited by Hans Schmidt. Munich-Duisburg: G. Henle, 1971.

Bengtsson, Ingmar, and Alf Gabrielsson. "Analysis and Synthesis of Musical Rhythm." In *Studies of Music Performance*. Edited by Johan Sundberg. Stockholm: Royal Swedish Academy of Music, 1983.

Bilson, Malcolm. *The Emergence of the Fantasy-Style in the Beethoven Piano Sonatas of the Early and Middle Periods*. D.M.A. dissertation, University of Illinois, 1968. Ann Arbor, Mich.: University Microfilms, 1968.

Brendel, Alfred. *Musical Thoughts and Afterthoughts*. Princeton: Princeton University Press, 1976.

Buelow, George J. "Rhetoric and Music." In *New Grove Dictionary of Music and Musicians*, vol. 15, 793–803.

Burney, Charles. *A General History of Music*. 4 vols. London, 1776, 1782, 1789, and 1789. Reprint, 4 vols. in 2. Edited by Frank Mercer. New York: Harcourt, Brace, 1935. Reprint, New York: Dover, 1957.

——. *Tagebuch einer musikalischen Reise durch . . . Hamburg . . . 1772/1773*. Facsimile. Edited by Richard Schaal. New York: Bärenreiter, 1959.

Christmann, Johann F. *Elementarbuch der Tonkunst*. Speyer, 1782–89.

Cooper, Kenneth. *The Clavichord in the Eighteenth Century*. Ph.D. dissertation, Columbia University, 1971. Ann Arbor, Mich.: University Microfilms, 1972.

Cramer, Johann Baptist. *84 Etüden für Klavier*. Vienna: Haslinger [1826].

——. *Selection of Studies by J. B. Cramer, with Comments by L. van Beethoven, and Preface, Translation, Explanatory Notes, and Fingering. . . .* Translated and edited by John South Shedlock. London: Augener [1893].

——. *21 Etüden für Klavier: Nach dem Handexemplar Beethovens aus dem Besitz Anton Schindlers*. Edited by Hans Kann. Vienna: Universal, 1974.

Czerny, Carl. *Complete Theoretical and Practical Piano Forte School*, Op. 500. 3 vols. Translated by J. A. Hamilton. London: Cocks [1839]. Vol. 4, *The Art of Playing the Ancient and Modern Piano Forte Works*. London: Cocks [1846].

——. *Erinnerungen aus meinem Leben*. Edited by Walter Kolneder. Strasbourg: Éditions P. H. Heitz, 1968.

——. *Die Kunst des Vortrags der älteren und neueren Klavier-kompositionen*. Vol. 4 of *Vollständige . . . Pianoforte-Schule*, Op. 500. Vienna: Diabelli, 1846.

———. *On the Proper Performance of All Beethoven's Works for the Piano*. Chapters 2 and 3 of *The Art of Playing the Ancient and Modern Piano Forte Works*. London: Cocks, 1846. Facsimile. Edited by Paul Badura-Skoda. Vienna: Universal, 1970. Page numbers in the present book refer to those of the Universal edition (bottom center of each page) rather than to the original numbers.

———. "Recollections from My Life." Translated by Ernest Sanders. In *Musical Quarterly* 42 (1956): 302–17.

———. *Über den richtigen Vortrag der sämtlichen Beethoven'schen Klavierwerke: Czerny's "Erinnerungen an Beethoven" sowie das 2. und 3. Kapitel des IV. Bandes der "Vollständigen theoretisch-practischen Pianoforte-Schule op. 500."* Facsimile. Edited by Paul Badura-Skoda. Vienna: Universal, 1963. Page numbers in the present book refer to those of the Universal edition (bottom center of each page) rather than to the original numbers.

———. *Vollständige theoretisch-practische Pianoforte-Schule*, Op. 500. 3 vols. Vienna: Diabelli, 1839.

———, ed. [32] *Sonates pour le piano, édition revue, corrigée, métronomisée et doigtée par Ch.* [Carl] Czerny, [from 1862] *im Einverständniss des Originalverlegers berechtigte Ausgabe*. 2 vols. Bonn: Simrock [1856–68].

Daube, Johann Friedrich. *Der musikalische Dilettant: eine Abhandlung des Generalbasses*. Vienna: Kurzböck, 1770–71.

Dies, Albert Christoph. *Biographische Nachrichten von Joseph Haydn*. In *Haydn: Two Contemporary Portraits*. Translated by Vernon Gotwals. Madison: University of Wisconsin Press, 1968.

Drake, Kenneth. *The Sonatas of Beethoven as He Played and Taught Them*. Bloomington: Indiana University Press, 1981.

Duckles, Vincent. "Johann Nicolaus Forkel: The Beginning of Music Historiography." In *Eighteenth-Century Studies* 1 (1968): 277–90.

Fallows, David. "Tempo and Expression Marks." In *New Grove Dictionary of Music and Musicians*, vol. 18, 677–84.

Forbes, Elliot, ed. *Thayer's Life of Beethoven*. 2 vols. Princeton: Princeton University Press, 1964.

Fuller, David. *Mechanical Musical Instruments as a Source for the Study of Notes Inégales*. Cleveland Heights, Ohio: Divisions, 1979.

———. "Notes inégales." In *New Grove Dictionary of Music and Musicians*, vol. 13, 420–27.

Gottsched, Johann Christoph. *Auszug aud des Herrn Batteux schönen Künsten aus dem einzigen Grundsatze der Nachahmung hergeleitet. Zum Gebrauch seiner Vorlesungen mit verschiedenen Zusätzen und Anmerkungen erläutert*. Leipzig, 1754.

Gotwals, Vernon, trans. *Haydn: Two Contemporary Portraits* (includes G. A. Griesinger's *Biographische Notizen über Joseph Haydn* [Leipzig: Breitkopf and Härtel, 1810] and Albert Christoph Dies's *Biographische Nachrichten von Joseph Haydn* [Vienna, 1810]). Madison: University of Wisconsin Press, 1968.

Graue, Jerald C. "Johann [John] Baptist Cramer." In *New Grove Dictionary of Music and Musicians*, vol. 5, 19–21.

Harding, Rosamund Evelyn Mary. "The Metronome and Its Precursors." Part 1 of *Origins of Musical Time and Expression*. London: Oxford University Press, 1938.

Helm, E. Eugene. "Carl Philipp Emanuel Bach." In *New Grove Dictionary of Music and Musicians,* vol. 1, 844–63.

——. "The 'Hamlet' Fantasy and the Literary Element in C.P.E. Bach's Music." In *Musical Quarterly* 58 (1972): 277–96.

——. *Music at the Court of Frederick the Great*. Norman: University of Oklahoma Press, 1960.

Henschel, George. *Personal Recollections of Johannes Brahms*. New York: A.M.S. Press, 1978.

Hill, Christopher C. "Rhetoric." In *New Harvard Dictionary of Music*. Edited by Don Michael Randel. Cambridge: Harvard University Press, 1986.

Hiller, Johann A. *Anweisung zum musikalisch-zierlichen Gesange*. Leipzig, 1780.

Hosler, Bellamy. *Changing Aesthetic Views of Instrumental Music in 18th-Century Germany*. Ann Arbor, Mich.: UMI Research Press, 1981.

Houle, George. *Meter in Music, 1600–1800: Performance, Perception, and Notation*. Bloomington: Indiana University Press, 1987.

Hummel, Johann Nepomuk. *Ausführliche theoretisch-practische Anweisung zum Piano-Forte-Spiel*. Vienna: Haslinger, 1828.

——. *A Complete Theoretical and Practical Course of Instructions on the Art of Playing the Piano Forte*. London [1828].

Johnson, Douglas, Alan Tyson, and Robert Winter. *The Beethoven Sketchbooks: History, Reconstruction, Inventory*. Berkeley and Los Angeles: University of California Press, 1985.

Jonas, Oswald. *Introduction to the Theory of Heinrich Schenker: The Nature of the Musical Work of Art*. Translated and edited by John Rothgeb. New York: Longman, 1982.

Kalib, Sylvan, trans. *Thirteen Essays from the Three Yearbooks: "Das Meisterwerk in der Musik" by Heinrich Schenker: An Annotated Translation*. 3 vols. Ph.D. dissertation, Northwestern University, 1973. Ann Arbor, Mich.: University Microfilms, 1981.

Kämper, Dietrich. "Zur Frage der Metronombezeichnungen Robert Schumanns." In *Archiv für Musikwissenschaft* 21 (1964): 141–55.

Kerman, Joseph, and Alan Tyson. *The New Grove Beethoven*. New York: W. W. Norton, 1983.

Kirkendale, Warren. "New Roads to Old Ideas in Beethoven's *Missa Solemnis*." In *Musical Quarterly* 56 (1970): 665–701.

Kirkpatrick, John. "New Looks at Old Music." Revision of an informal talk at a reception given by the Alberta Registered Music Teachers Association for examiners of the Royal Conservatory of Toronto and of the Western Board of Music, at Edmonton on Sunday, 11 June 1972. Typescript.

——. "Performance as an Avenue to Educational Realities in Music." In *College Music Symposium* 4 (1964): 39–46.

Kirnberger, Johann Philipp. *The Art of Strict Musical Composition* (translation of *Die Kunst des reinen Satzes in der Musik* [Berlin, 1771–79]). Translated by David Beach and Jurgen Thym. New Haven: Yale University Press, 1982.

———. *Die Kunst des reinen Satzes in der Musik.* Berlin and Königsberg, 1776–79. Facsimile. Hildesheim: Georg Olms, 1968.

Koch, Heinrich Christoph. *Introductory Essay on Composition: The Mechanical Rules of Melody, Sections 3 and 4* (from his *Versuch einer Anleitung zur Composition* [Leipzig, 1782, 1787, 1793]). Translated by Nancy K. Baker. New Haven: Yale University Press, 1983.

———. *Musikalisches Lexikon.* Frankfurt am Main, 1802.

Köhler, Karl-Heinz. "The Conversation Books: Aspects of a New Picture of Beethoven." In *Beethoven, Performers, and Critics.* Edited by Robert Winter and Bruce Carr. Detroit: Wayne State University Press, 1980: 147–61.

Kolisch, Rudolf. "Tempo and Character in Beethoven's Music." In *Musical Quarterly* 29 (1943): 169–87 and 291–312.

Kramer, Jonathan D. *The Time of Music: New Meanings, New Temporalities, New Listening Strategies.* New York: Schirmer Books, 1988.

Kramer, Richard A. "Beethoven and Carl Heinrich Graun." In *Beethoven Studies,* vol. 1, edited by Alan Tyson, 18–44. New York: W. W. Norton, 1973.

———. "Notes to Beethoven's Education." In *Journal of the American Musicological Society* 28 (1975): 72–101.

Krebs, Carl, ed. *Beethoven Sonatas for the Piano.* 2 vols. New York: G. Schirmer, 1953.

Lakoff, George, and Mark Johnson. *Metaphors We Live By.* Chicago: University of Chicago Press, 1980.

Leitzmann, Albert. "Beethovens Bibliothek." In *Ludwig van Beethoven: Berichte der Zeitgenossen, Briefe und persönliche Auszeichnungen,* 379–83. Leipzig: Insel-Verlag, 1921.

Levy, Janet M. "Texture as a Sign in Classic and Early Romantic Music." In *Journal of the American Musicological Society* 35 (1982): 482–531.

Lindley, Mark. "Keyboard Technique and Articulation: Evidence for the Performance Practices of Bach, Handel, and Scarlatti." In *Bach, Handel, Scarlatti: Tercentenary Essays,* edited by Peter Williams, 207–43. London: Cambridge University Press, 1985.

Lockwood, Lewis. "Beethoven's Early Works for Violoncello and Pianoforte: Innovation in Context." In *Beethoven Newsletter* 1 (1986): 17–21.

MacArdle, Donald W. "Anton Felix Schindler, Friend of Beethoven." In *Music Review* 24 (1963): 50–74.

Maniates, Maria Rika. "'Sonate, que me veux-tu?' The Enigma of French Musical Aesthetics in the Eighteenth Century." In *Current Musicology* 9 (1969): 117–40.

Marpurg, Friedrich Wilhelm. *F. W. Marpurg's "Anleitung zum Clavierspielen" (Berlin, 1755) and "Principes du clavecin" (Berlin, 1756): Translation and Commen-*

tary. Translated by Elizabeth L. Hays. 2 vols. Ph.D. dissertation, Stanford University, 1977. Ann Arbor, Mich.: University Microfilms, 1977.

——. *Kritische Briefe über die Tonkunst*. Berlin: Birnstiel, 1759–64. Facsimile. 2 vols. Hildesheim: Georg Olms, 1974.

Marx, Adolf Bernhard. *Ludwig van Beethoven, Leben und Schaffen*. Berlin, 1859. 5th ed. 3 vols. in 2. Leipzig: Adolph Schumann, 1902.

Mattheson, Johann. *Critica musica*. Hamburg, 1722.

——. *Der vollkommene Capellmeister*. Hamburg, 1739. Facsimile. Kassel: Bärenreiter-Verlag, 1954.

——. *Johann Mattheson's "Der vollkommene Capellmeister": A Revised Translation with Critical Commentary*. Translated by Ernest C. Harriss. Ann Arbor, Mich.: UMI Research Press, 1981.

Mersenne, F. Marin. *Harmonie universelle, contenant la Théorie et la Pratique de la Musique*. Paris, 1636. Facsimile. Paris: Éditions du Centre national de la Recherche scientifique, 1975.

——. *Harmonie universelle: The Books on Instruments*. Paris: S. Cramoisy, 1636–37. Translated by Roger E. Chapman. The Hague: M. Nijhoff, 1957.

Mozart, Leopold. *A Treatise on the Fundamental Principles of Violin Playing* (based on the first and third editions of *Versuch einer gründlichen Violinschule* [Augsburg, 1756 and 1787]). Translated by Editha Knocker. 2d ed. London: Oxford University Press, 1951.

Mozart, Wolfgang Amadeus. *The Letters of Mozart and His Family*. Translated and edited by Emily Anderson. London: Macmillan, 1985.

——. *Wolfgang Amadeus Mozart: Briefwechsel und Aufzeichnungen*. Edited by E. H. Mueller. 2 vols. Vienna: Perneder, 1949.

Neubauer, John. *The Emancipation of Music from Language: Departure from Mimesis in Eighteenth-Century Aesthetics*. New Haven: Yale University Press, 1986.

New Grove Dictionary of Music and Musicians. 6th ed. Edited by Stanley Sadie. 20 vols. London: Macmillan, 1980.

New Harvard Dictionary of Music. Edited by Don Michael Randel. Cambridge: Harvard University Press, 1986.

Newman, William S. *Beethoven on Beethoven: Playing His Piano Music His Way*. New York: W. W. Norton, 1988.

——. "Beethoven's Pianos versus His Piano Ideals." In *Journal of the American Musicological Society* 23 (1970): 484–504.

——. "A Chronological Checklist of Collected Editions of Beethoven's Solo Piano Sonatas since His Own Day." In *Notes* 33, no. 3 (March 1977): 503–30.

——. "Emanuel Bach's Autobiography" (translation of the 1773 autobiography with commentary). In *Musical Quarterly* 51 (1965): 363–72.

——. *The Sonata in the Classic Era*. 2d ed. New York: W. W. Norton, 1972.

——. *The Sonata since Beethoven*. New York: W. W. Norton, 1972.

——. "Tempo in Beethoven's Instrumental Music: Its Choice and Its Flexibility." In *Piano Quarterly* 116 (Winter 1981–82): 22–29, and 117 (Spring 1982): 22–31.

——. "Yet Another Major Beethoven Forgery by Schindler?" In *Journal of Musicology* 3 (1984): 397–422.

Nottebohm, Gustav. *Beethoveniana*. Leipzig: C. F. Peters, 1872. Reprint. New York: Johnson Reprint Corporation, 1970.

——. *Zweite Beethoveniana*. Leipzig: C. F. Peters, 1887. Reprint. New York: Johnson Reprint Corporation, 1970.

Quantz, Johann Joachim. *On Playing the Flute*. 2d ed. Translated and edited by Edward R. Reilly. New York: Schirmer Books, 1985.

——. *Versuch einer Anweisung die Flöte traversiere zu spielen*. Berlin, 1752. Facsimile. Wiesbaden: Breitkopf and Härtel, 1988.

Ratner, Leonard G. *Classic Music: Expression, Form, and Style*. New York: Schirmer Books, 1980.

Richter, Sviatoslav, and Mstislav Rostropovich. *Beethoven: The Sonatas for Piano and Cello*. Philips compact disc set 412 256-2 (two discs).

Rosenblum, Sandra P. *Performance Practices in Classic Piano Music: Their Principles and Applications*. Bloomington: Indiana University Press, 1988.

Rothschild, Fritz. *Musical Performance in the Times of Mozart and Beethoven: The Lost Tradition in Music, Part 2*. New York: Oxford University Press, 1961.

Rothstein, William. "Heinrich Schenker as an Interpreter of Beethoven's Piano Sonatas." In *19th-Century Music* 8 (1984): 3–28.

Rousseau, Jean-J. *Dictionnaire de musique*. Paris, 1768.

Rudolf, Max. *The Grammar of Conducting*. 2d ed. New York: Schirmer Books, 1980.

Saint-Lambert, Michel de. *Principles of the Harpsichord* (*Les principes du clavecin* [Paris: Christophe Ballard, 1702]). Translated by Rebecca Harris-Warrick. New York: Cambridge University Press, 1984.

Schenker, Heinrich. *Thirteen Essays from the Three Yearbooks: "Das Meisterwerk in der Musik."* Translated and annotated by Sylvan Kalib. Ph.D. dissertation, Northwestern University, 1973. Ann Arbor, Mich.: University Microfilms, 1981.

Schering, Arnold. "Carl Philipp Emanuel Bach und das 'redende Prinzip' in der Musik." In *Jahrbuch der Musikbibliothek Peters, 1938*, 45 (1939): 13–29.

Schindler, Anton. *Beethoven as I Knew Him* (annotated translation of the 1860 *Biographie von Ludwig van Beethoven*). Edited by Donald W. MacArdle and translated by Constance S. Jolly. London: Faber and Faber, 1966.

——. *Biographie von Ludwig van Beethoven*. Münster: Aschendorff, 1840, 1845, 1860, 1871 (4th ed. is a reprint of 3d ed., 1860). (For a description of the contents of each edition see Donald MacArdle's annotated translation of the 1860 ed., *Beethoven as I Knew Him*, 29n.1.)

——. "Für Studirende von Beethoven's Clavier-Musik." In *Niederrheinische Musik-Zeitung für Kunstfreunde und Künstler* 20 (May 20, 1854): 156–57.

——. *The Life of Beethoven*. Translated and edited from Schindler's *Biographie von Ludwig van Beethoven*, 1st ed., 1840, by Ignaz Moscheles. London, 1841. Reprint. Boston: Oliver Ditson [1842?].

Schulenberg, David. *The Instrumental Music of Carl Philipp Emanuel Bach.* Ann Arbor, Mich.: UMI Research Press, 1984.

Selfridge-Field, Eleanor. "Beethoven and Greek Classicism." *Journal of the History of Ideas* 33 (1972): 577–95.

Shedlock, John South, trans. and ed. *Selection of Studies by J. B. Cramer, with Comments by L. van Beethoven, and Preface, Translation, Explanatory Notes, and Fingering* . . . . London: Augener [1893].

Solomon, Maynard. *Beethoven.* New York: Schirmer Books, 1977.

Somfai, László, ed. *The Centenary Edition of Bartók's Records* (complete), 2 vols. Hungaroton LPX 12326–38.

Sonneck, Oscar, ed. *Beethoven: Impressions by His Contemporaries.* New York: G. Schirmer, 1926.

Stadlen, Peter. "Schindler and the Conversation Books." In *Soundings* 7 (1978): 2–18.

——. "Schindler's Beethoven Forgeries." In *Musical Times* 118 (1977): 549–52.

Sulzer, Johann Georg. *Allgemeine Theorie der schönen Künste.* 2 vols. Leipzig, 1771, 1774. Revised 1778–79 and 1786–87. Enlarged 2d ed., 4 vols. Leipzig, 1792–94. "Register" appears in a separate volume, 1799. Facsimile of enlarged 2d ed. Hildesheim: Georg Olms, 1969.

Thayer, Alexander Wheelock. *Ludwig van Beethovens Leben.* 5 vols. Translated by Hermann Dieters and edited by Hugo Riemann. Leipzig: Breitkopf and Härtel, 1907.

Tovey, Donald Francis. *A Companion to Beethoven's Pianoforte Sonatas.* London: Associated Board of the Royal Schools of Music, 1931.

Tovey, Donald F., and Harold Craxton, eds. *Beethoven Sonatas for Pianoforte.* 3 vols. London: Associated Board of the Royal Schools of Music [1931].

Türk, Daniel Gottlob. *Klavierschule, oder Anweisung zum Klavierspielen für Lehrer und Lernende, mit kritischen Anmerkungen.* Leipzig and Halle, 1789.

——. *School of Clavier Playing or Instructions in Playing the Clavier for Teachers and Students* (based on the first edition of his *Klavierschule,* 1789). Translated by Raymond H. Haggh. Lincoln: University of Nebraska Press, 1982.

Tyson, Alan. "Ferdinand Ries (1784–1838): The History of His Contribution to Beethoven Biography." In *19th-Century Music* 7 (1984): 209–21.

——. Review: "Cramer, Johann Baptist, *21 Etüden,* ed. 'from Beethoven's copy' by Hans Kann. With keyboard exercises by Beethoven (Universal, Vienna, 1974)." In *Music and Letters* 58 (1977): 247–49.

——. "Steps to Publication—and Beyond." In *The Beethoven Companion.* Edited by Denis Arnold and Nigel Fortune. London: Faber and Faber, 1971.

Walther, Johann G. *Musikalisches Lexikon.* Leipzig, 1732.

Wegeler, Franz Gerhard, and Ferdinand Ries. *Beethoven Remembered: The Biographical Notes of Franz Wegeler and Ferdinand Ries.* Translated by Frederick Noonan. Arlington, Va.: Great Ocean, 1987.

——. *Biographische Notizen über Ludwig van Beethoven von Wegeler und Ries.* Edited by Alfred C. Kalischer. 2d ed. Berlin: Schuster and Loeffler, 1906.

Winter, Robert, and Bruce Carr, eds. *Beethoven, Performers, and Critics*. Detroit: Wayne State University Press, 1980.

Wolf, Ernst W. *Musikalischer Unterricht*. Dresden, 1788.

Zuckerkandl, Victor. *Sound and Symbol: Music and the External World*. Translated by Willard R. Trask. Bollingen series 44. New York: Pantheon, 1956.

Index

Ries, Ferdinand, 53, 55, 69, 149; on Beethoven's playing, 8, 9n.19, 54–55; on Beethoven's teaching, 148–49; on Beethoven's tempo flexibility, 53–55; on Beethoven's Variations Op. 34, 148–49; compared with Schindler, 69; corroborating Schindler, 149n.9; as melodist, 46; *Notizen,* 54; pianism of, 54; studies with Beethoven, 54
ritardando, Czerny on, 85–86
Romantic era: and Beethoven, 46–47; and metronome, 13
Romanticism, 123
Rosenblum, Sandra P., 131n.57; on agogic expression, 72; on Beethoven's cultivation of legato, 44; on Beethoven's metronome marks for Op. 106, 53n.33; on cantabile lines, 45; on caricature, Schindler's, 72; on classicism, 52n.30; on Czerny's editions of Beethoven's sonatas, 61–62; on Czerny's metronome marks, 62; on Daube, 156n.4; on form and feeling, 52n.30; on fortepiano, 5n.12; on metronome marks, 57n.48, 61n.55; on musical character, 52n.30; on Schindler, 65, 71; on slurs and bowing/tonguing, 112n.125; on tempo flexibility, 52n.30
Rostropovich, Mstislav, 132–33
Rothstein, William, 107n.116
Rousseau, Jean-Jacques, 129n.154
Rudolf, Max, on metronome marks, 65

Saint-Lambert, Michel de, 24; on harmony, 163; on measure, 163; on melody, 163; *Les principes du clavecin,* 163–64; on rhetoric and music, 163–64
Salieri, Antonio, 47, 49, 50
scansion: Mattheson on, 127; and rhythmic accent, 130; Schindler on, 151
Schenker, Heinrich, on slurs for phrasing, 107
Schering, Arnold, on "singing," 117n.133
Schilling, Gustav, 74
Schindler, Anton Felix, 45n.15, 90; on analogy, 158; on Beethoven, 80; on Beethoven's accentuation, 129–31; on "Beethoven's" annotations to Cramer's Etudes, 124–26, 154–55; on Beethoven's concern for tempi, 65; on Beethoven's declamation, 66, 157–58; on Beethoven's metronome marks, 70; on Beethoven's Op. 13, 96n.102; on

Beethoven's playing, 8, 66, 151; on Beethoven's poetic programs, 71; on bowing/tonguing, 130; on caesura, 67n.70, 71–72, 124; on caricature, 66; on Clementi, 52, 123–24; compared with Czerny, 69, 77–78; compared with Ries, 69; on Czerny, 67, 69, 72, 78; on declamation, 52, 66, 71, 123, 157–58; on declamatory style, 74; on emphasis, 122; on fermata, 72; forgeries, 68, 72, 154; on "free performance," 74, 123–24; on "grammatical accent" in Beethoven, 130; on instrumental music, 52, 123–24, 155; on listening to singers, 130; on longs and shorts, 124, 155; on "melodic accent" in Beethoven, 130; on metronome, 9, 20, 54, 66, 69; on musical character, 130, 158; on music as speech, 123; personality of, 68–69, 72, 77, 154, 155; on poetic meter, 155; on prosody, 52, 123–24, 155; on rhetorical pause, 67n.70, 72; on rhetoric and music, 72–78, 97, 123, 155; on "rhythmic accent" in Beethoven, 129–30; on technique, 154; on tempo and character in Beethoven, 9; on tempo flexibility, 65–68, 69–74, 77–78, 80n.84, 120, 133; on *tempo rubato,* 66; on the two principles [zwei Principe], 71; on Weber, 72–73
Schott (publisher, Mainz), 53, 69, 70
Schröder-Devrient, Mme. Wilhelmine, 80n.83
Schulenberg, David, on Mattheson, 34n.40
Schulz, J. A. P., 33n.37
Schumann, Clara, and metronome marks, 63
Selfridge-Field, Eleanor, on Beethoven and Greek classicism, 2n.1
Seyfried, Ignaz von, on Beethoven's conducting, 79–80
Shakespeare, William, 40
silence, as marker of Beethoven's syntax, 131
simplicity, physical vs. psychological, 160–61
Simrock, Nikolaus (Bonn), 44; editions of Beethoven, 61, 62, 87n.94, 88, 89, 93, 96
slurs: Beethoven on, 45; Czerny on, 103–5; double, Türk on, 118n.134; Haydn's, 111; longer, 47, 110; measure-length, 104, 111, 117; Mozart's, 111; for phras-

Library of Congress Cataloging-in-Publication Data

Barth, George, 1950–
    The pianist as orator : Beethoven and the transformation of keyboard
style / George Barth.
        p.   cm.
    Includes bibliographical references (p.   ) and index.
    ISBN 0-8014-2411-9 (alk. paper)
    1. Piano music—18th century—History and criticism.   2. Piano
music—19th century—History and criticism.   3. Beethoven, Ludwig
van, 1770–1827.   4. Music—Philosophy and aesthetics.   I. Title.
ML700.B38   1992
786.2'09'033—dc20
                                                          92-52743